MISSISSIPPI TERRITORY

IN THE

WAR OF 1812

By

MRS. DUNBAR ROWLAND

REPRINTED FROM

Publications of the Mississippi Historical Society

CENTENARY SERIES, VOLUME IV

CLEARFIELD

Excerpted From
Publications of the Mississippi Historical Society
Centenary Series, Volume IV
Jackson, 1921

Reprinted with permission
Genealogical Publishing Company
Baltimore, 1968

Reprinted for
Clearfield Company, Inc. by
Genealogical Publishing Co., Inc.
Baltimore, Maryland
1996, 1999, 2005

Library of Congress Catalogue Card Number 68-29152
International Standard Book Number: 0-8063-0301-8

Made in the United States of America

PREFACE.

In this short history I endeavor to give a truthful account of the part played by the Mississippi Territory and its soldiery in the Campaign against the British and the Creek Nation during the War of 1812. Many historians fail to surround the war in this part of the Republic with its actual environment and the reader gets no more than a hazy idea of its locality. Excepting the defense of New Orleans the scenes of action lay principally in the Mississippi Territory. Without clear knowledge of this fact the reader cannot place the local color and fails to grasp the relative significance of events in the development of the states of the lower South.

While I write with the express purpose of emphasizing the activities of the troops of the Mississippi Territory and of drawing attention to many erroneous statements and omissions concerning them, yet it is my welcome task to record the brilliant exploits and valor of all troops who took part under General Andrew Jackson in the campaign against the Creeks and British.

In the story of the coast campaign against Great Britain and her allies the strong spirit of American nationality prevailing in the far southern section during this period is insistent and compelling. In view of the weak defense maintained in this region, had this spirit been less active the war in all probability would have been as lacking in valor here as it was in the North.

The documentary and printed sources to which I have had access, many of which have been collected by the Mississippi Department of Archives and History, are as follows:

Original Letters and Correspondence of Gen. F. L. Claiborne, 1813-14.
Letter-books and Journals of Gov. David Holmes, 1809-20.
Miscellaneous Mississippi Territorial Archives, 1813-15.
Correspondence of Judge Harry Toulmin, 1813-15.
Original Letter-books of Gov. W. C. C. Claiborne, 1801-16.
Newspaper Files, *Washington Republican, 1813-15.*
Original Letters of Gen. Andrew Jackson, 1813-15.
Historical Memoir, by Major A. L. Latour.
The History of Alabama, by Albert James Pickett.
Mississippi as a Province, Territory and State, by J. F. H. Claiborne.
The Creek War, by H. S. Halbert and T. H. Ball.
Life of Andrew Jackson, by John Spencer Bassett.
Life of Andrew Jackson, by James Parton.
Life of Andrew Jackson, by John Henry Eaton.

10 Preface.

History of Louisiana, by Alcée Fortier.
Colonial Mobile, by Peter J. Hamilton.
Military History of Mississippi, by Dunbar Rowland.
Encyclopedia of Mississippi History, by Dunbar Rowland.
History of Louisiana, by Charles Gayarré.
Harper's Encyclopedia of United States History.
Encyclopedia Britannica, Eleventh Edition.

In the preparation of the work I am indebted for valuable historical assistance to Dr. Dunbar Rowland, and for helpful criticism to Judge R. H. Thompson and Hon. J. R. Preston, officers of the Mississippi Historical Society. To these and to Mr. Hermes Knoblock for assistance in reading the proof and to Miss Kittie R. Sanderson and Miss Maria Shelton, who have been faithful and efficient in copying the manuscript, I am deeply grateful.

MISSISSIPPI TERRITORY IN THE WAR OF 1812

The publication by the Mississippi Historical Society of the roster of Mississippi soldiers who participated in the Southern Coast Campaign of the War of 1812 furnishes the writer an opportunity to publish with it a short history of the part taken by the troops of the Mississippi Territory in the second struggle for American Independence. In this lively and momentous episode during the last hostilities between the United States and Great Britain a number of distinguished sons of the Mississippi Territory, along with several thousand brave troops mustered within its borders, bore a conspicuous part. The most prominent figures in this period of the Territory's history were Governor David Holmes, General Ferdinand L. Claiborne and Major Thomas Hinds, whose patriotism and valor were as pronounced and ardent as that of any of the leaders of the American Revolution.

The campaign in the South closed with the Battle of New Orleans, January 8, 1815, and whether unfortunate and unnecessary as some historians think this last conflict between the newly established Republic and the mother country may have been, it certainly divested the latter of any desire to renew hostilities, or to set up pretexts by which England might construe the terms of the Treaty of Ghent to her own advantage.

"The battle," says a contributor to the *International Encyclopedia*, "though fought after the Treaty of Ghent was signed, was full of results of the utmost importance to the young Republic." The historian Shouler has, also, observed that it was "the only battle of the war that made any impression on the European mind." It is admitted by able historians that the war in other sections had been, to a large extent, without renown and that this successful climax not only strengthened Madison's administration but weakened the Federalist party beyond hope of recovery. It cannot be disputed that the spirit exhibited by the Mississippi, Tennessee, Kentucky and Louisiana troops in the southern conflict aroused and quickened the national conscience throughout the new Republic which was, at least during the war, at a low ebb in the New England States. The operations of the War of 1812 in the lower South were conducted by troops from Tennessee, Mississippi, Kentucky and Louisiana. As an historical setting it might be well in tracing the record of the troops of the Mississippi Territory to note that General Jackson began his aggressive campaign against the British within the confines of that Territory, Mobile having been included in the annexation of 1812. The soldiery throughout this region, whether formerly Tory or patriot, had by this time become thoroughly attached to the American government. Throughout the administrations of Winthrop Sargent and W. C. C. Claiborne, the first governors of the Territory, and from the time of Aaron Burr's expedition, to the period when Governor Holmes directed the destinies of the new Territory, its military organization had been a matter of pride, and had, during Governor Holmes' administration, become a reliable and efficient defense. Statistics in the military archives of the State of Mississippi show that from its large territorial militia detachments could at any time be drawn for prompt service in the United States Army.

The older population of the Mississippi Territory was planted during the colonial period in the Natchez District near the towns of Natchez, Port Gibson, Woodville, Old Greenville, Liberty, Washington and other smaller communities, all of which were surrounded by wealthy slave-holders who represented a social life in many respects as advanced as any in the Republic. The large slave and landholders were amassing immense fortunes which attracted the attention of the outside world. Their private libraries were filled with the classics and literary clubs were the order of the day. Many of the most aristocratic families were Federalists, but later the principles of the Whig party were imbibed by a considerable number of this class. However, the political doctrines taught by Thomas Jefferson, Calhoun, and Jackson, and still later by Jefferson Davis, were destined to enthrone democracy permanently in this section. But here at the very dawn of the nineteenth century democracy, nationalism and patriotism were making their appearance and being intensified each day.

The seat of war in the campaign against the Creeks and British during the War of 1812

The eagerness of the militia to defend their country's claims and the initiative, courage and ardor displayed in the face of danger were no more due to the austerity of pioneer life, which equipped men constantly for the roughest experiences of war, than to the fact that the older Southern States had contributed a goodly share of their best blood to the population that was taking root in the Gulf region, infusing into it constantly the fervid patriotism that had characterized the Continental Army. France and Spain, too, on their several leave-takings, had contributed fragments of the illustrious soldiery of Louis XIV and Charles X to their far western empire. In this way can be explained the presence of the high-bred type which flowered in many communities of the lower South during the first decades of the nineteenth century.

In the person of General Ferdinand L. Claiborne, who appears so conspicuously in this narrative we recognize the same type that prevailed in Virginia and the Carolinas. From the *Encyclopedia of Mississippi History* have been taken the following biographical data which briefly outline his early career:

Claiborne was a native of Sussex County, Virginia, brother of William Charles Cole Claiborne, second governor of the Mississippi Territory. His military service began February 23, 1793, when he was appointed ensign in the First Sub-legion under General Anthony Wayne. He joined the army in Ohio, was promoted to lieutenant in June, 1794, took part in the famous battle on Maumee River, was assigned to the First regiment in 1796 and promoted to captain, October, 1799. He was stationed in the recruiting service in Richmond and Norfolk after the close of the war in the Northwest and subsequently returning to that region served as acting adjutant-general of the army. January 1, 1802, he resigned and removed to Natchez, where he became a merchant and married a daughter of Colonel Anthony Hutchins. He was elected to the general assembly in 1804. After the close of his brother's administration he was appointed colonel of the militia regiment of Adams County to succeed Osmun and was selected to command the detachment that marched to the support of General Wilkinson for the Sabine campaign in 1806. In the fall of 1807 Governor Williams revoked his commissions as magistrate and colonel on account of troubles between them. Governor Holmes asked the President to commission him brigadier-general of the militia of the Territory; the Legislature joined in the request in 1809 and he was so commissioned in 1811, his appointment being proclaimed by the governor, September 28. He had charge of the organization of the Mississippi militia regiment for the United States service in 1812 and served as colonel of the same, September 6, 1812, to February 23, 1813, at Baton Rouge. March 1, 1813, he was commissioned brigadier-general of volunteers in the United States service, and in that rank continued at Baton Rouge organizing a brigade of Mississippi and Louisiana volunteers until ordered to Fort Stoddart[1] where he arrived July 30, 1813, to guard the frontier against the Creeks.

---

[1] Sometimes spelled Stoddert.

With the tide that flowed from the older American colonies to the Natchez District—a name that had clung to the region from early colonial days—came another adventuring youth, young Thomas Hinds, from Berkeley County, Virginia. He came upon the scene about the time the country was designated by Congress as the Mississippi Territory in honor of the great river in whose embrace it lay many leagues to the north and south.

The new Territory had a number of small flourishing towns and, though Natchez, Vicksburg and Washington held higher rank historically, none other was of more importance than the county seat of Jefferson County, "Old Greenville," named for Henry Green, a colonial settler from Virginia. It was to this place that young Hinds came when but a youth of nineteen. As early as 1798 the place, through which the old Natchez Trail ran, had contained a popular tavern, and on American occupation soon became a thriving village. Many distinguished men in the early history of the State spent a portion of their time here, among them Joseph E. Davis, brother of Jefferson Davis, George Poindexter, Christopher Rankin and Edward Turner. Here, also, lived for a time General Andrew Jackson, who was afterwards to become the military hero of the South.[2]

Greenville was destined to remain a memorable spot in the life of General Jackson since it was near the town that he was married to

---

[2] In a summary of the early life of General Jackson many facts of which are gathered from Spark's *Memories of Fifty Years*, the *Encyclopedia of Mississippi History* states: "Andrew Jackson was one of those rare creations of nature which appear at long intervals to astonish and delight mankind. His early life was very obscure and he himself was uncertain of his birthplace though he believed it was in South Carolina. . . . . His mother, was 'a little dumpy, red-headed Irish woman.' When Andy left home to go to Tennessee she told him, 'Never tell a lie, nor take what is not your own, nor sue anybody for slander or assault and battery. Always settle them cases yourself.' . . . . Jackson was a restless and enterprising man. . . . . In business he was cautious. He was a remarkable judge of human character and rarely gave his confidence to untried men. Notwithstanding the impetuosity of his nature upon occasions he could be as cool and as calculating as a Yankee. . . . He was in the habit of trading with the low country, that is, with the inhabitants of Mississippi and Louisiana. Jackson had a store at Bruinsburgh near the mouth of bayou Pierre in the Mississippi Territory in Claiborne County. At this store, which stood immediately upon the bank of the Mississippi, there was a race track for quarter races (a sport Jackson was very fond of) and many an anecdote was rife in the neighborhood of the skill of the old hero in pitting a cock or turning a quarterhorse."

Mrs. Rachel Donelson Robards,[3] an amiable and attractive lady for whom he had formed a deep and sincere attachment while in Nashville, Tennessee. This ripened into a devotion that brought about their marriage. The marriage took place at the residence of Mr. Thomas Marston Green at whose home Mrs. Robards had often been a guest. She owned a plantation near that of Mr. Green but it is not strange that she preferred the home of her warm and cultured friends for the important event of her marriage. The happy union which lasted until Mrs. Jackson's untimely death at "The Hermitage" a short while before General Jackson's inauguration as President of the United States was the subject of numerous tender references by Parton in his *Life of General Jackson*.

The ties of friendship between the Green and Jackson families were strengthened by several intermarriages, the representatives forming a part of a social circle that observed the customs and reflected the amenities of a well-ordered society. In these homes were to be found books and all the refinements of civilization, the owners dispensing a hospitality second only to that found in the older colonial states.

But "Old Greenville" was not without its frontier element, and among the many stories that still survive of the place none is more thrilling nor was better calculated to stir the blood of the inhabitants than the one that describes a party of rough riders coming into court one morning bringing the head of Samuel Mason, the noted outlaw. And here tradition disputes the records as to the identity of the head; the reward, however, was paid for it and the country breathed more freely at the thought of its burial place across the river. As an offset to the tales of murder and rapine that crept into the early courts of the old town was the presence of Protestant churches and schools whose influence was strongly felt in the life of the

---

[3] Mrs. Andrew Jackson was Rachel Donelson, the only daugther of Colonel John Donelson, a pioneer settler of Sullivan County, Tennessee. He had removed from Virginia with his family in the year 1779 to Sullivan County near Long Island, at present Kingsport. The Donelsons were among the most prominent people in the early history of this county. Colonel John Donelson, the father of Rachel, was influential in negotiating Indian treaties, having been associated with General Joseph Martin and Colonel Isaac Shelby in shaping the treaty at Long Island July 9, 1783. Many daring exploits are narrated of him in his expedition to the Cumberland Settlements. Two of the brothers of Thomas Marston Green married nieces of Mrs. Jackson. The Green family, distinguished in Virginia, came to the Mississippi Territory when it was a colonial possession of Spain.

people, engendering a deep piety markedly noticeable in succeeding generations. Here, too, sprang into existence the famous Jefferson Troop of Horse, a military organization composed of the flower of the community in whose blood still coursed a strain of the cavaliers of King Charles. It was into this environment that young Hinds of Virginia had cast his lot, and like all youth he was influenced and molded by the life around him.

The call to military life was very strong in many localities throughout the confederation of States at that period; everywhere young men were anxious for military preferment and it was not long before Thomas Hinds became first lieutenant of the Jefferson Troop of Horse. He is described as a youth of prepossessing appearance, with dark, flashing eyes, slender, graceful figure and good address, coupled with a certain mastery of speech and confidence of manner that arose not only from temperament but from his having been acquainted with the best social customs of an older civilization. He soon became very popular in the new community, and the fact that after only a few years residence in the place he won the heart and hand of the daughter of Thomas M. Green[4] is proof of his having become a social favorite. In addition he was what was termed one of the "rising" young men of the new Territory. In 1806 he was happily married to Miss Malinda Green. His marriage strengthened the already warm attachment between himself and General Jackson, with whom he was in after years to come in close contact in some of the most thrilling episodes of the history of the State and of the country. His connection with this influential family also opened up many opportunities for position in the civil service, and he was not without a due appeciation of such honors. A few years after his marriage he was made a member of the General Council and in 1811 was appointed Chief Justice of the Orphans' Court. His association with Andrew Jackson during his early years at "Old.Greenville" had influenced him deeply, and it was not long before his young wife and her family discovered that he was enamoured of Jackson's profession, that of soldiering, to the exclusion of all others. He continued captain of the Jefferson Troop until promoted to higher honors on the field of battle.

---

[4] The descendants of Thómas Marston Green still reside in their ancestral home at Church Hill in Jefferson County.

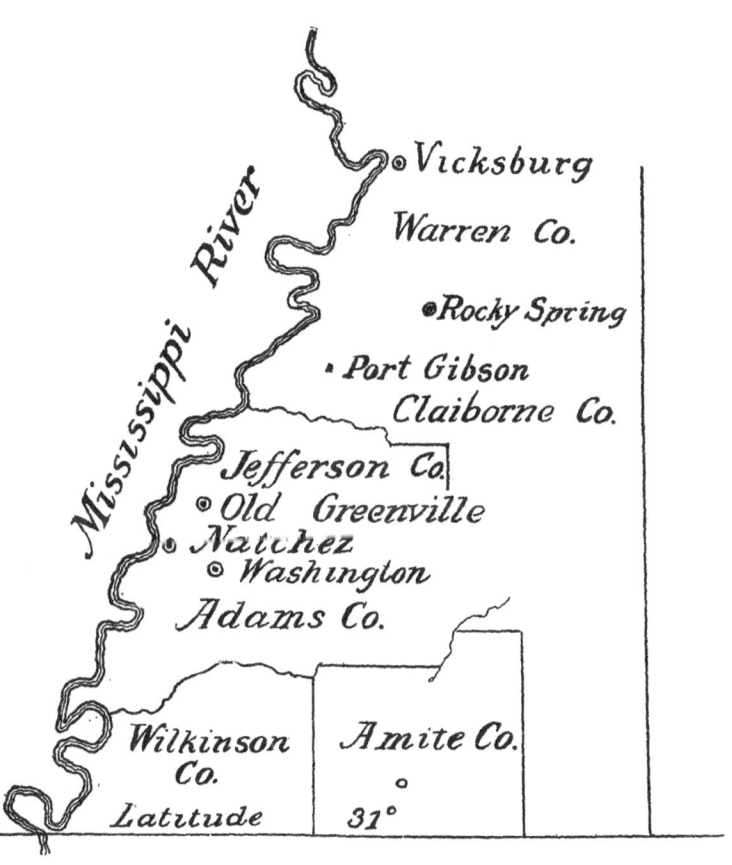

Early map of the western portion of the Mississippi Territory showing the river counties and towns.

It was now that the Mississippi Territory was to have a share in the national struggle for complete independence of English control and interference. The Mississippians began the struggle at their own doors. The British, through the great Shawnee chieftain Tecumseh, incited the Creeks to make war upon neighboring Americans, and thus began what is known as the Creek Indian War, recognized by historians as one of the most most moving chapters of the War of 1812. As a goad and spur to the Coast Campaign under Jackson against the British it was of the utmost importance.

It was not with Jackson, however, but with General Claiborne, commander of the Territorial Army of Mississippi, that young Thomas Hinds saw his first military service—with his cavalry at Natchitoches and later in opposing the advance of Aaron Burr into the Territory. Connected by marriage with the Claibornes both the General and his brother, W. C. C. Claiborne, had watched with keen interest the career of the young soldier. After Mississippi had given the latter to Louisiana as its first American govenor he continued to follow with enthusiasm the career of the Mississippi cavalryman through the War of 1812 which ended in the South with the battle of New Orleans as a brilliant climax.

Leading up then to hostilities on the Southern Coast, the Creek Indians waged a bitter and blood-thirsty war against the Mississippi Territory. Especially were they unrelenting after they discovered that it was a war for self-preservation and the possession of their native lands. Their various feats of daring and self-sacrifice in behalf of their homes and country compare favorably with the qualities that characterized the white combatants opposing them. Cruelty to their victims, however, including even women and children, places them in the lowest scale of civilization.

The history of the Creek War not only gives a part of the story of the war in the South but also reveals the strength and position of the military organizations of the Mississippi Territory when its troops were needed for further service along the Coast. Historians have treated very slovenly the part taken by the Territory in Jackson's Coast Campaign against the British, Parton in his *Life of Andrew Jackson* being so inexcusably inaccurate as to confuse General Ferdinand L. Clairborne with Governor W. C. C. Claiborne of Louisiana. From his pages one would suppose that the headquarters of the military operations of the Creek War and of the entire Coast Campaign was in New Orleans. Though Governor Claiborne was keenly alive to the situation the facts are, that, up to the time that New Orleans became the object of attack, the Mississippi Territory was, with the exception of the expedition in forcing the British out of Pensacola, the scene of action, and it was on Governor Holmes that the weight of responsibility fell more heavily than it did on any governor in the lower South.

It was thoroughly recognized by the people of the American Republic that at the inception of hostilities between their nation and Great Britain in 1812 it was the latter's policy to attach to its standards the various Indian tribes throughout the country extending into the far Southwest.[5] Among the Creek branch of the great Muscogee tribe of Indians which was the most potential in the Southern section of the country the United States agent of Indian affairs, Colonel Benjamin Hawkins, had kept peace in a tolerable fashion at least for many years, but while he was very popular with the Creeks, personally, they were rebellious and defiant at times in their attitude toward the white settlers of the country. Every concession granted in the way of transportation privileges, especially the great wagon route—though consented to—through the midst of their country, rendered them more dissatisfied each day. The constant stream of emigrants passing through their lands daily over the old Federal road out into the inviting hills and vales of the Mississippi Territory that reached from the Mississippi River on the west to the Alabama streams that watered the western borders of Florida, alarmed and filled them with apprehension as to their future. The fate of the Natchez to the west of them, too, seemed to forecast a day when the pale face would over-run and take possession of their country.

The English welcomed the growing dissatisfaction of the Creeks, recognizing in them a useful ally, and lost no opportunity of warning them through various emissaries of the danger that would arise from the growing population that made up the Tombigbee, Alabama

---

[5] In *The British Campaigns at Washington and New Orleans* by *Subaltern* the author says: "It is well known that at the period to which my narrative refers an alliance offensive and defensive subsisted between the government of Great Britain and the heads of as many Indian nations or tribes as felt the aggressions of the settlers upon their ancient territories and were disposed to resent them."

and Tensas settlements of the Mississippi Territory. In the person of the famous Tecumseh,[6] a savage of most unusual type, they had found an ally who needed no urging. Born about 1775 in the Miami Valley in the ancient abode of his tribe, whither his parents had returned after a sojourn among their kindred in the beautiful Tallapoosa country, he was a pure product of his race at its best. Endowed by nature with manly instincts and possessing the noble virtues of patriotism, love of race and country, and the recipient of the gentler Moravian theology, he was, notwithstanding, a savage still. Always an ally of the British, it was with the hope, one can easily believe, of using that power to assist him in his larger and more worthy purpose of regaining the ancient possessions of his race that he labored so enthusiastically. His scheme of uniting all the western tribes in a great Confederacy bore no fruit, but was ever in his heart and colored his thoughts in death.

The Choctaw branch of the Muscogees, which had for its most dominant ruler the celebrated medal chieftain Pushmataha was known to be friendly to the Americans and was more dependable than

---

[6] The name Tecumseh is thought by some students to mean "meteor," by others "flying panther." It was sometimes spelled Tecumtha. The *Encyclopedia Britannica* gives the following short biography of the famous chieftain: American Shawnee chief, was probably born in the old Shawnee village of Piqua, near the site of Springfield, Ohio, between 1768 and 1780. While still a youth he took part in attacks on settlers passing down the Ohio and in widely extended hunting expeditions or predatory forays to the west and south; and he served in the Indian wars preceding the Treaty of Greenville in 1795. About 1800 his eloquence and self-control made him a leader in conferences between the Indians and whites. After 1805 the Indians of the North-West became aroused by a series of treaties calling for new cessions of their territory and by the prospect of war between Great Britain and the United States. This presented to Tecumseh and his brother Tenskwatawa (i. e., the Open Door), popularly called "the Prophet," the opportunity to put into operation a scheme which followed the ambitious dream of Pontiac. With some scattered Shawnee clans as a nucleus, the brothers proceeded to organize, first near Greenville, Ohio, and later on the White and Tippecanoe Rivers in Indiana, "the Prophet's town," which was based on a sort of communism and was apparently devoted to peace, industry and sobriety, but their actual plan was to combine all of the Indians from Canada to Florida in a great democratic confederacy to resist the encroachment of the whites. Tribal organizations were to be disregarded, but all warriors were to be represented at periodical assemblages where matters of interest to all Indians were to be definitely decided. The twofold influence that was to dominate this league was the eloquence and political ingenuity of Tecumseh and the superstitious reverence aroused by "the Prophet." This programme alarmed the whites along the north-western border. In the course of the next three years Governor William Henry Harrison of Indiana held interviews with each of the brothers, and during one of these, at Vincennes in 1810, the respective leaders narrowly avoided a hostile encounter.

the Chickasaws, who had more than once, since their fierce and victorious encounters with Bienville, shown a tendency at times to repel the advances of the Europeans. Between these tribes, however, there was a bond of sympathy; they spoke the same language and were often allies in war, while neither regarded the Creek with admiration nor confidence and lived in continual fear of his fierce wrath. The Chickasaws, influenced by the growing friendship for the white race so perceptible on the part of the Choctaws, and the powerful Colbert family of half-breeds in their own midst, remained at peace with the Mississippi Territory.

It was the impetuous and warlike Creeks boasting a Confederacy of their own, an alliance that dated back for many years and having for its burning purpose self-protection and perpetuation as a race, who were now to make war for their rights and liberties as they took them to be. Alas! that unfair methods should have attended a noble purpose!

The Spanish[7] in possession of Pensacola through the victory of Don Bernardo de Galvez were for the time in sympathy with the British

---

Nevertheless "the Prophet" and Tecumseh reiterated their determination to remain at peace with the United States if the Indians were unmolested in their territory, and if all cessions beyond the Ohio were given up by the whites. The treaty of Fort Wayne in 1809, which called for the cession to the whites of some three million acres of land in central Indiana, was a direct challenge to this programme, and when, during Tecumseh's absence in the South, Harrison made a hostile move against "the Prophet's" town, the latter ventured to meet him, but was defeated on the 17th of November, 1811, in the famous battle of Tippecanoe, which broke the personal influence of "the Prophet" and largely destroyed the confederacy built up by Tecumseh. Tecumseh still professed to be friendly toward the United States, probably because his British advisers were not ready to open hostilities, but a series of border outrages indicated that the fatal moment could not long be postponed. When in June, 1812, war broke out Tecumseh joined the British, was commissioned a brigadier-general in the British army, and participated in the skirmishes which preceded General William Hull's surrender at Detroit. He took an active part in the sieges of Fort Meigs, where he displayed his usual clemency toward his prisoners. After the battle of Put-in-Bay, when Colonel Henry Proctor began to retreat from Malden, Tecumseh bitterly reproached him for his cowardice and finally forced him to join battle with Harrison on the Thames River on the 5th of October, 1813. In this battle Tecumseh was killed, as traditionally reported, by Colonel Richard M. Johnson of Kentucky, although this has never been fully substantiated. Like Pontiac, whom he doubtless imitated consciously, he had a wonderful eloquence and a power of organization rare among the Indians. His brother, "the Prophet," remained with a small band of Shawnees and died west of the Mississippi in 1834."

[7] The rumor that a Spanish naval force was with the British fleet proved to be false, yet from every indication it is clear that but for internal troubles Ferdinand VII would have materially aided the British in their invasion of the Southern Coast of the American Republic.

and were continually seeking to arouse the martial spirit of the Creeks, urging them to make war on the white settlers along the Tombigbee in the Mississippi Territory. These did their full share in strengthening the new Creek Confederacy. The eagerness of the people of Georgia, too, to see the compact entered into between that State and the United States in 1802 to extinguish the Indian title to certain lands was not lost on the Indians and this with other grievances cited had caused a restlessness and dissatisfaction among them that readily deepened into a fixed resentment under the spell of Tecumseh's fiery and eloquent appeals. Much magnetism and learning have been ascribed to this celebrated chieftain as an orator. Not only was he physically a splendid specimen of his race, but historians also agree that he was "masterful in manner, eloquent in speech and learned in the lore of treaties."

While the warriors of many tribes to the north were already in possession of his plans, Tecumseh, who had recently visited the tribes west of the Mississippi and on Lakes Superior, Huron and Erie, inciting them to hostilities against the whites by appeals both of religion and of personal gain, came south in the summer of 1811 with a view of attaching the southern tribes to the "Prophet's" army. His task, though a delicate one of much diplomacy and intrigue, was not in vain. Alexander McGillivray,[8] the noted half-breed, sometimes styled the "Emperor of the Creeks," in whose veins ran the blood of the best races of Europe, might have proved a match for Tecumseh in advising against the war, but the mighty barterer and tradesman and what could be considered a diplomat and scholar among savages was dead, and there was none other strong enough to effect peace.

One obstacle loomed high in the pathway of the ardent Tecumseh —the powerful Choctaws were still in open sympathy with the Americans and no Confederacy formed in the South would be safe or lead to victory without their aid. At the intertribal councils neither the prophets' incantations nor the inducement of personal gain could

---

[8] Alexander McGillivray, perhaps the most remarkable half-breed Indian of America, was the son of Lachlan McGillivray who came from Scotland when a youth of sixteen, tradition says from a titled home. He came first to the Carolinas and joined the Indian traders in 1735. Later he met the beautiful young Princess Sehoy in the Creek Nation and was married to her about 1738. Princess Sehoy was the daughter of Captain Marchand, a French officer who at one time commanded Fort Toulouse on the Coosa River. The mother of Sehoy was a Creek of the "Clan of the Wind."

affect the imperturbable Pushmataha and his loyal assistants, Moshulitubee and Houma Mingo. To all appeals there was but one answer, that "never in their history had a Choctaw shed the blood of a white man in war." The attitude of the Choctaws meant much to the American cause and while for the first months there was occasional alarm, amounting at one time to a panic, in the main security throughout the war was felt even along the borders of the Mississippi Territory. The following interesting account of Tecumseh's visit to the Creek Nation, which the author places in the autumn of 1812, is taken from Harper's *Encyclopedia of United States History:*

He addressed the assembled Creeks for the first time in the lower part of what is now Autauga County, Alabama, late in October. Soon afterwards, having addressed the Creeks at different points, he approached a great council called by Colonel Hawkins, United States Indian agent, at Toockabatcha, the ancient Creek capital, where fully 5000 of the nation were gathered. Tecumseh marched with dignity into the square with his train of thirty followers, entirely naked, excepting their flaps and ornaments, their faces painted black, their heads adorned with eagle's feathers, while buffalo tails dragged behind, suspended by bands around their waists. Like appendages were attached to their arms, and their whole appearance was as hideous as possible, and their bearing uncommonly pompous and ceremonious. They marched round and round in the square, and then, approaching the Creek chiefs, gave them the Indian salutation of a handshake at arm's-length and exchanged tobacco in token of friendship. So they made their appearance each day until Hawkins departed.

That night a council was held in the great round-house. It was packed with eager listeners. Tecumseh made a fiery and vengeful speech, exhorting the Creeks to abandon the customs of the pale-face and return to those of their fathers: to cast away the plough and loom and cease the cultivation of the soil, for it was an unworthy pursuit for noble hunters and warriors. He warned them that the Americans were seeking to exterminate them and possess their country; and told them that their friends, the British, had sent him from the Great Lakes to invite them to the war-path. The wily Prophet, who had been told by the British when a comet would appear, told the excited multitude that they would see the arm of Tecumseh, like pale fire, stretched out in the vault of heaven at a certain time, and thus they would know by that sign when to begin the war. The people looked upon him with awe, for the fame of Tecumseh and the Prophet had preceded them. Tecumseh continued his mission with success, but found opponents here and there. Among the most conspicuous of them was Tustinuggee-Thlucco, the "Big Warrior." Tecumseh tried every art to convert him to his purpose. At length he said, angrily: "Tustinuggee-Thlucco, your blood is white. You have taken my Redsticks and my talk, but you do not mean to fight. I know the reason; you do not believe the Great Spirit has sent me. You shall believe it. I will leave directly and go straight to Detroit. When I get there, I will stamp my foot upon the ground and shake down every house in Toockabatcha."

Strangely enough, at about the time Tecumseh must have arrived in Detroit, there was heard a deep rumbling underground all over the Alabama region, and there was a heaving of the earth that made the houses of Toockabatcha reel and totter as if about to fall. The startled savages ran out, exclaiming: "Tecumseh is at Detroit! Tecumseh is at Detroit! We feel the stamp of his foot!" It was the shock of an earthquake that was felt all over the Gulf region in December, 1812. At the same time the comet—the blazing arm of Tecumseh—appeared in the sky. These events made a powerful impression on nearly the whole Creek nation, but it did not move the "Big Warrior" from his allegiance to the United States.

Though bitterly disappointed in his failure to attach the Choctaws and the Peace Party of the Creek Nation to his cause, the untiring Tecumseh, tall, dignified and graceful, arrayed in royal robes and flaunting his regal head-dress with its significant red plume, continued in the Creek country and pursued his aims, accomplishing in a large degree his purpose just as he had done at Vincennes on the Wabash and in the Detroit country. Each day the war spirit of this fierce Muscogee tribe grew until it finally yielded to the advocate's subtle spell who, in sowing the seeds of war along the Tallapoosa with the hope of benefiting his own race, was willing enough for some of the harvest of the Red Flower to go to his English friends.

Allowing that it was the sudden flaming up of patriotic fires half a century old, it was British gold, also, that now played a part in kindling strife between the American and Indian, and the Creek whose ancestors' ferocity had struck terror to many a frontier hearthstone proved that he still needed no military training in the various diabolical forms of savage warfare.

It is thought by some historians, viz.: Lossing, Drake and Parton, that Tecumseh paid a second visit to the Gulf tribes at which time he had with him his brother, the "Prophet." Many conflicting statements of local authorities and students have furnished material for investigators and historians concerning this visit south and, while a number of authors agree on some points, none seem able to determine with any degree of certainty how often he came among the Creek Indians. Halbert, one of the latest and best interpreters of Indian life among the southern tribes, leans, I think erroneously, to Beckwith's opinion that he came only once, in 1811. Ramsey, Pickett and Moore have taken the position that he paid a second visit. J. F. H. Claiborne, too, is an ardent supporter not only of a second visit but of an express purpose on the part of Tecumseh to enlist them for the British, even to the extreme point of resenting any other opinion of the matter, attributing the tardiness of the militia of the Mississippi Territory in attacking the Indians as a part of the British forces to the attitude taken by Colonel Benjamin Hawkins, agent of

Indian affairs.[9] However, this author was destined in later years to become a subject for much satire by the painstaking if prosaic investigator, Halbert, who not only found in the accomplished historian's "rich flowers of speech" a source of amusement, but becomes downright impatient with many of his statements especially doubting his translation of Tecumseh's speech and even going so far as to say that it not only rested on no authority but did not reflect credit on the famous Indian orator and statesman. But giving Halbert due credit for having studied his subject minutely, one cannot forget that Pickett agreed with J. F. H. Claiborne in his estimate of Colonel Hawkins' attitude. Still, it must be admitted that the Alabama historian generally used with great care and caution his original record sources, nearly all of which were furnished him by Claiborne.

The object of Tecumseh's visit is a more important matter and it is logical to believe that since the Indians were federating everywhere in the north and joining the "Prophet's" army with a view of aiding the British this was the counsel, if not the dictation, of the able Tecumseh to the southern tribes, especially to the Creeks, who were more sympathetic with his scheme and purpose than any other of the Muscogee family.

In vain, then, did Colonel Hawkins strive to keep the peace between the Mississippi Territory and the Creek Indians; but even in the lower country where his influence was stronger with them than in the upper portion he failed, nor did he hesitate to lay on the whites the major part of the blame for the sudden participation in the war.

The Creek country, including the upper and lower divisions, reached from the Oconee River in Georgia to the Alabama River. It was an attractive well-watered region and with a population of 10,000 had established fifty-two towns. It was well supplied with warriors familiar with the use of firearms and *en masse* highly skilled in all native methods of warfare. The people of the Territory, especially those of the Tombigbee, Mobile and Alabama settlements, were never wholly at ease in the thought of having them as such close neighbors.

Here it would be well to give the reader some specific knowledge

---

[9] Benjamin Hawkins was born in Bute County, North Carolina (which was changed to Warren County in 1779), on August 15, 1754, and died at his residence in the Creek Nation, in the exercise of his functions as Superintendent of Indian Affairs, on June 6, 1816. For an extended sketch of Colonel Hawkins see Wheeler's *History of North Carolina*, pp. 426–432.

of the military situation in the Mississippi Territory during the year 1812. The following summary from the *Encyclopedia of Mississippi History*, with such editing as is necessary, will give the reader an insight into affairs in the Territory from a local standpoint.

Governor David Holmes, at the town of Washington,[10] then the seat of government of the Mississippi Territory which included what is now Alabama as well as the present state of Mississippi, received on Sunday, June 20, 1812, letters from the Tombigbee region assuring him that part of the Creek Nation of Indians was determined on war. These letters were from Colonel James Caller, Colonel Joseph Carson and Major John McGrew, officers of the Territorial militia. They were dated June 14, and had come to the Governor by express, the horseman charged to travel with the greatest possible speed. The route lay through the Choctaw Nation whose attitude in case of war was then open to doubt. This doubt, however, was later dispelled by the attitude of their leading chieftain, Pushmataha.

Governor Holmes had, also, to consider at this time the organization of the Spanish coast country between the Pearl River and Perdido, annexed to his territory by Act of Congress, also the revolution in and about San Antonio in which some Mississippians were actors, and above all the danger of war with Great Britain. He had, before the addition of the Mobile strip, a military organization representing thirteen regiments of militia. In the Tombigbee-Alabama settlements, threatened by the Creeks, Colonel James Caller was the commanding officer of militia. At Fort Stoddart in the same region there was a detachment of United States troops under Major John Bowyer, and Cantonment Washington was the headquarters of Colonel Leonard Covington whose advice the Governor immediately asked.[11] The action taken by Holmes and Covington, which began the participation of Mississippi in the war of 1812, was to request Major Bowyer to send out a full company of regulars to an advanced point on the frontier. Another dispatch to Colonel Caller instructed him to send a party of mounted militia with

---

[10] Natchez was the first capital of the Mississippi Territory. During W. C. C. Claiborne's administration the capital was moved by act of the Legislature, February 1, 1802, to the little town of Washington, six miles east, where it remained until 1820.

[11] Covington, Leonard, native of Maryland; entered the United States army in 1792, in the light dragoons; was promoted rapidly to lieutenant and captain; had a horse shot under him at Fort Recovery, Ohio, and was distinguished for gallantry at the battle of the Maumee, 1794. Resigning in 1795, he returned to Maryland, and was elected to congress from the St. George district. He returned to the service when there was danger of war with England in 1809, as colonel of light dragoons, and was for a time stationed in Mississippi Territory, where Governor Holmes called him in consultation at the beginning of the Creek war. He was promoted to brigadier-general August 1, 1813, and called to the Canadian frontier, where he participated in the unfortunate campaign of General Wilkinson, and was mortally wounded in the battle of Chrysler's field, November 11, 1813, dying three days later. He was riding a white charger, cheering his men to attack the British intrenchments, when he fell. At that time his wife and six children were making their home with Alexander Covington near the town of Washington, where they continued to reside. Levin, a son of General Covington, became judge of probate of Adams County; a daughter married the well known geologist and author, B. L. C. Wailes. Alexander Covington, a brother of the general, was a native of Prince George's, Virginia, resided in Mississippi forty years, was a man of great intelligence and social powers, served as county judge many years, and died at Warren City, October 16, 1848, aged 71 years.

the regulars, also to detail from the 6th, 8th, 9th and 12th regiments of militia, one major, six captains, six lieutenants, six ensigns, 360 privates, with the competent number of noncommissioned officers "to be held in readiness to march at the shortest notice." This detachment was intended to unite and act with the regular troops in case the Indians should enter the country in considerable force with hostile intentions. The militia were generally unarmed. Colonel Caller was directed to obtain 200 stands of arms from Major Bowyer. The rendezvous of the militia was to be at Fort St. Stephens. It does not appear, however, that this battalion as a whole was called into the field at this period. The Creeks were yet under the control of the peace party; the murderers of white settlers had been punished and quiet restored for a year on that frontier.

The express from James Monroe, Secretary of State, announcing the declaration of war with Great Britain, was addressed to Governor Holmes on June 19, 1812, and received by the Governor by way of Cantonment St. Tammany, July 11, 1812.

On July 14 the Governor issued his general orders announcing the declaration of war and as commander-in-chief making such disposition of the militia of the Territory as he deemed best calculated to protect the citizens thereof and to maintain order and make war upon the enemy with all the effect that the Territory's forces and ability would permit. The confidence with which he relied on the spirit of nationalism among the Mississippi militia is apparent throughout his orders and messages. That portion of his communication to the legislature on November 3, dealing directly with the war, is quoted here in full:

The weighty and important duties that have devolved upon the executive branch of our local government in consequence of the eventful and momentous crisis that has occurred in the national concerns of our country, render the meeting of the legislature at this time peculiarly gratifying to me and highly interesting to your constituents.

The people of the United States from their situation, from the nature of their political institutions which have solely in view the liberty and happiness of the citizens, and from the strictly neutral and impartial course pursued towards the belligerents of Europe by their government, might in justice have expected to remain undisturbed by the contending powers. But truth and justice are not the attributes of governments founded upon tyranny or supported by corruption. Pride, avarice, and an insatiable ambition ever prompt them to extend their baneful influence and effects, unrestrained by the rights of others, and regardless of the happiness of those they profess to protect.

No nation ever endeavored with more sincerity than the United States to avoid the war in which she is now engaged. The aggressions, insults and outrages upon our lawful commerce and rights of sovereignty, were borne with until longer forbearance would have constituted the crime of submission. No efforts on the part of our government could divert Great Britain from her determined purpose of attempting to crush American commerce, and if possible American independence. Propositions which could have been accepted by her without in the least degree wounding her national pride, but evidently calculated to promote her best interests, were rejected upon pretenses too palpably erroneous for any one to believe that they were advanced with sincerity. Her disposition to depredate and insult seemed to increase with every effort on our part for amicable adjustment. The American government became sensible that the honor and rights of the nation demanded that expostulation, remonstrance, and all other measures short of actual war should cease, that the alternative of an honorable resistance or a base surrender of incontrovertible rights was placed before them. To have doubted as to the correct course under such convictions would have been dishonorable to themselves and disgraceful to their constituents. War, therefore, was resorted to as the only measure that could be taken to rescue the nation from abject degradation. This important change in our national affairs made it the duty of the Chief Executive of the Territory to take such measures for the defences of the country, and to aid in the war against the enemy, as his powers and the existing laws would authorize. Under this impression I issued an order on the 14th of July last directing a portion of the militia to be held in readiness for immediate service. At that time it was uncertain when this force would be required, but I considered that some preparatory measures were called for by the existing state of public affairs. On the sixth of September in pursuance of a requisition made by the authority of the general government, an additional number was directed to be selected for actual service, and the whole of the force detailed from the regiments west of Pearl River amounting to about seven hundred were ordered to rendezvous at Cantonment Washington. It is with much satisfaction, I assure you, Gentlemen, that on this occasion the militia of the Territory from every quarter evinced a degree of patriotism and determination to support the rights of their Country highly honorable to them as citizens and as soldiers.

In this spirit the first detachment of Mississippi militia in the service of the United States was placed in readiness.

In his orders the Governor called for details from militia regiments as follows: From the 1st Regiment (Amite County), one company; from the 2d Regiment (Wilkinson County), one company; from the 3d Regiment (Adams County), three companies, including the volunteer companies of Captains Becket and Painboeuff; from the 7th Regiment (Baldwin County), one company; from the 4th, 5th, 10th, 11th and 13th Regiments (Jefferson, Claiborne, Warren, Franklin, Marion Counties), each parts of a company. The previous orders to the 6th, 8th, 9th and 12th Regiments (Washington, Baldwin, Wayne and Greene) exempted those counties from this detail. In addition to these details the cavalry troops were to be in readiness to take the field whenever ordered.

Ferdinand L. Claiborne, recently appointed brigadier-general of militia, was entrusted with the execution of the order and General Wilkinson, in command of the United States Military Department, was asked to supply the necessary equipment. General Claiborne reported August 18, 1812: "It will be particularly gratifying to your excellency to be informed that the requisition has been filled principally by voluntary enrolment." The arms, ammunition and camp equipage were delivered at Natchez landing by steamboat, September 19, 1812, and a little later in that month about 600 men were in camp at Cantonment Washington. A further detail of 300 was then called for. On November 3, the regiment began its march to Baton Rouge with General Claiborne in command with the rank of colonel. Captain A. H. Holmes, brother of the Governor, was inspector of the regiment during its organization. The period of service for this command, which was known as "the detachment of Mississippi militia in the service of the United States," was six months. The legislature that winter by resolution acknowledged and praised the response to the public call. When the term of service was near expiration the greater part of this command re-enlisted in the regiment to be mentioned later.

Another organization under the orders of the Governor in the year 1812 was a battalion in the Mobile region under Colonel Joseph Carson. At Natchez a volunteer company was formed by men legally exempt from military duty, which the Governor assigned to patrol duty.

Though to all appearances secure in the military defense of the State and even more in the long peace that had been maintained, the people of the Mississippi Territory, the pioneer settlements along the Tombigbee and Alabama especially, were not without some apprehension that trouble could be expected from the Creeks any day.[12] The "Prophet's" army, urged and assisted by the ardent Tecumseh, had for the past year been actively engaged in hostilities with many

---

[12] As far back as both French and Spanish possession sparse settlements had been established along these rivers. To this hiding-place Tories and loyalists came in great numbers and lived amicably with the wealthy and influential natives and half-breeds. No civil form of government existed among them; all taking their chance as thoughtlessly as the birds in a fanciful Elysium where neither priest nor king prescribed. With the coming of the Americans these settlements increased rapidly, and at the period of this history numbered about 2000 with as many slaves. The people in their manners and mode of life, though now governed by the laws of the Territory, were unlike those of the high-bred communities of the older counties near Natchez and along the Mississippi. The spirit of nationalism, however, was very strong among them, even the Tory by this time having become loyal to the young Republic. Border contact with the Indians had established in many instances close social relations between the two races and intermarriage occurred frequently, especially between prominent American settlers and the aristocratic descendants of Lachlan McGillivray, the later being thought eligible for any social distinction desired. "To this circle belonged," says Pickett, "the Taits, Weatherfords, Durants, the proud Linders and the Mims."

warriors in aiding the British, and by midsummer of 1813 war-clouds, too distinct to be mistaken, had gathered in the Southern country.[13] Tecumseh had fallen in battle, but his counsel was treasured deep in the hearts of the Creeks, and with them war had become an obsession. The historian, Anderson, attributes the suddenness of its approach to the unfortunate execution of three Indians by the whites for the murder of a converted Indian boy. Other local incidents have, with a great deal of gravity, been made to appear as the sparks that started the flame, reminding one of the part that the question of slavery played in our Civil War, which, with compromise failing, was inevitable sooner or later in defense of Constitutional liberty.

---

[13] The following letter from Judge Toulmin at Fort Stoddard to General F. L. Claiborne reflects the state of affairs among the Creeks during the month of July, 1813:

"You have done me the honour to request my opinion relative to the hostile disposition of the Creek Indians.

"My own apprehensions on this subject have grown out of transient circumstances as they have occurred, but are not founded on what would be deemed legal evidence.

"I may safely say that I am sufficiently satisfied—but as I would not express opinions which may influence on so important an occasion the conduct of others without bringing into view the grounds and reasons of those opinions—I will endeavour to trace back the impressions which have been made upon my own mind and will lay before you the result.

"1. I think it is about two months since Col. Hawkins informed me that he anticipated civil war among the Creeks—which was notoriously originating in a good degree in the vigorous measures taken by the heads of the nation to punish those of their tribe who had made war on the people of the United States.

"Where the cause of the white people was the primary source of domestic disturbance in the nation, it was reasonable to suppose that the interest and safety of white people would be materially involved in the progress and issue of those disturbances. Col. Hawkins accordingly soon after sent his family from the nation and has since removed himself.

"2. A few weeks after this Gen. Wilkinson was about to pass through the nation but found the prospect of disturbances so alarming that he halted for a guard. As soon as he had an opportunity, he made himself acquainted with the spirit prevailing in the Indian nation and satisfied that the hostilities were intended, he sent an express back to me with a letter on the subject—a copy or the substance of which I immediately did myself the honour to transmit to you, to Genl. Flournoy, to Govr. Holmes and to Col. Bowyer. This letter evinced his conviction that we were on the eve of an Indian war and that immediate measures of defense ought to be adopted.

"3. Mr. Saml. Manae, a half breed, well known to all persons conversant with the Creek nation, whose veracity I have never heard impeached and who has certainly as much at stake as any man in the country, assured me that he had had a conversation with High Head, one of the chiefs who has lately been at Pensacola and who was then on his way—in which High Head acknowledged to him that their object was to make war on the American people, that they had no animosity against the half-breeds, but wished to have them as partners in the general scheme, and that as to going to war with their own people they had no

Passing on from the first signs of hostilities between the whites and Indians, it is evident from much of the record sources of that period that there was in the spring of 1813 a definite war-party formed among the Creeks, and that their old Confederacy had been revived and strengthened. By July 25 the noted half-breed chieftain, William Weatherford, was an acknowledged member of the party. He was of the famous McGillivray clan and a sympathizer of the Creeks. His Indian name, though he was more often called "the Red Eagle," was Hoponika Futsahia, which Woodward interprets as Truth Maker. It is said by partial biographers that he counselled against war and

---

idea of the kind but merely wished to put about eight chiefs out of the way, who had signalized themselves by their anxiety to preserve peace with the whites.

"4. The letter from the Choctaw chief, Mushshulatubbe to Mr. Geo. Gaines fully corresponds with the account given by Mr. Manae. He had sent messengers into the Creek nation who had clearly ascertained their hostile disposition towards the people of the United States and had seen them dancing the war-dance, a national ceremony preparatory to warlike operations. No suggestions existed that their hostilities were intended against other Indians. They avowed that they were to be against us:—and some few restless, misguided Choctaws had unhappily imbibed the spirit of the Muscogees.

"5. It is a fact concerning which, I believe, there is no doubt that some of the Creeks have participated in the northern warfare from the time of its commencement. They have committed murthers on our peaceable citizens in their passage to and from the north. Some of them and particularly the Little Warrior have been put to death since their return. Their friends, their confederates and their relatives survive. These are the men who have organized the present confederacy and overthrown the legitimate government of the Creek nation. They are well known to the British and have been patronized by them. The Little Warrior was furnished with a letter from a British General to the Governor of Pensacola containing as *they* say a requisition for arms and ammunition, and as *he* says, merely an introduction and recommendation of them to his notice. On the strength of this, however, they applied for ammunition and have obtained it. Whilst in Pensacola, they avowed their intention of making war on the American people:— they danced the war-dance:—they told the Governor that 19 towns had joined them, and that in those towns there were 4800 men.

"6. A party of the Indians going to Pensacola attacked the post rider and robbed him of his mail. They shot at him and killed his horse. They carried the mail to Pensacola and said that they had killed the post rider. They refused to give it up, when the governor informed them that he would send it to Mobile.

"7. There is a general impression that hostilities are meditated against the United States. No one travels thro' the Creek Nation. All intercourse between this country and Georgia has ceased. The carrying of the mail is completely suspended.

"8. The general commotion through the Creek nation is a matter of notoriety. Their plantations are, in a great degree, neglected and uncultivated:—and the houses of all who resided near the road are abandoned. This state of things seems a prelude to war.

"I believe that all the circumstances which I have stated can be established on oath:—and under this belief—I submit it to you, Sir, whether I am not warranted in the opinion that war exists between a part of the Creek nation and the people of the United States."

for some time held aloof. Many other notable half-breeds, as in the instance of Moniac, refused to take the "black drink."[14] The mixture nevertheless, was brewed and none, be he ever so far removed in blood, dared at the risk of his life to decline to partake of it. War then on the part of the Creeks for the extermination of the Americans was fully determined on. The Almibamos in the upper district especially were fierce in their attitude, these having been for some time bitterly resentful of the encroachments on their hunting grounds. The deposition of Samuel Moniac taken by Judge Harry Toulmin, though not considered seriously by some historians, on account of the half-breed's open disapproval of Tecumseh, indicates a well formed plan to attack from the Tensas to the Southern Coast. The struggle among the Indians everywhere to regain their lost territory in North America was soon to begin in earnest in the South.[15]

---

[14] This drink was a kind of tea made of the leaves of the Ilex Cassine or holly of the Gulf States. After a visit to the country in 1777, William Bartram, in his description of the Creek rotunda, which was erected upon an artificial mound, gives an elaborate account of the ceremonies in the rotunda connected with partaking of the "black drink." He states that the chief first puffed a few whiffs from the sacred pipe, blowing the whiffs ceremoniously upward towards the sun, or, as it was generally supposed, to the Great Spirit, and then puffing the smoke from the pipe towards the four cardinal points. The pipe was then carried to different persons and smoked in a similar manner by them in turn, after which the drink was solemnly presented to each warrior present.

[15] The condition of affairs just prior to the encounter of Burnt Corn Spring is reflected in the following letter from Captain J. L. Kennedy, addressed from McIntosh Bluff, July 24, 1813, to General Claiborne:
"I arrived at this place on the 21s of this instant from *Mobile Point*, & the first time I have been absent one hour since I have entered the army, and found the whole country deserting their Homes on the account of the Indians— The *War Party* in the creek Nation have killed all the chiefs that were friendly to the U. States. Col. Hawkins has left the Nation and about two hundred and eighty men are now in Pensacola obtaining ammunition from the Spanish Government on an order from Canada. The whole of the Creek Nation is for *war* except those who have fled to us. They have robbed the mail which they have taken to Pensacola—we have sent men to Pensacola, and find that the Indians intend to attack the Tensas settlements on their return home. The inhabitants have called on me—but I have not the power to protect them. I have been to see Captain Dent and he has spared all the men he can from his *command*. I shall cross today with all the militia I can muster and the Volunteers to Tensas, where I shall form a junction with Caller and we intend to attack the Indians on their return from Pensacola. I would give the world for my Company, which is now at the *Point*. I have eighty the finest fellows you ever saw and now it is the time to make *my fortune*. *Distruction* and ruin awaits this country without you arrive in eight days, the inhabitants are without arms or ammunition—cant you leave your Baggage under a proper command and reach us with your Troops. We have sent to Col Bowyer at the Point but General Flournoy is still sick at the Bay of St. Lewie. I have sent Sergeant Byord with *this* together with *Judge Toulmin's letters*. My furlough is out the last of this month and I must then return and join my Company at *Mobile Point* a second *time*.

32

It seems a coincidence that they were allied with a nation that was, also, seeking to recover possession of some portion, at least, of a like territory, for it is quite evident that the British at this juncture were using the Creek Indians against the American Republic. A state of civil war existing between Tecumseh's followers and the peace party in the Nation to some extent retarded the preparation for hostilities, though it is certain that the "Dance of the Lakes" was in progress by the prophets, many of whom in their zeal meeting death at the hands of the unbelievers, as the peaceful Indians were styled.

The first definite act of armed warfare between the inhabitants of the Mississippi Territory and the Creek Nation was the battle of Burnt Corn on July 27, 1813. The Creeks, numbering about 300 picked warriors, had gathered in camp at the Holy Ground according to information given out by General James Wilkinson, who was soon to leave for his new post in Canada, General Flournoy taking his place as commander of the United States troops in the South. The party moved on from the camp towards Pensacola, whither they were going for a supply of arms and ammunition promised them by the Spanish and to come in touch with the British in the Southern seas. Planning at the Holy Ground, according to the testimony of Mrs. Ward, whom they had captured and held as a prisoner, to attack the white and half-breed settlements on the river, it is logical that they meant to use their ammunition on their return in carrying out their threatened purpose.

The Creeks were under the command of Peter McQueen, a noted war chief, Jim Boy, one of the most chivalrous, gallant and humane warriors of his tribe,[16] and the despicable Prophet Joseph Francis, commanding in the order named: the Tallassees, Atossees and Alibamos, a proud Confederacy that had given themselves the name of "Red Sticks," a military organization that was to win the reputation of fighting men of great valor and steadfastness of purpose. It was a part of the old Confederacy that reached back past the day when eight mighty tribes made a treaty with Oglethorpe in 1732, doubtless brought about by the rough treatment of De Soto, who passed through

---

[16] This Indian chief's name is sometimes given as High Headed Jim. By some he was thought to have been the little boy Sonata, befriended by the McGirths, a frontier family whom he helped to escape at Fort Mims. His devotion to Mrs. McGirth and her daughters and the humanity evinced in his treatment of the white prisoners laid him open to much suspicion on the part of the Red Sticks.

the Muscogee Nation in 1540. The Creeks to this day call the war in the Mississippi Territory in 1813 the "Red Sticks War" and have always been proud of the title. Their war clubs were painted red and they wore the significant red feather among the white plumes in their head-dress.

Before the initial battle fought between this strong nation and the Americans to settle their many differences is described, it is due the former to give here a short history of this branch of the famous Muscogee race. Occupying a region that reached from the Atlantic to the Tombigbee and Alabama, including portions of the States of Georgia and Alabama and all of Florida, the Seminoles there having been a kindred tribe, they had developed a civilization that held the forms and customs and was marked by many of the best characteristics of the most advanced tribes on the Western Hemisphere. However, it must be admitted that the Creeks exhibited a ferociousness that did not characterize the neighboring tribes—the Natchez, Choctaws and Cherokees, though no tribe existed that did not have this trait well enough developed and all in war resorted to the massacre.

This branch of the Muscogees was nicknamed "Creeks" by the Europeans on account of the many streams that flowed through their country. Referring to an older generation a writer says:

> The men of the Creek Confederacy were well-proportioned, active and graceful; the women were smaller, exquisitely formed and some of them were very beautiful. In summer both sexes went without clothing excepting a drapery of Spanish moss that was fastened at the waist and fell to the thighs. The principal people painted their faces and bodies in fanciful colors and fops sometimes appeared in beautiful mantles of feathers or deer-skins and on their heads were lofty plumes of the eagle and the flamingo. The houses of the chiefs stood upon mounds sometimes in the form of a great pavilion and the inside of their winter dwellings were daubed with clay. Hunting, fishing and cultivating their fertile lands were their employment for they seldom made aggressive war. They were skilful artisans in making arms, houses, barges, canoes, and various kinds of ornaments. They made pottery for kitchen service and some of it was very ornamental. Fortifications were constructed with moats and walled towns and grand and beautiful temples abounded. They made mats of split cane with which they covered their houses and upon which they sat. These resembled the rush carpeting of the Moors. In their temples, dedicated to the worship of the sun, were votive offerings of pearls and rich furs. They regarded the sun as the superior deity and in all their invocations they appealed to it as to God. To it they made sacrifices of grain and animals. The chief, while living, was held in the greatest veneration as priest and king. As a symbol of devotion to him of the entire strength of the nation, the sacrifice of the first-born male child was required while the young mother was compelled to witness the slaughter of her child. Their marriages were attended with great displays of ornaments and flowers and at the setting of the sun the bride and groom and their friends prostrated themselves before that luminary and implored his blessing. Like

the Iroquois, the civil power in their government was widely distributed; and like the Iroquois the Creeks were an exception in their approach to civilization to all the Indian tribes of North America. Such were the Creeks or Muscogee Indians when first seen by Europeans.[17]

The English, in the main, had been the Creeks' choice of the Europeans, the English governors, Johnstone, Browne and Chester of Pensacola having kept the peace with them by the most extravagant use of presents such as blankets, rum and gew-gaws. During the Revolutionary War they were stanch allies of England and many Tories sought their towns in efforts to stir them up against the frontier settlements. A burning patriotism and love of country were chief characteristics of the race. In 1802 they began ceding their lands to the United States, their dissatisfaction increasing with every concession made to the white race. Though long kept in peace by the colonizing whites, their martial spirit was pronounced and just prior to their outburst with the people of the Mississippi Territory they had been engaged in a fierce civil war.

Colonel Benjamin Hawkins saw in the Creeks of his day many evidences of their former high state of civilization, though the historian Claiborne sets aside as very doubtful Hawkins' estimate and brings the Muscogee to this region at a later day from the northwest, affirming that a superior race had met De Soto. The Muscogees claimed that their race came out of the bosom of the Nanih Waiya and reverently regarded the great mound beside which they first dwelt as their mother.[18] As the Muscogees were sun worshipers it is natural to believe that there was a day when this sacred mound was used as a temple for the worship of the sun by the various tribes, while there are many evidences that it was also used as a national center for tribal councils. But while all Muscogee tribes have regarded the Nanih Waiya (Ishki chito, the "Great Mother") as the place of their creation, another legend, as told by Peter Folsom, one

---

[17] Bartram writing of Creek culture in 1777 says, "Some of their favorite songs and dances they have learned from the Choctaws, but it seems that these people are very eminent themselves for poetry and music; every town among them strives to excel each other in composing new songs, and by a custom among them they must have one new song for exhibition at every annual busk."

[18] Nanih Waiya or Nuniah Waiya, the sacred mound of the Choctaws, is the most important of the prehistoric mounds in the State of Mississippi. It is located in Winston County on the west side of Nanih Waiya Creek near the Neshoba County line.

Mississippi Territory in War of 1812—Rowland. 35

of their race, treats of their migration to the South from the far Northwest. Though the Choctaw and Creek branches of the great Muscogee race had now drifted far apart, hardly acknowledging their consanguinity, both protested that they would never leave their "Mother," the sacred Nanih·Waiya, while the patriotic Creek showed that he was always ready to fight for the land of his nativity.

Returning to the story of the battle of Burnt Corn, the exposed condition of the pioneer settlements along the Tombigbee and Alabama Rivers deserves attention, for it was there that the militia and the volunteer troops of the Mississippi Territory bore the brunt of the war several months before General Andrew Jackson arrived on the scene.

Pickett in his description of the exposed eastern border, while he seems ignorant of the military strength of the Mississippi Territory and of the part taken by Governor Holmes in prosecuting the war, gives the reader a clear idea of the condition of the sparse settlements that, notwithstanding Colonel Hawkins' optimistic views, were really in danger of momentary attack from their fierce neighbors. These had been "taking the war-talk," brandishing their war-clubs and making their towns red for many days. A rumor had flashed through the white settlements, too, that they had publicly danced the ceremonial war-dance, the famous "Dance of the Lakes" taught them by Tecumseh, which meant immediate battle. Consequently the party of painted and armed warriors moving to Pensacola from the Holy Ground was easily taken for belligerents.

The troops that hastily gathered to intercept the war party were called out by Colonel James Caller, the senior militia officer on the frontier stationed in Washington County, now in Alabama. This force, composed of a handful of militia, was reinforced at Fort Glass by a company of volunteers under the famous border hero, Sam Dale, whose marvelous adventures in the Southwest rank with all such feats as "The Charge of the Light Brigade." Walter G. Creagh, another valiant frontiersman, was second in command. These were joined later by the celebrated half-breed, Captain Dixon Bailey, whose association, training and patriotism had allied him with his white kinsmen. The whole force numbered only one hundred and eighty men, many of whom were drawn from the struggling element of society who, though fond of the chase and rough and ready in a frontier bout or joust, were unused to actual war.

In no sense were they a match for the band of 300 picked and armed warriors sent on a deadly war mission. On their road to Pensacola the Creeks on July 27 reached the famous spring on Burnt Corn Creek, soon to become the scene of battle. The place is described with almost infinitesimal minuteness by the patient fact-gatherer, Halbert. On coming to the secluded spot, the Indians threw themselves from their smoking ponies and hurriedly formed a camp, where they rested and feasted with no thought of imminent danger. When the hastily gathered troops of Colonel Caller cautiously approached and, quietly dismounting, charged them, the idling party was taken completely by surprise. The Indians instantly flew to arms and returned the fire of their white assailants without a moment's hesitation. After an unsuccessful resistance, they fled in wild disorder into the canebrakes and undergrowth fastnesses from which with sharp eyes they soon discovered the weakness of their foe, the number being less on account of the absence of many of Colonel Caller's men who were still pursuing the fleeing savages. The victors were busy looting the camp, appropriating their findings and carrying off the best horses when the wrathful Creeks secreted in the thickets of cane poured a volley of rifle balls into the party. Sweeping from their hiding places, they reassembled and gave open battle to the Americans, attacking them with guns, war-clubs and tomahawks with such sudden fury that consternation reigned supreme among the occupants of the camp.

So fierce was the onslaught of the infuriated Creeks that the raw militia could not reassemble their broken ranks though constantly urged by their Colonel to face the foe. Greed, too, had possessed some of them, and, though they dreaded the scalping knife of the brutal Creek, they hoped to get away with the horses and other loot, trusting to his poor marksmanship, which had never been an accomplishment of which he could boast when the rifle was the weapon in question. In vain their leader urged them to reform and give battle to the redskins but only eighty men could be found willing to contend with the savage horde. These, commanded by Captains Dale, Bailey and Smoot, faced the enemy unflinchingly, giving blow for blow and for a time forcing them back, when the heroic Dale was struck in the left side by a rifle ball which lodged near the backbone. He continued to fight desperately until compelled to quit the field. The battle lasted about three hours, the Indians fighting with a fierce tenacity. When the encounter was over the Americans had retreated, but not without carrying off many of the pack-horses, probably not concerning themselves about the fighting, since war had not been openly declared, and, notwithstanding the Creeks' reputation for cruelty, the hardy pioneer thought little of him as a soldier.

It is generally conceded by historians—and the writer admits it, that the Indians worsted the frontier militia and the volunteer forces at the battle of Burnt Corn. The victory, whatever there was of victory, belonged to the Creek warriors. But when one takes into consideration the long peace that had existed between the white people and the Indians and the growing contempt on the part of the former for the latter as a rival of any sort, also the fact that the Indians were now ready in spirit for war, having secretly determined on it for many months, it is not surprising that the hurriedly mustered forces of Colonel Caller were unprepared for serious fighting. Certainly in later engagements with the foe no act of recreancy has been recorded, but to the contrary a spirit of reckless daring that partook more of hazard and adventure marked the career of the frontier soldier dwelling remote from the older communities of the Mississippi Territory. Like all such spots in America these frontier river settlements were breeding places of romantic and chivalrous adventure.

Participants in the Burnt Corn engagement reappear in later fierce combats where we find Dale, Bailey, Smoot, May, Armstrong, Baldwin, Lewis, Glass, Henry, Hollinger, Bullard, and Bradberry conspicuous for courage of the highest order. These, with many other better trained but not more chivalrous troops, from the older population of the Territory near Natchez, fought heroically for American freedom and make up the famous roster of the Mississippi soldiers in the War of 1812 presented with this narrative. Though late, it is well that their names and deeds be recorded in history. As one historian has said in substance, the vanquishers of the Pequots, King Philip, Pontiac and the Narragansetts have been crowned with laurels; but of the soldiery of the Mississippi Territory, who conquered the fierce Creek Nation, little or nothing has been said.

The Creek War, one of the fiercest and most extensive ever engaged in by the Indians of North America, took place wholly within the confines of the new Territory. Its people bore the brunt of it, suffering the tragedy of the burnt home, murdered wife and child, and the dangers of the battlefield; yet to Jackson's Tennessee troops—valiant and invincible, it is gladly admitted—partial historians have given the honor of the victory.

A close study of this and some other periods of American history causes the thought to arise that the bold effrontery with which the average American historian knowingly tampers with truth is enough sometimes to make one doubtful of the integrity of our civilization.

Throughout the Creek War Mississippi troops mainly were engaged in the conflict; and since the 1st Regiment of Mississippi Infantry, United States Volunteers, made so vital a part of the army gathered to quell the Creek uprising, its formation and officers will here be given from the *Encyclopedia of Mississippi History*, whose statements are based on original records:

This regiment was organized at Baton Rouge, beginning in January, 1813, with the re-enlisting members of the Mississippi regiment mentioned, as a nucleus, recruited by volunteers from the Territory. Cowles Mead[19] was first commissioned as Colonel and Joseph Carson as Major but Mead soon resigned and Carson was made Colonel and Daniel Beasley, General Claiborne's aide, was appointed Major. Lieut. W. R. DeLoach was Adjutant; Lieut B. F. Salvage, Quartermaster; William R. Cox, Surgeon's Mate. The companies were commanded by Captains Philip A. Engle, Archilaus, Wells, Randall Jones, William Jack, William C. Mead, Benjamin Dent, Hutton Middleton, Abram M. Scott, James Foster, L. V. Foelckil, C. G. Johnson, and Hans Morrison. The First Lieutenants were James Bailey, Richard Bowman, A. L. Osborn, William Morgan, J. D. Rodgers, W. R. DeLoach, Theron Kellogg, A. Montgomery, John Camp, Alexander Calvit, John Allen, Robert Layson and Benjamin F. Salvage. Second Lieutenants, Kean Caldwell, Charles Moore, Charles Baron, W. M. Osborn, N. Lockridge, R. C. Anderson, George Dougherty, Robert Swan, James Luckett, George H. Gibbs, Robert Burton and D. M. Callihan. Ensigns, Stephen Mays, Y. R. McDonald, Benjamin Blanton, Benjamin Stowell, William S. Britt, Isaac W. Davis, Robert Davis, Charles West, Samuel Guest and Richard Smith (Register of the Army, 1813). A morning report dated at Liberty, July 18th, lists the Captains as Jack, Engle, Jones, Mead, Painboeuff, Dent, Scott, Middleton, Johnson, Foster, Brandon, and Morrison with an aggregate present and absent of 402.

This regiment and a Louisiana regiment,[20] organized at the same time and place, formed a brigade which General Ferdinand L. Claiborne of Natchez was assigned to command, he, as has already been stated, being commissioned Brigadier-General of Volunteers in the United States service in March, 1813. On his staff were Captain Joseph P. Kennedy, Brigade Major; Lieutenant Alexander Calvit, Aide; and Dr. John Kerr, Surgeon.[21]

---

[19] Mead resigned to make a canvas for Territorial delegate to Congress, an action which resulted in his defeat for that office.

[20] The history of the service of the Louisiana Regiment is so meager that it is impossible to tell whether it served as a whole or not during the Creek war. Some Louisiana volunteers however were with General Claiborne in the war zone. To these he refers in terms of warm praise.

[21] The same, probably, who became surgeon-general of Jackson's army during the defense of New Orleans. The family was prominent in the Mississippi Territory, David Ker (sometimes spelled Kerr and pronounced Car), having been Judge of the Territorial Supreme Court in 1802.

Mississippi Territory in War of 1812—Rowland. 39

The latter part of July, Brigadier-General Ferdinand Leigh Claiborne, commanding at Baton Rouge, was ordered by General Flournoy to take the whole army hastily to Fort Stoddart to defend the country in event of trouble, not only between the Mississippi Territory and the Indians, but on the southern coast between the Republic and Great Britain with Spain for an ally of the latter.

Claiborne reached Mount Vernon on July 30, having patriotically mortgaged his lands to supply the soldiers with additional comforts. With the same high heart and *amor patriae* which had won him, when a youth of twenty, a lieutenancy in Wayne's great army on the far Northwest frontier, he was still serving the American government.

On the eastern frontier he found the inhabitants very much alarmed over the Indian invasion—a topic discussed everywhere. Many of the people had deserted their homes and were occupying rough, hastily built block-houses all over Clarke County and in the forks of the Tombigbee and Alabama Rivers. After making a distribution of his troops as best to defend the frontier, he began the construction of Fort Madison, dispatching Colonel Carson with 200 troops to the fork, where wandering bands were reported to be daily committing depredations. Colonel Scott was sent to Old Fort St. Stephens with headquarters in a block-house built by the French and afterwards held by the Spaniards. The companies of Captains Jack and Middleton were sent to garrison a stockade east of the Alabama River, called Fort Mims, a fort that was soon to become the scene of one of the most tragic events of the war.

Although Colonel Joseph Carson with the 1st Regiment of Mississippi Infantry, United States Volunteers, was now in the river country and General Ferdinand L. Claiborne had been inspecting the forts, the encounter of Burnt Corn between the Creeks and the frontier soldiery of the Mississippi Territory for a time filled the settlers everywhere in the Tombigbee, Tensas, Alabama and Mobile regions with grave concern, causing them to keep more closely within the stockades.[22] Though many of the families of the detached settle-

---

[22] A summary of the stockades, and forts, according to Halbert and Ball (a number already standing and others erected to provide for hostilities with the Creek Indians), are as follows.:
1. "Fort St. Stephens, established by the French, probably about 1714, held afterwards by the Spaniards, who made there a settlement about 1786, given up by the Spaniards to the Americans in 1799, has been already mentioned. So far as the Creek Indians were concerned, this was considered an impregnable fortress. As this locality, the old St. Stephens, will be again more fully men-

tioned, it needs no further notice here, only the statement that it was on the west bank of the Tombigbee, on a high bluff, at the head of sloop navigation.

"2. Fort Stoddart, as established by United States troops in July, 1799, has also been named, with its stockade and bastion. As this was for some years a government post, held by the United States troops, and became a port of entry where the Court of Admiralty was held, it was of course a strong point. In 1804 Captain Schuyler of New York was commander here, with eighty men, Edmund P. Gaines was Lieutenant, and Lieutenant Reuben Chamberlain was paymaster. At Fort Stoddart duties were exacted on imports and exports. Four miles west of Fort Stoddart was Mount Vernon.

"3. Passing down the river, a strong fort was located at Mobile called Fort Charlotte. Another was also constructed here, Fort Bowyer.

"4. Going now northward, on the east side of the Alabama, two miles below the 'cut off,' a quarter of a mile from the Tensaw Boat Yard, was the ill-fated Fort Mims. This was built in the summer of 1813 and will be again noticed. When the erection of this stockade was commenced is uncertain, perhaps in July, and, according to Pickett, its last block house was never finished.

"This might be called No. 1 of the stockades erected especially for protection against the Creeks but the former notation will be continued.

"5. Fort Pierce was a small stockade some two miles south-east of Fort Mims. It took its name from two brothers, William Pierce and John Pierce, who came from New England and made there their home in Spanish times. William Pierce was a weaver and John Pierce a teacher.

"6. Crossing the Alabama and coming into the new Clarke County, we reach Fort Glass, built some time in July at the home of Zachariah Glass by himself and his neighbors, Nah-hee, called a Tory Creek, an intelligent Indian, employed in the Creek war as a scout, assisting, it is said, in the building.

"7. Fort Madison was in the north-east corner of section one, township six, range three east of the St. Stephen's meridian, on the water-shed line, which was then the eastern boundary of Clarke County. It was north of Fort Glass only two hundred and twenty-five yards, and the two stockades constituted one locality, being the center of the quite large Fort Madison neighborhood. The first store in this region was about due east from Fort Madison, on the Alabama River, distant six miles, opened, probably, in 1812; and one of the first grist mills was built about the same time, perhaps about four miles north; and in 1813 the first cotton gin in the vicinity was erected some two miles north. This was one of the seven principal settlements in the then new Clarke County and the region west of the Alabama. As is evident from the mention of the store and the mill and the gin, and the plantations that were opened around these, it was an important locality for these settlers to hold.

"Fort Madison contained not quite an acre of ground, having been sixty yards square. A trench three feet in depth was dug around the outside and bodies of pine trees cut about fifteen feet in length were placed perpendicularly in the trench side by side, making thus a wall of pine wood twelve feet in height. Port holes were cut at convenient distances so as to enable the inmates to look out, and in case of an attack to fire upon the besiegers. In about the same way all these stockades of 1813 were constructed. They were lighted at night by means of the abundant pitch pine placed upon scaffolds, covered with earth, erected for the purpose. Additional securities were added at Fort Madison and an improved method of lighting introduced. Within this enclosure, bearing the name of the President of the United States, were the tents and cabins of the settlers of that neighborhood, and after its erection, the date not certain, Fort Glass was occupied by the soldiers.

"8. Fort Sinquefield was about ten miles north of Fort Madison, on the western side of Bassett's Creek, a large stream of water for a creek, on section thirteen, township eight, range three east, a smaller stockade built very much in the same manner. It was about five miles south-east from the present town of Grove Hill, formerly called Macon, the county seat of Clarke County. This fort stood on a tableland or height of ground extending for a mile north and south. Eastward is a gentle slope which terminates finally in the Bassett's Creek valley. Westward are deep valleys and narrow, between large, high ridges of land. No actual hill is within miles of this locality, yet the ascent from the valleys to the top of the ridges or table, might be called going up hill. The spring which supplied this stockade with water is south of west, in one of the deep valleys, distant two hundred and seventy-five yards.

"Ninety feet distant from the once stockaded ground, in a northwest direction, are some graves. A few rods eastward of the fort ground is supposed to be an old burial place, although here the traces of the graves were not distinct in 1879. One of the principal highways of Clarke County runs directly by this locality, but, as it has been for many years a family home, no traces of the stockade outlines can be found here which are still so distinct at Forts Glass and Madison.

"9. Fort White was a small stockade a short distance northeast of the present Grove Hill.

"10. Landrum's Fort was eleven miles west from Fort Sinquefield; on section eighteen, township eight, range two east.

"11. Mott's Fort was in the same neighborhood. These both were small.

"12. Going now to the Tombigbee River and northward, Fort Easley was on section ten or eleven, township eleven, range one west, at what is now called Wood's Bluff. This fort was named, as were nearly all others, from a prominent settler in the neighborhood, and the bluff took its name from Major Wood, an officer in the Burnt Corn expedition. This stockade was on a small plateau containing about three acres. On the side next to the river the bluff is almost a perpendicular wall, there is 'a bold spring of water flowing from its side,' and the descent is quite abrupt from this plateau above and below the stockade ground, making this fort a naturally strong position.

"General Claiborne visited this stockade about the last of August, having received a report that it would be attacked by the Indians. It is possible that some of the Creeks started this report to call attention away from the real fort which they designed to attack, that Fort Mims, which was fifty miles south and twelve miles east from Fort Easley.

"13. Turner's Fort was some eight miles south and five west, in the west bend of the Tombigbee River, near the residence of Abner Turner. This fort was built of split pine logs doubled, and contained two or three block houses. It was held by the citizens of the neighborhood, thirteen men and some boys forming the garrison that expected to protect the women and children. Two or three miles distant, on the river, was a Choctaw reservation known as Turkey Town, called by the Choctaws, 'Fakit Chipunta,' Little Turkeys. In this stockade were members of the Turner, Thornton, Pace, and other families, early settlers in what became the delightful West Bend neighborhood. Here for a time resided Tandy Walker, who is mentioned in the Gaines records, who was 'a most experienced and daring backwoodsman;' but in the summer of 1813 he was connected with the affairs at Fort Madison.

"The inmates of the two forts, Turner's and Easley's, held religious services in their fort life. At Fort Easley a camp-meeting was held, probably in August, which some from the other stockades attended. The 'love feast' on Sunday morning was held outside the fort, but guards were stationed to give warning if any attacking party of Indians appeared.

"14. Passing, now, down the river on the west side, five miles below Coffeeville, about a mile from the river, was Cato's Fort.

"15. Still further west, in Washington County, was Rankin's Fort, quite a large stockade, and the most western one of the River Group.

"16. McGrew's Fort was in the corner of section one, township seven, range one west, about three miles north of Fort St. Stephens, in Clarke County five miles north and eighteen west from Fort Madison. It is claimed that the area here enclosed with palisades was about two acres. Some of the posts were remaining in 1879, and around the fort locality was an old field. Here two brothers, William McGrew and John McGrew, British Royalists then, refugees, probably from the Atlantic coast, made an early settlement near the Tombigbee River. McGrew's Reserve, an old Spanish grant, is still a landmark in Clarke County. These brothers left the reputation of having been exemplary men, and of having become good Americans. How many families were in this fort is not known.

"17. Six miles south from Jackson, at Gullet's Bluff, was Fort Carney, on the line of travel to Mount Vernon. This fort was built by Josiah Carney, who settled on the river in 1809.

"18. Three miles south of Fort Carney, near Oven Bluff, was Powell's Fort, where were about six families, including those of John McCaskey, James Powell, and John Powell.

"19. Lavier's Fort, written sometimes by mistake or misprint Rivier's, was built, so far as has been ascertained (the only authority is an aged colored man, Dick Embree), near the residence of Captain Lawson Lavier, who traded with the Choctaw Indians. It was built by himself and a few neighbors, but its locality is not known. Pickett names it, but no resident of Clarke County was found, in 1877, who knew anything of it.

"20. At Mount Vernon, to which as General Claiborne's headquarters we now come, and where was a United States arsenal, were two forts. An arsenal was maintained, here until 1861, and since 1865 this has been held as a United States post, where a few officers and soldiers may always be found. Near the parade ground are some of those beautiful trees known as live oak, and the long-leaf pine growth extends a long distance northward. The landing place on the river known as Arsenal wharf or Fort Stoddart, four miles distant, the early United States 'port of entry' is distant from Mobile by the river channel forty-five miles, and five miles further north by the river brings one to the head of the Mobile River, the union of the Alabama and Tombigbee. The Mobile River, of the formation of which, judging from the school maps of Guyot and others, many must be ignorant, is fifty miles in length. Mount Vernon is distant now from Mobile by railroad only twenty-nine miles. As a place supposed to be very secure the two forts there, in the summer of 1813, are said to have been 'packed.' How many people were in these different stockades at any one time is not certain. But after the alarm caused by the massacre at Fort Mims there were at Forts Madison and Glass more than one thousand citizens and soldiers. At Fort Carney there were about four hundred. Rankin's Fort contained five hundred and thirty. How many hundred were at St. Stephens and at Mount Vernon is not known.

"In these river settlements there were at that time, it has been already stated, about two thousand whites and two thousand blacks, taking for the basis of authority the United States census of 1810.

"Besides these twenty or twenty-one forts, so called, which were in the line of the river settlements proper, two forts, named Roger's and Patton's were constructed in what is now Wayne County, Mississippi; Patton's Fort at Winchester and Roger's Fort, six miles above. There was little use for these, however, and no real need, for the Creeks were not likely to cross the Tombigbee and go into the Choctaw territory. In fact, families of Clarke County instead of trusting themselves in the stockades and enduring the inconveniences of thus living, for even a few weeks, crossed the Tombigbee and selected camping grounds far enough west to be, as they thought, out of danger. Among some such was the family of Mrs. Cathell, a widow with four sons and four daughters, having come into Clarke County from Georgia in 1812. Two of her sons went as soldiers against the Indians. She dreaded to have them leave her, saying that she had lost two brothers in the Revolutionary War and she felt sure these sons would fall in the coming conflict. And they did fall with so many others at Fort Mims. Disliking fort life for herself, as she had experienced it in her girlhood in the War of the Revolution, she with the other members of her family and ten or twelve other families crossed the river and went into camps."

ments were half-breeds, this distinction, if any distinction can be attached to the possession of a strain of savage blood, availed them little so long as they affiliated with their white kinsmen. Those of mixed blood stood even more in dread of the war party than the white settlers, since to them was meted the severest punishment for refusing to "take the war talk." Peace had been maintained between the two neighboring peoples so long that there was still much doubt in the minds of many of any permanent hostilities. Close confinement, too, in the forts grew irksome to the hardy frontiersmen accustomed to the largest freedom, and eager to improve their homes and lands. Halbert and Ball say:

After the battle of Burnt Corn, which did not terminate as the whites had hoped, as the settlers of this exposed and isolated river region gathered more fully into their various stockades, the inhabitants on the Tensaw and along Little River, many of them being of mixed and of Creek blood yet dreading the fury of the war parties of the Creek Nation, gathered around the residence of a settler named Samuel Mims, an old Indian countryman, one mile from the Alabama River, two miles below the cut-off and one fourth of a mile from the Tensaw boat-yard. Here where before the Burnt Corn action, many families had gathered, they erected a stockade nearly square, enclosing about an acre, built very much as was Fort Madison and the other stockades and entered through a large eastern and a western gate. In this enclosure were several buildings, the home of the Mims family being near the center. One of these buildings was known as Patrick's Loom-house and having some extra picketing attached to this, the inmates called it the "Bastion."

Both Pickett and Halbert describe Fort Mims, erected during the summer of 1813, as a military post under very lax discipline, for the moment utterly unprepared for the sudden attack upon it which with the coolest deliberation had been planned by the Creeks. Filled no less with Tecumseh's counsel than with revenge at the memory of the affair on Burnt Corn Creek, they had strengthened their Confederacy, making no secret now of having danced the significant war-dance. They had been well supplied with arms and ammunition by the Spaniards at Pensacola, who, judging from every circumstance and the swiftness of Governor Manique's congratulations sent to William Weatherford, now the recognized leader of the war party,[23] had assisted them in planning the attack on Fort Mims.

---

[23] Weatherford is thought by Halbert to have joined the war party about August 25, just five days prior to the massacre of Fort Mims, and while it appears absurd and preposterous to think that an opponent of a movement that had been fomenting for months, if not years, should at the last moment become its leader, we give his views on account of Weatherford's prominence in this narrative.
In speaking of a correspondence between General Flournoy and General Claiborne, dated August 25, 1813, Halbert says:

In spite of conflicting opinions as to the war spirit of the Creeks, the Burnt Corn expedition had its weight and preparations for war went steadily on. Governor Holmes had greatly strengthened the military defenses of the Mississippi Territory and the numerous stockades were daily inspected by General Claiborne, commanding at Mount Vernon. On August 7 he visited Fort Mims in person and advised the utmost caution on the part of Major Beasley. The latter continued to view the whole situation with an optimism highly colored by Colonel Hawkins' views, and even if there were trouble his sense of security and contempt for the source are evident in his reply when the cautious and gallant half-breed scout, Jim Cornells, after reconnoitering the Fort for several miles along the river, returned and announced that a band of Indians were approaching, that it was "only a gang of red cattle." "Red cattle" was a sobriquet, if not an epithet, that the white settlers contemptuously applied to the Creeks.

Major Daniel Beasley, in command of the garrison at Fort Mims, has been presented by Halbert and others as wholly unfit temperamentally and on account of his free use of intoxicating liquors for such a responsible position. Other historians have sought to exonerate him.

"Some time between the dates of these two letters, it is evident that Weatherford joined the war party, for before August closed we find him at Fort Mims; General Woodward places it in 1813, but does not name the month. And it may be here observed that Tecumseh seems to have had no influence over Weatherford. Woodward says that Sam Moniac and Weatherford, returning from a trip into the Mississippi Territory, where they had been 'trading in beef cattle,' found several chiefs assembled—it is said on Tallewassee Creek, a mile and a half from the Alabama River—and taking the 'black drink.'

"These chiefs told Weatherford and Moniac that they must join them or be put to death. The following are Woodward's own words: Moniac boldly refused and mounted his horse. Josiah Francis, his brother-in-law, seized his bridle. Moniac snatched a war club from his hand, gave him a severe blow and put out, with a shower of rifle bullets following him. Weatherford consented to remain. He told them that he disapproved their course, and that it would be their ruin, but that they were his people, he was raised with them, and he would share their fate.' General Woodward names among these chiefs Hopie Tustanuggee, or Far Off Warrior, a Tuskegee, their eldest or principal chief, 'the one' says Woodward 'looked upon as the General,' and who was killed at Fort Mims; Peter McQueen; Jim Boy or High Head Jim; Josiah Francis or Hillis Hadjo, 'the new made prophet,' probably the same who is called Joseph by General Wilkinson; Seekaboo, the Shawnee prophet; and several others. He says that Weatherford offered some advice to these chiefs, but they declined to follow his suggestions. The reasons which Weatherford assigned for joining the war party, as detailed at some length by Woodward, are very creditable to Weatherford's humanity. He thought he would thus be the means of preventing not a little bloodshed."

DRAWING OF FORT MIMS,

Found among Gen Claiborne's manuscript papers.

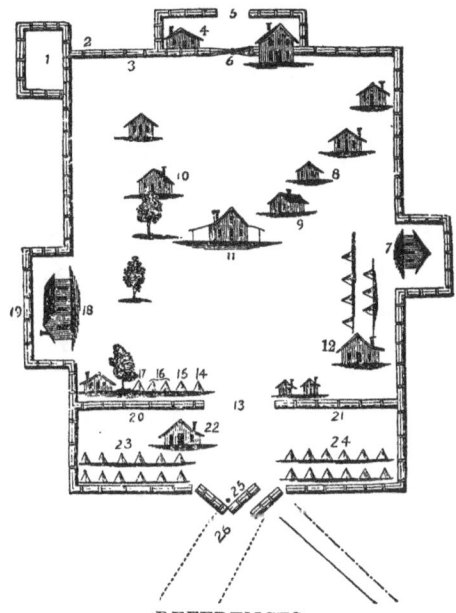

REFERENCES.

1 Block House.
2 Pickets cut away by the Indians.
3 Guard's Station.
4 Guard House.
5 Western Gate, but not up.
6 This Gate was shut, but a hole was cut through by the Indians.
7 Captain Bailey's Station.
8 Steadham's House.
9 Mrs. Dyer's House.
10 Kitchen.
11 Mims' House.
12 Randon's House.
13 Old Gate-way—open.
14 Ensign Chambliss' Tent.
15 Ensign Gibbs'.
16 Randon's.
17 Captain Middleton's.
18 Captain Jack's Station.
19 Port-holes taken by Indians.
20 21 Port-holes taken by Indians.
22 Major Beasley's Cabin.
23 Captain Jack's Company.
24 Captain Middleton's Company.
25 Where Major Beasley fell.
26 Eastern Gate, where the Indians entered.

Certainly he did not lack physical courage. That he shared largely in the doubt manifested in some quarters of any serious hostility on the part of the Indians as to lead to actual war is evident. It is clear, too, that he regarded the battle of Burnt Corn as much ado about nothing. Though making light of the situation, the whites in the main still kept within the fortresses erected for their safety. It is said that at Fort Mims they were permitted to stroll far beyond the gates and with the exception of the anxiety shown by General Claiborne in his message of August 29 to Major Beasley the people seemed lulled into an unaccountable sense of security, a condition that overtakes men sometimes when in imminent danger. At Fort Mims, to which place had been brought a few days previous a supply of whiskey, "some of the inmates," writes Pickett, "had become inactive and free from alarm and had abandoned themselves to fun and frolic." All historians paint the scene as something of a holiday festivity.

Led by the sphinx-like Weatherford—a descendant of the beautiful Princess Sehoy, in whose veins ran the blood of McGillivray—and by his trusted confederates Peter McQueen and the "Prophet" Francis, the Indians decided to make the attack at noon in retaliation for the assault of the whites at Burnt Corn, which also had been fixed at that hour. The horrible massacre took place on August 30. The day has been described as beautiful and placid, with golden shafts of summer sunlight burnishing forest, field and water. The usual drum-beat, which had been instituted as a call for twelve o'clock dinner, had sounded, falling with a double significance on the ears of the thousand grim warriors who in the coverts of the forest awaited this signal for the attack. Just as many have done before, the occupants of the Fort were engaged in the feast and the dance, totally unconscious of danger, when the painted and befeathered warriors of Weatherford, who commanded the attack, stealing from the deep woods and tall cane-brakes, stealthily approached the Fort.[24] In a moment, clashing

---

[24] In connection with Weatherford's attack on the Fort the following letter from his grandson, Charles Weatherford of Mt. Pleasant, Alabama, dated October 7, 1890, to Mr. T. H. Ball will prove interesting:
"Sir—Your letter of the 2d inst. came to hand yesterday. Sir, your subject has become stale. The name of Billy Weatherford is almost forgotten, superseded by the names of such men as Lee, Jackson and Grant. With the death of my father, Charles Weatherford, Sr., who is about ninety-five years old, the name of Weatherford will become commonplace. My father is the oldest and only living

with the gay, hilarious chatter and laughter, the yells of the savages arose on the air. Original records of General Claiborne, used by Pickett, say in substance that the sand had washed against the eastern gate and that on August 30 it was swinging wide open. As Weatherford and his warriors sped swiftly towards it, Major Beasley ran forward and vainly essayed to close it. The Indians struck him fiercely with their clubs and tomahawks and supposing him dead rushed over his body into the Fort. In a dying condition the stricken officer crawled behind the gate, where he shortly expired. While in the throes of death, all historians record that he, to the last, tried to rally his men, persistently calling to them to save the Fort. Whatever may have been his offense in the neglect of duty, that he died bravely none will dispute.

---

child of the notorious, and so called bloody-handed, Billy Weatherford. And I, sir, am the only living child of Charles Weatherford, Sr. Now, sir, you know who and what I am.

"My grandfather, Billy Weatherford, died in 1826.

"I was born in 1834, therefore what I have to say will only be hearsay and from many lips, some prejudiced and some partial.

"According to the most authentic information, Weatherford did not desire the massacre at Fort Mims. About the middle of the afternoon of that sadly memorable day Weatherford met his half brother, David Tate, about twelve miles above Fort Mims, and told him of the massacre and spoke of it with much regret. He told Tate that he tried to prevent it; but under the excitement his warriors threatened his life if he interfered. Tate did not belong to the hostile party.

"Now as to Weatherford's being mounted at the time the engagement began, circumstances prove that he was not. I had an aunt who was a refugee in Fort Mims. I have often heard her say that she saw Billy Weatherford as he came in the gate at full run, at the head of his warriors, jump a pile of logs almost as high as his head. (Weatherford stood six feet two inches.) She said, as he sprang over the logs he saw Captain Dixon Bailey who was a bitter enemy, to whom he shouted, 'Dixon Bailey, to-day one or both of us must die.' So I judge by this that he was not mounted at the time of the engagement. But in the evening (afternoon) of that day, when he met Tate, Weatherford was mounted on the veritable black horse. I believe it is a recognized fact that all warriors of note ride either a milk-white or raven black steed. Now, sir, I, being a man of peace, and altogether unlike my grand sire, ride an old sorrel mare.

"The aunt of whom I have spoken as being a refugee, in Fort Mims at the time of the massacre was Mrs. Susan Hatterway (nee Stiggins) who hated Billy Weatherford with a thorough hatred. My aunt's husband was killed early in the fight. She had no children. And when she saw that the fort would be reduced to ashes she took hold of a little white girl, Elizabeth Randon, with one hand, and a negro girl named Lizzie, with the other, and said to them, 'Let us go out and be killed together.' But to her surprise she saw one of the busy and bloody warriors beckon her to him. On approaching she recognized him. It was Iffa Tustunnaga, meaning Dog Warrior. He took her prisoner with the two children. He took them to Pensacola, and gave them over to some of their friends, where they remained until the war closed, when they returned to their homes in Alabama.

Mississippi Territory in War of 1812—Rowland.   47

Though scattered here and there in the wildest state of disorder and confusion, the brave defenders of the Fort snatched their guns and knives and began a terrific battle with the foe. Leading and cheering them was none other than the heroic Captain Dixon Bailey, already referred to for his bravery at Burnt Corn. He was now aided by his brothers, James and Daniel. Of the royal blood of Sehoy also, his stern eye did not quail even in this dread hour before the fierce gaze of the haughty Weatherford, nor of that of the Creek leader's far-famed grandfather, the elder "Red Eagle," known as the fiercest warrior of the Muscogee tribe. With one blow of his trusted gunstock he struck down one of their beaded and feathered prophets frantically leading an assault. Striving by his side in heroic defense

---

Soon after the close of the war my aunt married Absalom Sizemore. She died near Mount Pleasant in 1865.

"When Elizabeth Randon grew to womanhood she married Algier Newman, and lived many years on the Alabama River just below Fort Claiborne in Monroe County. Excuse me for the digression.

"I will get back to my subject by saying that Lucy Cornell's story must have been merely to embellish the story. But it would not have surprised me if he had done so. All great warriors do such things.

"I believe the name has always been spelled Cornells.

"Billy Weatherford was married three times, twice under the Indian law. His first wife, my grandmother, was Mary Moniac, originally spelled McNac. She died in 1804 at Point Thloly, which is in Lowndes County. His second wife was Sapoth Thlanie. I never heard where or when she died. His third and last wife was Mary Stiggins. They were married under the white law in 1817. She died near Mount Pleasant, Monroe County, 1832.

"I had an anecdote told me once by the mother of the late Colonel William Boyles, of Mobile, which is the only one that I have never seen in print. Mrs. Boyles was a widow and lived near Billy Weatherford in Monroe County. She kept what was called at that time a wayside tavern. Weatherford, in going to and from his plantation, passed right by her door. They were warm friends and she frequently invited him to eat a meal with her. On this particular day she invited him to eat dinner. Just before the meal was ready four strangers rode up and asked for dinner. All were soon seated at table, and discussion commenced, in the course of which the strangers wanted to know where that bloody-handed savage, Billy Weatherford lived. Mrs. Boyles said Weatherford's eyes sparkled. She shook her head at him to say nothing. The talk went on. Three of the strangers expressed a wish to meet Weatherford, assuring Mrs. Boyles they would kill the red-skinned, bloody-handed savage on sight. (Weatherford was fair, with light brown hair and mild black eyes.) Dinner being over, the gentlemen walked out on the gallery. To the surprise of the strangers, the man with whom they had sat at table stepped into the midst of the crowd and said: 'Some of you gentlemen expressed a wish while at table to meet Billy Weatherford. Gentlemen, I am Billy Weatherford, at your service!' But Mrs. Boyles said she never saw men more frightened than were the three belligerently disposed gentlemen. Not one of the trio was entitled to a raven black or a milk white steed. They quailed under the glance of the Red Eagle's eye. The fourth gentleman, who had said but little, stepped forward and shook hands with Weatherford, and introduced himself as Colonel David Panthon."

of the Fort, until death claimed them both, were the brave Captains Jack and Middleton commanding companies of the Mississippi volunteers, all of whom perished in the first hours of resistance. General Claiborne had sent these two companies, drawn from the best population of the Territory, to help guard the Fort in event of trouble. The loss of these gallant spirits was a serious one to the army and to the communities from which they had volunteered. They were among the first to resist the Indians and their heroic efforts at one time, for a few moments, checked the work of the savages. But confusion prevailed everywhere and the lack of order served to increase the panic. The author of *In Clarke and Its Surroundings*, in a vivid if crude description of the scene, writes:

> The officers bravely endeavored to drive the Indians from the gateway but bravery was now of no avail. Officers and soldiers fell in vain attempts to counteract the results of a want of vigilance in the past. Help or hope there was none and soldiers, women, children, Spaniards, friendly Indians fell together in heaps of mangled bodies, the dying and the dead, scalped, mutilated, bloody, to be consumed ere long by fire or to become food for hungry dogs and buzzards. In vain the young men, no longer dancing with the girls, and also the aged men and the boys, fought the unrelenting savages with desperate fury. In vain did the brave Captain Bailey, left as the commanding officer and who lived through all the carnage, animate the inmates to a resolute resistance. In vain did the women load the guns, bring water from the well and do all that it was possible to do in sustaining the courage of the men.

The massacre had lasted between two and three hours when there was a slight cessation of hostilities, to be immediately renewed some historians assert, when the Indians had been reinforced and led by the illustrious Red Eagle.[25] It was at this time that one of the main buildings of the Fort was set ablaze by the fire laden arrows from the bow of the fierce Shawnee chieftain, Seekaboo. The cunning device never proved more effective and the Fort with the exception of a block-house and a few pickets soon went up in flames.

The sickening details of the massacre that have left an eerie shadow on the pages of our early history will not be dwelt on further. In the afternoon of the ill-fated August 30, the ghastly tragedy of Fort Mims was concluded. "Not even in the Sepoy Rebellion," says one historian, "did human eyes behold a more revolting spectacle." Surpassing in frenzied fierceness the ravage of Wyoming Valley, and similar in many respects to the massacre of Fort Rosalie at Natchez

---

[25] Weatherford always denied that his grandfather, the elder Red Eagle, led the Indians in this second assault on Fort Mims.

nearly a hundred years previous, when the French in its region were practically exterminated, it takes rank as one of the most inhuman pieces of butchery ever perpetrated in the history of the American Indian. The deed had been so tragic and had been committed so suddenly that in view of the large admixture of blood between the two races and the long peace maintained few could account for it. As brutal as the nature of the Creeks was known to be, few believed that they were still as much the savage as this recent deed had proved. Loyola's Jesuits had for nearly a century taught them Divine law, but, though the sincerest lovers of freedom—with an aspiration it is true that partook largely of that of the lion's impulse for mastery of the forest—they still were, except in a few instances, unresponsive to lasting Christian instruction. However, we can realize how strong must have been the national spirit of the Muscogee. Though bound to the white race by the linking of proud names in both Muscogee, European and American genealogy, in the final reckoning the names of McGillivray, Bailey, Cornell, McGirth, Tunstall, Tait, Durant, Moniac, Smith, McQueen, Ficher and many more of American significance were as names written in sand in comparison with names and faiths sacred since the Great Spirit commanded the Muscogee to come out of the bosom of the Nanih Waiya—names and faiths which must now be defended at every cost and sacrifice.

As an instance of the irony of fate, while the Spaniards at Pensacola were urging the Creeks to exterminate the Americans, members of their own race and creed at Fort Mims, in a suppliant attitude and in the very act of making the sign of the cross, were mercilessly tomahawked by the brutal hands they were aiding.

There has been much controversy relative to the number of Indians engaged in the massacre. Pickett and some others place the strength of the attacking party at one thousand. Many local authorities, and some historians also, have disputed about the number of inhabitants slain. Halbert, who follows Pickett in most statements, fixes the number of whites killed during the massacre, including men, women and children, at five hundred. A number having fled at the outset, it would be safe to say that near these figures would be found the truth. Pickett's list,[26] taken from Claiborne's papers of inhabitants

---

[26] Pickett's list of those who escaped from Fort Mims is as follows: Mrs. McGirth and her daughters, a friendly Indian named Socca, Hester a negro woman,

that escaped, with an additional one made later, is given in a note for the benefit of those who, like the patient, minutiae-loving, fact-gleaner, Halbert, take pride in holding their apples in both hands. In all this gruesome picture of savage warfare, from the entrance into the Fort to the last fiendish blow, only one single act has been cited by historians to lighten the dark chronicles of the red man, that being the protection, already referred to, given by the valiant young chieftain, Jim Boy, to Mrs. McGirth and her family, who had found and nourished him when a child forsaken and starving. With the exception of this sincere mark of gratitude no other act, unless we accept as authentic the instance of the protection afforded Mrs. Susan Hatter-

---

Samuel Smith of mixed blood, Lieutenant W. R. Chambliss, Dr. Thomas G. Holmes, Lieutenant Peter Randon, Sergeant Matthews, Josiah Fletcher, Martin Rigdon, Joseph Perry, Jesse Steadham, Edward Steadham, John Hoven, ——— Jones, and ——— Maurice. This last name can now be corrected from a newspaper record. A. J. Morris died at Heflin, Alabama, April 5, 1891, nearly one hundred years of age. He is supposed to have been the last survivor of the inmates of Fort Mims. Five are mentioned in the *Birmingham Age Herald*, by a special correspondent, L. E. M., as escaping through the pickets together. These were Martin Rigdon, Samuel Smith, Joseph Perry, Jesse Steadham, and A. J. Morris, and all these, it is said, went to Mount Vernon after several days wandering. These names are all in Pickett's list. "To these," says Halbert, "may be added, according to Dr. Clanton, Stubblefield, Cook, Montjoy, Aaron Bradley and Elemuel Bradford. Dr. Clanton's authority was Samuel Smith. Pickett's informers were Dr. T. G. Holmes, Jesse Steadham and Peter Randon. On the authority of Judge Meek may be added the name of James Bealle, and on the authority of Rev. J. G. Jones of Hazlehurst, Mississippi, the name of private Daniels of Jefferson County, Mississippi. There have already been given on good authority the additional names of Mrs. Mims, David Mims, Alexander Mims and Joseph Mims; also of Mrs. Susan Hatterway, Elizabeth Randon, and Lizzie the colored girl. So that, in addition to the fifteen of Pickett, without counting the McGirth family of seven or eight, we have the names of fourteen others, making in all some thirty-six survivors out of five hundred and fifty-three. There were probably a few others whose names are yet unknown, and some of the hundred colored people were probably taken away by the Indians, of whom there would remain no traces. About fifty seems to be a fair estimate of those who survived the horrors of that day and night.

"The escape of Lieutenant Chambliss," continues Halbert, "as given by Pickett, was remarkable. After passing out from the stockade and the Indians around it, he at length took refuge in a log-heap. To this in the night, some Indians set fire and when it seemed that he could no longer endure the smoke and the heat, something called the Indians away and he escaped.

"Captain Dixon Bailey, although severely wounded, left the Fort with others, taking with him his little child, but he never reached a human habitation. Judge Meek states that some time after there was found in the swamp a gun having the name, Dixon Bailey, cut in the stock, and by it were the bones of a man and a child. Pickett states that a negro carried a child of Dixon Bailey's in the effort to escape and that becoming bewildered in his excitement he ran back among the Indians who immediately killed the trembling boy as he was calling on his father to save his life."

way and two children by Dog Warrior, indicates that there was any intention on the part of the savages to spare the helpless women and children of the Fort,[27] though Weatherford claims, it is said, to have urged that these be left unmolested.

An incident preserved in behalf of the negro race makes a strong appeal: this being the instance of the negro Hester's devotion to the white race and her heroic effort, though severely wounded, to apprize General Claiborne of the calamity that was overtaking the Fort. In comparison with the savage and inhuman behavior of the Indians, the conduct of the slave, inferior though her race was to the red man's in many of the nobler aspirations, may be pointed to as interpretative of racial characteristics. Association with the white race had affected and improved her nature. Even here on this marge and limit of civilization, where the white man was lax in many rules that were with common consent made for him, we find the negro slaves, as a whole, reflecting in some degree his best virtues and instincts, while the red race of America was slow to receive the impress of the Christian civilization.[28]

The news of the dreadful massacre at Fort Mims was borne over the country as fast as horse and rider could travel and aroused not only the hot indignation of the people of the Mississippi Territory but of Americans throughout the Republic. Hearts everywhere were anxious for the safety of the white race in this far Southern section. Particularly in the Southern States the horrible deed was denounced, since Virginia, North and South Carolina had sent many representatives to the beautiful and fertile Mississippi country. Other States from Connecticut and Maine down to Kentucky had furnished numerous names to the list of immigrants who had settled the Territory.

When the news of the atrocity committed by the Indians was verified, vigilance committees were formed throughout the Mississippi

---

[27] See note on page 45-46 of this narrative.
[28] Another instance of the heroism and devotion of the negro race should be cited, the story running that one Samuel Smith, a survivor of the massacre, related to Dr. A. B. Clanton for publication an incident depicting the courage and loyalty of a negro man who by the side of Captain Dixon Bailey and his brothers valiantly assisted in the defense of Fort Mims. "A large and powerful negro man," says this eye witness, "wielding an ax killed more Indians than any other man in the Fort but he fell at last covered with wounds from knife and club and tomahawk."

Territory and the new State of Louisiana, the name of Harmon Blennerhassett, the unhappy dupe and confederate of Aaron Burr, appearing on the one formed at Port Gibson, Claiborne County, Mississippi, where the unfortunate family had made a hiding place for itself, calling the retreat "La Cache."

It was through the talented Mississippian George S. Gaines, who displayed unusual leadership in helping to enlist the Choctaws' aid in the American cause, that General Andrew Jackson was first apprised of the dreadful catastrophe at Fort Mims. The news, as has been stated elsewhere, spread consternation throughout the Southern States and the brave Tennesseans, remembering their own frontier experiences with the Cherokees and Chickasaws, determined to assist the Mississippi Territory in her hour of need. The gallant force that volunteered in her defense contained such spirits as Sam Houston and Davy Crockett.

Communication with the Governors of the adjoining States was opened up by Governor Holmes, who lost no time in strengthening the military defense of the Territory and putting it on a war footing. His messages and orders abound with patriotic utterances, such as "Patriotism, humanity, every motive of self preservation and every honorable feeling that binds man to man demands our utmost exertion."

The massacre at Fort Mims filled no hearts, perhaps, with more sorrow than those of General Ferdinand L. Claiborne and his Mississippi volunteers. The troops of the detachment dispatched with all haste to the scene were horror striken at the sight that met their eyes, and on beholding the butchered bodies of their friends and relatives "breathed out vengeance," says an eye witness, against the perpetrators of the appalling deed.

The brave and gallant Claiborne had left nothing unprovided for in the protection of the frontier, which would have been complete had his instructions been carried out. He had been everywhere on the Territorial boundary as far as the Choctaw line, sometimes riding seventy miles a day, and was often compelled to take the initiative, so restricted had his movements been by General Flournoy. After the dreadful disaster of Fort Mims, Claiborne began to be more self-assertive and aggressive and determined at any cost to protect the Mississippi Territory from an invasion by the ferocious and merciless

Creek Indians. Always counseling the greatest care on the part of the forces garrisoning the various forts, he now began active operations against the Creek war party. A favorite with the Mississippi militia, he always retained their confidence under the worst possible conditions, before and after they had entered volunteer service, an instance of his influence being shown on the occasion when he had determined to lead his regiment into the Indian country and attack the capital city of Holy Ground. Though the terms of his troops had expired and they were barefooted, hungry and half clothed, their crops at home ungathered, and the low price of cotton making it certain that their families would suffer for the necessities of life, he called the volunteers back into service and led them to victory in one of the most decisive battles that was fought for the safety of the Territory. And in this connection it is a fact worthy of record here that throughout the war not a shadow of disloyalty nor a trace of mutiny can be found in their service with Claiborne nor later with Jackson.

The attitude of Major-General Flournoy at this time would have chilled the soldierly ardor of a commander less brave than Claiborne. Cautious to the verge of timorousness, he, while a man of ability and worth in many respects, more than once had interfered with and thwarted a number of brilliant exploits planned by General Claiborne early after the fall of Fort Mims, exploits that would have summarily put an end to the Creek hostilities. Claiborne, knowing how imminent was the danger to the frontier settlements from the Indians, was determined to protect not only Mobile, but the entire Southern section. To all his appeals for immediate action against the destroyers of the garrison at Fort Mims, with his troops writhing under inaction and nursing with an implacable spirit their grievance against the Indians for the brutal massacre at Fort Mims, with the war already established and a certainty of Great Britain's and Spain's assistance thereto, he had received the following meticulous and tantalizing reply from the commander at Mobile:

"I do not wish you to engage in any rash enterprise. You must act on the defensive." Compare such a diffident spirit with the martial one that called forth such fervid utterances as "Seize Pensacola and you disarm the Indians. It is the real heart of the Creek Confederacy;" "At all hazards, I wish you would enter the Creek Nation;"

"I would advise a stroke at the root of all present distress—Pensacola." Such confidence of speech not only reveals the military ardor of the Mississippi soldier, but conclusively proves that he had a clear understanding of the situation. Being denied the expeditions planned for the use of combined forces, in squads of 100 and less, and sometimes single-handed and alone, the Mississippi troops under this brave discerning officer met the Indians throughout the months of September, October, November and December and overwhelmed them in every instance after the fatal event of August 30. Placed in the vicinity of Mobile to guard that place against an attack by the British, he was, also, keenly alive to the danger along the entire frontier. Dealing, however, with a superior who was evidently not in touch with the situation, his position was a trying one. Knowing the temper of the Mississippi volunteers, he feared nothing from the Indians if given the opportunity of quelling them. As the days passed in his correspondence with General Flournoy he evinces a confident, aggressive generalship, while a weak and vacillating judgment on the part of that officer is apparent, as is shown not only in the instance of his change of mind in the use of the Choctaw troops but in his lack of decision in so many other matters.

It was to General Claiborne more than to any other holding high rank in the army that Gaines and McKee looked for assistance in arranging the Choctaw alliance and in securing the active participation of Pushmataha in the war. It is thought by many local historians that had this renowned chieftain joined the war party the people of he Mississippi Territory could not in all probability have withstood the Creek invasion. The wisdom and judgment Governor Holmes displayed during the alliance with the Choctaws are also very apparent, and much credit is due this able official for the attitude of the Indians to the north of the Territory. With the Choctaws and Chickasaws friendly and General Claiborne now checking the advance of the Creek army Holmes felt that the safety of the people along the frontier was in a large measure assured, and his messages and orders reflect his relief.

If Claiborne had proved an obstacle to the invading foe, no less active and vigilant was Colonel Joseph Carson, whose volunteer forces were to lead many a fierce charge against Weatherford's warriors.[29] Both of these brave Mississippi commanders were fast driving the Indians from the frontier when General Jackson began active operations against them in the Northern District.

In addition to the message of Gaines, later official communications from Governor Holmes had brought news of the massacre at Fort Mims to the Tennessee capital and with his known impetuosity, though still weak from a wound received in a street duel with Thomas H. Benton, Jackson had gathered a large volunteer force of Tennesseans about him and hastened to the Mississippi Territory by way of Huntsville, now in the State of Alabama, joining his faithful subordinate, Colonel Coffee, who had preceded him.

General Claiborne, then in charge of the Mississippi defenses, was henceforth to be reinforced by General Jackson and his brave Tennesseans supported by United States regulars and numerous volunteers serving under Generals Coffee, Cocke, White and Floyd, the last mentioned commanding the volunteer forces from Georgia. These were to assist Jackson in his efforts to reduce the strength of the Creek Nation in such a manner as to render it of no assistance to the British.

It was about this time that young Thomas Hinds with the Mississippi Dragoons arrived on the scene. The following extracts from the *Encyclopedia of Mississippi History* relative to the furnishing of troops by Governor David Holmes will give the reader some idea of the organization of this troop of horse in the Mississippi Territory:

> Previous to the Fort Mims massacre, Governor Holmes ordered five companies of infantry and the cavalry to be in readiness to move at the shortest notice. The Mississippi Dragoons were among the first to respond. This famous cavalry battalion was composed of the Jefferson Troop commanded by Thomas Hinds before his promotion; the Adams Troop with James Kempe [30] captain, the Madison

---

[29] Colonel Joseph Carson of the Tombigbee settlements was one of the prominent men of the later Territorial period. He married a daughter of Abner Green of Adams County and consequently had influential connections in the Natchez district. He was commissioned as an attorney-at-law in 1807, was a member of the Territorial Council from 1809 to 1817; was attorney-general of the eastern district for many years, a militia officer, in 1813 was colonel of the 1st Mississippi regiment, United States Volunteers, on duty in the Alabama region. He forced the evacuation of the Spanish post on the Perdido River, April 27, 1813. In 1812 he was urged by his section as a candidate for congressional delegate. To him was accorded an admiration by Governor Holmes second only to that the Governor constantly expressed for Major Thomas Hinds.

[30] "James Kempe the grandfather of Mrs. Jefferson Davis, was a native of Castlefin, County Donegal, Ireland, and was one of the 'United Irishmen' of 1798, compelled to flee to America," wrote Anthony Campbell, the last survivor

Troop, J. G. Richardson captain and the Amite Troop, ———— Dunn captain—in all about 200 men.

In his General Orders issued at Liberty, Governor Holmes said:

> The commander-in-chief has witnessed with the utmost satisfaction the alacrity shewn by the cavalry in repairing to the standard of their country upon his call for their services. The corps is composed of men in whose patriotism and courage their fellow citizens must have the utmost confidence. Not soldiers from compulsion, or from necessity, they have placed themselves in the front ranks of danger to oppose a savage foe now threatening our country with destruction and devastation.

The battalion was composed of the very pick of the young manhood of the Mississippi Territory and notwithstanding the estimate placed on it by General Flournoy, commanding at Mobile, it was destined to take a leading part in the story of Jackson's Coast Campaign against the British. It was organized by order of Governor David Holmes for immediate use on the frontier to meet the Indian situation.

The cavalry were sent forward with the 3rd United States Infantry, which had been largely recruited by volunteers from the Mississippi Territory. Governor Holmes in a message that followed their arrival in the war zone announced that "the arrival of these troops renders the entire force on the eastern frontier efficient and reputable."

The infantry furnished by the Mississippi Territory were to coöperate when necessary with Jackson's army composed of East and West Tennessee troops and United States infantry. Later, Governor Holmes sent another regiment under the gallant Colonel Nixon.[31] Two more companies were sent to this regiment in February, 1814,

---

of these Irish immigrants in Mississippi. Henry S. Foote had it that he was born in Virginia. Kempe succeeded Benjamin Farrar as Captain of the Adams troop of horse and won distinction in the New Orleans campaign, not long after which he died, leaving several children. Says Foote: "Among the daughters who sprang from him was a Mrs. Howell, of whom, I am told, Mrs. Jefferson Davis is the daughter".

Kempe, who became a colonel of cavalry, died at Natchez in 1820, leaving a numerous family of sons and daughters. One of the daughters, as Foote said married William B. Howell, of Natchez, son of an old revolutionary officer and governor of New Jersey. Campbell wrote of these families, "What a clutch of true blues there will be between the blood of Howell and Kempe." See *Encyclopedia of Mississippi History*.

[31] Colonel Nixon was born in Virginia and after living some years in South Carolina removed in 1809 to the Mississippi Territory. He was among the first to offer his services in defence of his country. During the Creek War, Colonel Nixon at the head of a considerable force scoured the swamps of the Perdido and other streams and killed and captured many Indians. After he had accomplished all he could, he marched to the head of the Perdido, where he divided his command, sending Major William Peacock with the troops of the 39th to the boat yard on

from Colonel Neilson's regiment (Amite County) and Captain Rapalje's company from Washington. When the term of enlistment expired in April, 1814, the regiment was immediately recruited. On March 20, 1814, the Governor wrote to the colonel of the 3rd United States Infantry: "I have ordered six companies of infantry to be drafted and marched to the eastern frontier as expeditiously as possible." To Colonel Nixon the Governor wrote: "These six companies with the two that marched under the command of Major Swayze and as many more as can be prevailed upon will form your command." Though the Territory was sparsely settled every man who could bear a gun, as Governor Holmes noted in a message, was in the service at some period of the campaign in the South against the British.[32]

After the arrival of Major Hinds with his troop of horse, General Claiborne continued to throw his forces with the utmost confidence against the Indians. It was to the chivalrous, adventure-loving Dragoons that the latter entrusted the whole territory, employing the gallant troop of horse to scour the country in pursuit of the roving bands of Indians who were menacing the white settlements.

General Jackson addressed a letter to Governor Holmes in which he thanked him for the promptitude with which he assembled and marched this body of troops, especially commending the fine appearance of the Dragoons. Made up of the sons of the first families of the Mississippi Territory, the troopers bore themselves a trifle arrogantly but cheerfully and almost lightly amidst every privation and hardship.

Their haughty and self-confident air and manner did not meet with the approbation of the commander of the district at Mobile. Seeking military glory through adventure and chafing under restrictions, the

---

Lake Tensaw, while he marched the remainder of his command to Fort Claiborne. He was an excellent officer and served to the end of the war. He was a member of the convention that formed the first constitution of the State of Mississippi, and was, afterwards, frequently a state senator. He died in Pearlington, Mississippi, in 1824. He was a large, fine-looking man, with fair complexion, and was very popular.

[32] Jefferson Davis, President of the Southern Confederacy, writing of this period many years later said: " . . . . When news came of the approach of the British army to attack New Orleans, the sons of Wilkinson County went in such numbers to defend the city, that the county court held a draft to keep a certain proportion of the men at home, for police purposes. The records of the County probably contain the particulars of the event, of which I have only the recollection of what a child would hear."

high-spirited battalion acted as an irritant to the obtuse though touchy and testy Flournoy. General Claiborne regretted their inability to coöperate amicably with the commanding general of the district and deplored the communication which they addressed to that source, a remonstrance that must have been very tart, judging from the increased heat on the part of the commanding general. Knowing the real worth of the spirited troop of horse, he refused to take sides with the General in the controversy that followed. Both Claiborne and Jackson were always in perfect accord with the gallant young commander of the Dragoons. Throughout the fall of 1813 Claiborne depended on him at every turn in checking the movements of the wily foe, while General Jackson, perceiving his rare capacity as a cavalry officer and his ability as a leader, selected him to lead the army into Pensacola. Despite the attitude of General Flournoy, the adventurous, self-reliant Dragoons were to reap the glory they sought. Stung by the petty injustice of a superior at Mobile, the mettlesome and light-hearted battalion continued to follow Claiborne along the frontier and in the forks of the Tombigbee which immediately after the atrocity at Fort Mims became the scene of numerous bloody encounters between Mississippi troops and the Indians. Instigated by the revengeful "Prophet" Francis, his blood-thirsty warriors marched from settlement to settlement, making a holocaust of the deserted homes, killing all whom they met and carrying off the fattest cattle for the war feasts in which they were now constantly indulging.

It was on September 1, 1813, that the home of Ransom Kimbell, a pioneer settler from South Carolina, was attacked by Francis and his army, the Kimbell family with a party of friends and relatives having left the crowded stockade at Fort Sinquefield for more comfort in the farm house during the hot weather of August. It was in this unprotected condition that the entire party was surprised and fiendishly massacred by the "Prophet" and his warriors at 3 o'clock in the afternoon. The Indians advanced suddenly from the fastnesses of the dense summer forest, along Bassett Creek. The horrible deed was committed in the same spirit that prevailed at Fort Mims, the savages sparing neither old age nor the mother with the unborn child. Isham Kimbell, one of the two survivors, became a worthy citizen of Clarke County, where doubtless some descendant still resides who may well be proud of lineage from this strong and valiant-hearted pioneer folk who marked with untimely graves the trails that became open roads for other feet. Leaving the main party supposed to be still commanded by Weatherford, who like his grandfather was also called "Red Eagle," the "Prophet" Francis continued to operate in the forks of the Tombigbee, where, on the rich, alluvial lands, the hardy pioneers had established settlements, the more prosperous of them with the help of their slaves having opened large plantations. It was of these fair lands of promise that the Indians grew jealous, seeing in the cultivated fields and pastures the passing of the hunting-grounds and the buffalo trails that had been fixtures of their civilization. And now that they had taken the war path, the Creeks determined to exterminate the encroaching white settlements root and branch. Immediately following the murder of the Kimbells and their friends and relatives, the "Prophet" made a direct attack on Fort Sinquefield, to which the people in its vicinity had fled. The Fort was defended by a small company of troopers sent in haste by Colonel Carson from Fort Madison under the command of Lieutenant James Bailey, brother of the heroic Captain Dixon Bailey, who though maternally of savage descent had given his life at Fort Mims in behalf of the ideals of the civilization of the white race in America, having recognized in himself and in his children its superior claim.

Among the brave horsemen sent with Lieutenant Bailey in defense of Fort Sinquefield were James Wood, Isaac Hayden and James Smith. Few stories of the pioneer folk of America glow with more romance and adventure than those of the first settlers of this far southern region. Of the many daring feats daily performed the charge made by young Isaac Hayden near this Fort upon one hundred painted savages with a pack of dogs and a pair of pistols was an exploit so romantic and savoring even of the preposterous that it would, in all probability, have disconcerted a better trained soldiery than the "Prophet" Francis commanded. But one should not forget that the dogs with which the hero charged the Indians were pioneer dogs and that both dogs and men are taught to do their part in border life.

In the attack on Fort Sinquefield, the Indians did not display their usual strategy. While they very cunningly selected an hour when the gates of the Fort would be open, the inmates being engaged in a burial service of the Kimbell party massacred a few days before, they failed to remember that the happenings of the last few days had rendered every mind alert and ready for defense and that their daylight approach down hill from the woods would be instantly caught by sharp eyes on the lookout for trouble. Though frantically urged forward by the "Prophet" himself, the Indians failed to surprise the gallant Lieutenant Bailey, who with his small party of Dragoons conveyed the people safely to the Fort. Failing to overtake them and perceiving a few women at a spring, the Indians made a break in that direction. It was then that the valiant Hayden flew at them with every dog in the Fort, urging on his one hundred snarling canines and brandishing his pistols in such a clamorous and boisterous manner that the savages, abashed at the performance, stood stock still while with the exception of one which was overtaken and slain, the women passed in safety to the Fort. After several hours' fierce attack on the Fort, Francis and his army, amid a whir of bullets, retreated, leaving the excited defenders of the Fort victors though for the moment shaking with fear.

The next morning the inmates of Sinquefield made their way to Fort Madison, where they breathed more freely after their terrifying experience. Some attempted to carry along clothing and food and the journey became a painful one, filled as all were with fear of momentary attack by some lurking band of savages. It was with sad hearts, too, that they had left the new-made graves of their relatives and friends and it is little wonder that even such hardy spirits as theirs were depressed. In their own fireside superstitions, the stars had foretold their sorry plight, there was blood on the moon and the letter "W:" on the wing of the locust. It was a dark day in American history but it had its meaning. It was the advance of civilization to the far outer rim of its adventuring efforts; and scattered everywhere on the lonely frontier beneath the trees that had not as yet given up their forest depths were thousands of shallow graves, silent testimonials of the sacrifice of the first comers who cleared and made the fair land habitable for their race.

Tragic occurrences, such as have been related, were being daily reported to General Claiborne. The Creeks were now fully at war, and murder, rapine and pillage marked their pathway along the frontier.

After the verification of a constant rumor that a combined attack by the Indians was to be made on Fort Madison, General Claiborne ordered Colonel Carson and Major Hinds to quit that stockade and march to Fort St. Stephens as a place of greater safety.[33] Colonel Carson took with him about 500 settlers, men, women and children, with a view toward their better protection. It was natural, that any settlers still remaining in that section should feel alarmed at the evacuation of Fort Madison and so urgent were they in their entreaties for protection that General Claiborne, who had left the order discretionary with Colonel Carson, now hurriedly sent him a dispatch not to abandon Fort Madison if he felt sure his forces could protect it. Colonel Carson had already obeyed the order and for a short space Fort Madison was left without military defense, except that afforded by the eighty citizens who immediately enrolled themselves under the valiant Captains Austill and Dale. The latter was recovering from wounds he had received at Burnt Corn and was thirsting for revenge on the Indians. This force was not required to maintain the fort very long before Colonel Carson returned with his large company of women and children.

It was in this manner that General Claiborne with his small but trusted army moved for many days from place to place as the needs seemed more urgent. The forts were scattered and the Indians were roving in small predatory bands everywhere, and no one could tell where they would next concentrate their attack. Every settlement and every fort was appealing to Claiborne for protection and it was with the utmost care and the highest order of generalship that he prevented a repetition of Fort Mims.

General Claiborne was criticized by a few short sighted persons at the time for removing the garrison for several weeks from Fort Madison, but it is clearly seen that it was a move that he thought best to take until he could feel assured that the Indians were not gathering in such numbers that Colonel Carson could not maintain its defense.

---

[33] Colonel Carson was the military commander of the territory between the Alabama and Tombigbee Rivers in which region were located Fort Glass and Fort Madison and it was to General Claiborne with headquarters at Mount Vernon, forty miles distant, that he sent young Jerry Austill who later became a border hero with a special communication. The hardy youth traveled alone through a heavily timbered country filled with roving bands of Indians.

The situation at this time presented anything but a pleasing prospect. As yet the Choctaws, though allied with the Americans, had furnished no troops to the army and it was with much relief that the people heard that Pushmataha had visited St. Stephens with a proposal to enlist several companies of Choctaw troops for the American cause.

The celebrated chieftain met with much encouragement from General Claiborne and was accompanied to Mobile by Mr. George Gaines where the formal acceptance of the troops by General Flournoy took place. The commanding general, having by this time slowly but thoroughly embraced General Claiborne's view of the Indian matter, now no longer directed him to act on the defensive but, to his great relief empowered him to attack the Indians. The order, however, did not provide for an invasion of the Creek country so much desired by Claiborne.

After arriving home, Pushmataha, celebrated for his wisdom and discretion among the Choctaws, assembled the most powerful heads and rulers of the whole nation and with his convincing eloquence actively federated them with the Americans. The Chickasaws, too, were attached to the Americans through the efforts of Colonel McKee and John Peachland. It was as has already been observed, largely due to the statesmanship of Governor Holmes and General Claiborne that the aid of the Choctaws and Chickasaws was enlisted in the war, and their alliance with the American Republic was one of the master strokes in the successful defense of the Coast against British invasion.

It was during these days that Major Thomas Hinds with his Mississippi Dragoons was so closely associated with General Claiborne, both being engaged in service of the most strenuous and hazardous nature along the frontier and especially in the valley of the Tombigbee in keeping broken and disorganized bands of Indians from overrunning the entire country. The young cavalry officer, notwithstanding his breach with Flournoy, continued close to Jackson and Claiborne, and drew from them many warm expressions of praise.

While operating at this seat of war, the main body of the Indians usually kept within the dense, heavily-timbered swamps, sallying forth in companies sometimes numbering as many as a hundred, but very often composed of not more than a dozen warriors. During such forays and raids, conducted with the utmost suddenness, the Creeks picked off many of the bravest scouts of the American army and put to sudden death the inmates of many lonely farm houses. Scouting parties of the whites went frequently in search of the Indians and it was during one of these excursions that Carson lost some of his bravest men. The story of Beard and his friend Tandy Walker is one filled with the wildest adventure, resulting in the death of the former at the hands of a savage. The gallant young soldier, Bradberry, who had won fame as a good fighter at Burnt Corn, also lost his life in one of these forays. In a similar manner Colonel William McGrew had been killed previously. While pursuing a party of Indians over stream and through forests and field on the northern bank of the Tombigbee, he suddenly came upon them on Bashi Creek to find them more ready for battle than he dreamed. In the severe encounter that followed the brave man with three of his company was killed. Several days later when General Claiborne with Major Hinds and the Mississippi Dragoons were marching in pursuit of the Indians, who hovered in small bodies everywhere, he found and interred with military honors the bodies of these four heroes, pioneer Mississippians who had sacrificed their lives willingly in defense of their country. The loss of such lives was a serious blow to a young Territory whose population was scant and rural community life, to a large extend, unformed.

It was during the incessant guerrilla warfare, filled with pillage and murder by the Indians in the rich river settlements along the eastern borders of the Territory, that the famous Mississippi frontiersman, Sam Dale, again appears on the stage. A native of Rockbridge County, Virginia, descended from a line of border heroes, he was well fitted to act his part in the affairs of his adopted section. Having in a measure recovered from his wounds received earlier in the war, he sought the field once more with a determination to help General Claiborne drive the Indians from the country. Colonel Carson, who had returned to Fort Madison, was prevailed on to furnish him with a sufficient force to put his plans into execution, and he was provided with a detachment of thirty Mississippi volunteers from Captain Jones' company, while forty of the Clarke County militia were detailed to accompany him in his rather hazardous adventure. The expedition, though the soldiers were all poorly equipped and faced the late autumn days thinly clad and bare-foot, had to its credit the remarkable canoe fight on the waters of the Alabama in which four of Dale's party distinguished themselves as border heroes.

This hand to hand conflict was, perhaps one of the wildest ever staged in frontier history. For the gruesome tragedy the heavy American forest, beneath which glided the silent river, now at low water mark and wrapped in autumnal shadows, was selected. And was it not its solemn beauty appealing to their highest aspiration of a God that had made its wild, red children swear to defend it, "as long as the sun shall shine and there shall be water in the river?"

The description of the fierce struggle by local historians is filled with details of such a horrid nature that their hideous and revolting particulars will not be enumerated here, the heroic courage and devotion of the combatants of both sides being things of more moment.

Captain Dale and his little company, after putting to flight a small band of mounted Indians in the open, had formed the advance in crossing the river. Screened from view by the bank covered with tall cane, great forest trees and undergrowth, they were engaged in preparing a needed repast when they discovered gliding down the Alabama in slow, stately fashion an unusually large and handsome flat-bottomed canoe in which sat, with erect forms and dignified mien, a company of Indian warriors richly clothed in panther skins, their faces and strong bare limbs painted in the brilliant hues of the puccoon. With august decorum bearing their guns before them they were the personification of the Indian War Spirit at ceremonial moments. The solemn touch of dignity, acquired doubtlessly by long contact with the silent things of nature, vanished in a trice so soon as they discovered the Americans. They were now only painted savages filled with revenge and thirsting for the blood of the hated foe. What race, alas! has proved itself much better?

The boats of Captain Dale, which were under the command of the famous Jerry Austill, floated along the river in sight of the troopers who kept to the river bank in search of the enemy. They were near the home of the brave Dixon Bailey who had given his life in the defense of Fort Mims and the memory of that gallant soldier filled them with a hot desire to punish his slayers. Alarmed at the approach of the whites, the Indians rowed back to concealment in the mouth of Randon Creek. Discovering that the largest part of Dale's company had crossed the river to the western bank, the canoe emerged, while anxiety and watchfulness had taken the place of proud unconcern on the faces of its occupants. As it moved cautiously down the river Captain Dale and his little party fired upon the stately crew to which the proud warriors replied instantly, showing their readiness for battle. After several exchanges of rifle shots that resulted in little injury to either side, Captain Dale sprang into his small boat and called to his men to follow him; three instantly obeyed their leader as only this number could crowd into the tiny boat. The combatants drew nearer each other and the fight grew desperate. The fearless and valiant attacking party, besides their redoubtable captain, was composed of Jeremiah Austill, James Smith and the powerful and courageous slave Caesar, a half-breed Indian negro. This faithful creature, who had now taken charge of the little boat, rowed alongside the large canoe and with might and main held his craft in position while the battle raged. The Indians fought desperately for they knew that "Big Sam," as they called Captain Dale, was their antagonist. Many a brave story had they heard of this wonderful man both as a trader and a fighter. Still, they were not afraid to measure lances with him as was unconsciously shown in the grimly spoken challenge. "Now for it, Big Sam!" In and out of the water but more often with feet planted firmly in their boats, which the burly Caesar kept lashed together, the combatants fought with a fury known only to border warfare. When the close and deadly struggle came to an end the hero Dale found himself in the enemy's boat while eleven of the best warriors of the proud Muscogee tribe had paid the price of liberty. Both the living and the dead were covered with wounds and upon the breast of both Creek and Anglo-Saxon alike could well have been placed the Distinguished Service Cross. This hand-to-hand combat, fierce and daring as any known to history remains undimmed in comparison with the feat of the dauntless three who held the bridge in the days of ancient Rome. Henceforth Dale, Austill and Smith became names to conjure with in both Jackson's and Claiborne's army, while Caesar's desperate courage, as it was shown not only in action, but, also, in the dead silence that bound his lips broken only in his urging the use of the sword and bayonet, clearly proves that the heroic deeds of that day were not all confined to the free races. After the short but terrific battle, gathering up his little band, Captain Dale, whose exploits make some of the most colorful pages of Mississippi's history, marched back to Fort Madison. It was in this manner that the brave Mississippi soldiery, descended from good Revolutionary fighting stock and patriotic to the core, kept the Creeks at bay on the forks of the Tombigbee, along the Alabama, and up and down the southern frontier in the first months of the war.

General Claiborne had always felt that to rid the country of the Indians it would be necessary to deal them a concentrated blow on their own soil. He again urged General Flournoy to send him into the Creek Nation with a sufficient force to attack them in their strongholds and cripple their strength by destroying their towns. The large expedition planned by him in the early autumn had been frustrated by the over-cautious commander at Mobile whose indecision in matters of such vital importance appears little short of criminal. That General Flournoy had at last arrived at the same conclusion General Claiborne held regarding the trouble with the Creeks was very gratifying to the Mississippian, though the harsh war measures recommended by the commanding general, who had now gone to the other extreme in his views of the Indian situation, were not in keeping with Claiborne's code of ethics. Even when dealing with savages, though always to be feared in battle, no foe was ever taken undue advantage of by this knightly and kindly soul. Throughout the months of September, October and November, he had been busy in the Southern District, his brave volunteers fighting daily battles and guarding the defenceless inhabitants from sudden slaughter. With him for much of the time was Major Thomas Hinds and his eager-hearted Dragoons. These were taking their first lessons in warfare, a game in which they were destined to play a shining part in the very drama that was now being enacted. Even at this time their commander was becoming conspicuous for his courage and initiative, and of him General Claiborne confidently said to the old border hero Sam Dale "When you see danger ahead take Hinds with you."

At this place will be enumerated a number of fierce battles and encounters with the Creeks in which Jackson's troops were engaged. No truer nor more intrepid soldiery ever went out in defense of their country than the volunteer troops of Tennessee, and we rear on this page a signal monument to these defenders and lovers of liberty. But one cannot forget that border warfare of the severest nature had been conducted by troops of the Mississippi Territory throughout the Southern District before General Jackson's forces fought at Tallussahatchie, and that Mississippians in this section were everywhere engaged in the defense of the Republic. Even in the ranks of Jackson's own army, especially in the 3rd United States Regulars, large numbers of Mississippi troops had enlisted. Recruiting stations were established at several points in the Territory, and volunteers from the Mississippi Territory entered various commands and were largely instrumental in winning the victories that perched on the American banners in this section.

Jackson's campaign against the Creeks during the months of October and November opened with the battle of Tallussahatchie. A successful attack had been made at Littefutche led by Colonel Dyer with 200 cavalry sent out by General Jackson from Fort Deposit, where he had established headquarters, and foraging parties had captured a few Indians and negroes who were camp-followers of Weatherford's army. The Creeks learning that Jackson was near by, hastily collected their forces at the town of Tallussahatchie a short distance from his headquarters. After locating the town and the extent of its defense, General Jackson sent Brigadier-General Coffee with 1000 men to destroy the place. Half of the troops were to constitute the attacking party while the rest reconnoitered the Ten-Island country as preliminary to future movements. The Tennesseeans were well supplied with good rifles and were in their best fighting mood. A picturesque band of Creeks and Cherokees friendly to the whites, arrayed in the white head-dress which was their emblem of peace, led Coffee's men against the war party. The battle began at sunrise, the turbulent savages rushing out amid war-whoops and the beating of drums, their prophets breathing vengeance upon the invaders and on any of Indian blood who assisted them. They fought a losing fight without asking quarter from their well-armed foes. Not one would desert the field, but men, women and children all perished with their city. On November 3, 1813, General Jackson wrote to Governor Blount of Tennessee relative to the battle, "We have retaliated for the destruction of Fort Mims." In his report of the same day General Coffee said, "Not one of the warriors escaped to carry the news." The feat might be compared with the brave old deeds that marked Alexander's or Hannibal's campaigns, but wherefore?

Following the successful attack on the Indians by General Coffee, on November 3, 1813, General Jackson moved to Ten-Island where he erected Fort Strother. With an army of 1200 infantry and 1800 cavalry the 3rd United States Regulars being recruited with Mississippians, he moved on the town of Talladega, 30 miles away, where he raised the siege then going on at that place.

The town having been the rendezvous of a large number of Creeks friendly to the Americans was now beleaguered by wrathful Creek prophets who, for all their magic and black art, were no match for the astute disciple of peace who clothed in a shaggy hogskin passed through their ranks at night on all fours from the invested city. Grunting and rooting his way out of the town he bounded to his feet and fled to Jackson's camp to implore aid from that mighty pale-face. The Tennesseans received their envoy with shouts of laughter and applause and straightway marched to the relief of the beseiged redskins who—and here the laughter dies down into a sigh—passed out of the city over the bleeding bodies of one thousand dead warriors who had given their lives in defense of their race and civilization.

Writing of this battle to General Claiborne, General Jackson said:

> It is impossible to tell with any precision the loss they sustained. We counted, however, 299 dead on the field but this is known to fall considerably short of the number really killed. Could I have followed up that victory immediately the Creek War before this had been terminated but I was compelled by a double cause—the want of supplies and the want of coöperation from the East Tennessee troops—to return to this place.

A strong jealousy, historians all agree, existed between the East Tennessee and the West Tennessee troops which interfered at times with Jackson's operations in the Creek War, and explains this reference in his letter to the East Tennessee troops. Near the close of his letter to Claiborne, General Jackson makes this suggestive statement:

> It is not understood by the Government that this war is to be confined to mere temporary incursions into the enemy's country. Such movements might distress them but would produce none of those lasting and beneficial effects which I design to be produced.

On November 18, 1813, occurred what Halbert rightfully calls the

"Hillabee Massacre."[34] That staid historian characterizes it as a "deplorable action" and it was, indeed, little else than butchery. For American toops to have made war on a lower plane than did the savages was a poor expression of the Christian civilization claimed by the superior race. Negotiations were then pending for the surrender of the Hillabees, and it was a rude awakening for the helpless creatures, generally faithful to their vows, to find that "their scrap of paper" had been cast to the winds by the great Jackson. It is sincerely hoped that they located the right source on which to lay the blame. That Generals Cocke and White did not possess Jackson's and Claiborne's ideals is clearly shown in the reports of the Hillabee affair. While the spirit with which the two last mentioned waged war was as stern and invincible as Caesar's or Napoleon's, humanity and its kindlier purpose can be clearly discerned in their treatment of the helpless savages when at their mercy. Whenever an act on the part of the troops commanded by either of these great leaders took the form of mere butchery such conduct always received his severe condemnation. Both welcomed every honorable sign of surrender on the part of the Creeks and the flag of truce was borne more than once to the strongholds of the Muscogees.

That the Indians in some places were still having civil war among themselves and were in large numbers joining the party friendly to the whites is found in their scant records of the war. Still the spirit of self-preservation united the main part of the Creek Nation in a great army to resist with the most heroic efforts both Jackson and Claiborne. Notwithstanding desertions from their ranks this spirit grew stronger each day and inch by inch until finally overcome they resisted the despoilers of their towns and villages.

It was during the last week of autumn on November 29 that General Floyd with 950 Georgia militia supported by two friendly Indian chieftains, Mad-dog and Tookabatchee, with their following

---

[34] This battle was fought by General White with a thousand men of Major General Cocke's division of East Tennessee troops who carried out General Cocke's orders to attack the town while the Hillabee Indians were arranging terms with General Jackson for its surrender. As Jackson was regarded as the commander-in-chief of the Tennessee army one can readily understand why the Hillabees accused him of bad faith. His differences with General John Cocke who had brought a body of East Tennessee troops into the Mississippi Territory and the lack of co-operation with him on the part of that General do not bear particularly upon the main story but may be found in full in Parton's *Life of Andrew Jackson*, Vol. I.

of about 400 warriors attacked the town of Autossee one of the most attractive on the south bank of the beautiful and historic Tallapoosa. The city was situated near the Hickory Ground and the union of the Coosa. In the battle which also partook largely of a massacre the town was completely destroyed with several other inland villages, notable among them the Apple-grove, the birthplace of the renowned half-breed chieftain William McGillivray whose descendants were equally divided between the contending forces. In many of these skirmishes the fights assumed the proportions of real battle. The Indians whose country was being invaded and desolated were now fighting for the preservation of their race, homes and hunting-grounds and though savage and untutored, they were as much attached to their native heath as the Anglo-Saxon had ever been to his. While now rarely on the aggressive, as they had been earlier in the war, at Fort Mims and throughout the Southern District, no fiercer resistance was ever offered by a people than that with which they met Jackson when attacked on their own soil, and by superior numbers. To them by this time "Captain Jackson," as they called him, had loomed into a mysterious and prodigious power of evil to do them harm. But even as formidable as he appeared the Hillabee did not shrink from him in battle and more than once boasted of having put him to flight. In every encounter they met him with the indomitable spirit of a free people. The Georgians, too, led by General Floyd through the beautiful Callabee Valley, heard the sharp twang of their bows and felt the sting of their arrows.

At his camp at Pine Level in Clarke County General Claiborne received orders on November 10, from General Flournoy to quit that post for another field of action. Sharing his burning desire to make Pensacola the objective point, it was with eagerness that his troops broke camp on November 13, and moved forward to Weatherford's Bluff where they were to make preparations for General Jackson looking to an attack on Pensacola which was now believed by all to be the seat of trouble. On November 17, Claiborne crossed the Alabama River and halted at Weatherford's Bluff. Here his troops, cheerful despite the scantiness of food and clothing, fortified themselves for future action, Pushmataha's warriors practicing daily with the new rifles given them at Fort Madison, and, if tradition can be trusted, sallying forth to take a view of Burnt Corn, the fame of

Mississippi Territory in War of 1812—Rowland.   71

which had spread far into the Choctaw Nation. It was in a spirit of exultation that the great chieftain claimed that he put to flight a party of Creeks whom he found occupying the famous battle-ground. After constructing a strong fort to which his soldiers gave his magnetic name, Claiborne wrote to Governor Holmes giving him an account of the concentration of his troops and announcing his determination to intercept and break connection between the Indians and Pensacola. A letter, also, went to General Jackson congratulating him on his victories in the northern district and still another went to Governor Holmes expressing a fervent desire that all the troops should be hurled against Pensacola.[35]

The last battle of the year 1813 was to fall to General Claiborne and his Mississippi volunteer regiments. Carrying out his long cherished desire, he gathered a strong force about him composed almost entirely of Mississippi soldiery and a number of Louisiana volunteers and confided to them his determination to march to the enemy's capital. This fortress of two hundred houses, fortified after the Indian manner, bore the sacred name of Econachaca called, also, "Ikanchaka," the Holy Ground. "The fortress and town were erected" says the Mississippi historian, Claiborne, "by Weatherford on the south bank of the Alabama 125 miles from Fort Claiborne just after the massacre of Fort Mims." It was designed for a safe haven for the Creeks in time of trouble. A rude citadel, planted on a little peninsula jutting out into the river and set in the deep forest, it was surrounded on the land side by marshes, slashes and bayous. To it no path ran that the foot of the white man had ever trod. Guarded by 10,000 ungoverned and rampant savages, it yet—notwithstanding its wizard circles and the incantations of its holy men—was not im-

---

[35] In his letter to Governor Holmes Claiborne said:
"I am now on the east bank of the Alabama, thirty-five miles above Mims, and in the best part of the enemy's country. From this position we cut the savages off from the river, and from their growing crops. We likewise render their communication with Pensacola more hazardous. Here will be deposited for the use of General Jackson, a supply of provisions, and I hope I shall be ordered to cooperate with him. Colonel Russell of the Third U. S. Infantry has been ordered to co-operate with the Georgia troops, and is now on his march to this place. We have by several excursions alarmed the Indians, and the possession of this important position will induce them to retire. I have with me Pushmataha, who, with fifty-one warriors, accompanied by Lieutenant Calahan of the volunteers, will march this morning and take up a position to intercept more effectually the communication of the enemy with Pensacola."

penetrable to the conquering race that now sought it. It was here that, with the spirit of the Inquisition, the "Prophet" Francis ordered all prisoners to be burned at the stake, and it was here he boasted that no enemy of the Creek could tread without being blasted by the hand of the Great Spirit.

Unlike Weatherford, for whose fairness and courage he had always had respect, Francis had ever been an object of aversion to General Claiborne and to punish this heartless and wily fanatic in his own stronghold and put an end forever to his flummeries and wizardry was an undertaking espoused with as fervid zeal as ever fired the breast of a twelfth century knight. Every soldier in his command when fully acquainted with his purpose manifested his aspiration and battle spirit. Smarting under the injustice and petty spite of censorious critics and seeing in the expedition the adventure to which they had long looked forward, with spirits overflowing with love of adventure and patriotic fervor, the invincible volunteers, though their terms of enlistment had expired and the prospect was anything but inviting, voluntarily re-enlisted in the service.

While some of Claiborne's officers at first opposed an expedition into the Creek country, going so far as to petition him to desist from what seemed merely a quixotic enterprise, they concluded their petition with the soldierly utterance that "Be your decision what it may we shall cheerfully obey your orders and carry out your plans." The objections set forth in the memorial were of such a compelling nature that a purpose less firm than Claiborne's would have been shaken. The memorial drew his attention to the facts that it was winter and the cold, soaking rains had set in; the unknown and untrodden wilderness must be traversed; the impossibility of taking any supplies with them; the present condition of his army, without clothes, shoes or blankets—these and a number of other reasons, perhaps the most urgent and pathetic being that a total failure of crops that year had left their families in a destitute condition, were sufficient, it would seem, to have cooled his ardor for the expedition against the Creeks. But notwithstanding all this and the fact that the Tennessee troops and all others engaged in the service usually went home at the expiration of their term of enlistment, when Claiborne gave the order to break camp every man flew to his gun and took his place in the line of march.

Mississippi Territory in War of 1812—Rowland. 73

On the morning of December 13, Fort Claiborne was abandoned and the Mississippi army at their trusted General's command moved forward towards the Creek capital to confront not only the bitter Francis but the fierce Weatherford himself.[36] The frontier army of 1000 patriots was made up of Colonel Joseph Carson's Regiment of Mississippi Volunteers, the 3rd United States Regiment of Infantry, largely supplied with Mississippians, Major Cassell's valiant battalion of horse, a battalion of militia commanded by Major Benjamin Smoot in which Patrick May, Sam Dale, Creagh and Heard, border fighters who had already won their croix de guerre, were officers. These with 150 fine Choctaw warriors under the celebrated Pushmataha made up Claiborne's army. To this deft and adroit chieftain, now a brigadier-general in the United States Army, is due much of the enthusiasm with which the Choctaws participated in the invasion of the Creek country. The Mississippi volunteers were in gay, good humor, forgetting all their discomforts and anxieties once they were on the road. The army, represented by many of the best families of the Mississippi Territory bore itself with due appreciation of the fact. It boasted mainly Revolutionary ancestry and the young men possessed much of the manner and air of the cavalier. Through the pathless deep woods its columns wound their way, maintaining a martial bearing that would have compared favorably with that of any frontier army in the history of America. Much in the light of a crusader its valiant commander appeared imbued as he was with the spirit of freedom and filled with a sacred desire to plant the Cross of Christianity in the strongholds of the pagan.

On December 23, the troops approached the Holy City. Even as they advanced upon it prisoners both white and half-breeds were being bound to the stake awaiting the fagot and torch. The Indians, notwithstanding their claim of perfect security within their Holy of Holies, at the approach of Claiborne's army hurriedly began beating the war-drums and gathering their numerous forces into battle-line. The Mississippians could hear the heavy roll of drums as they entered the outskirts of the town. Through the swamps and over the bayous

---

[36] It is thought by Halbert after close investigation that Weatherford was never present at any battle but that of the Holy Ground after the Massacre of Fort Mims, though he does not hold to this opinion, in his sketch of Weatherford written many years before his later researches.

and lagoons surrounding the city the whole army steadily pushed its way, General Claiborne riding at the head of the cavalry. The troops behaved with great credit, Major Smoot especially on entering bearing himself in true military form. Major Cassells commanding mounted riflemen, alone suffered some criticism as to the manner of stationing his troops.

The subtle and inscrutable Weatherford ordinarily humane and mitigative but now cold and set in purpose and true to the maternal strain led his people in battle. In this splendid creature Claiborne met a foe not to be contemned.

The Creeks had done everything possible to make the Holy Ground impregnable but not even the fearless and daring Weatherford himself, whose personality fascinated them as no other, nor all the enchantments and sorceries of the "Prophet" Francis could save the sacred city from destruction. Actuated, if not by some premonition of danger, by a purpose well worthy of comment, they had removed their women and children to a place of safety across the river in a secluded, densely wooded covert that should, in connection with the Holy Ground, be marked by the patriotic societies of Alabama.

As Claiborne's troops poured into the city along the left bank of the river, the center column under Colonel Carson curving outward like a crescent, each face hard and set was filled with a purpose that could not be mistaken. For days they had marched through mud and water covering the flat, pine marshes while the bitter winds of late December chilled their half-clad bodies to the bone; still they did not flinch nor quail at the wild demoniacal clamor of the savages preparing for battle within the town. Amid a frenzied outburst of shouts and yells and beating of drums, the Creek warriors rushed out to meet the Americans, while smaller detachments from covert and ambuscade everywhere suddenly sprang forward and poured a discharge of rifle bullets into Carson's advancing ranks.[37] From the heavy log breastworks Indian gunmen continued to fire. These were more to be dreaded than those armed with bows and arrows whose misdirected missiles fell harmlessly into the ranks of Carson's companies in spite of the fierce and urgent commands of the sorcerers and prophets in

---

[37] Weatherford knew the Creek manner of fighting and did not try to restrain the noise in their preparation for battle though he himself was not given to savage customs.

their midst. These Creek seers and oracles have been described by historians as rushing about frantically, uttering piercing screams, while madly waving in each hand a cow's tail dyed a brilliant scarlet. Retiring suddenly behind some wall or structure, as if to work a spell, they would suddenly return to the open to urge with renewed vehemence their people to withstand the foe. It was, however, for their entire nation as well as for the Holy City, for which the Indians now fought, and not until the galling fire from Claiborne's men had begun to decimate their ranks did they begin a retreat. Not even then did they suddenly fall back but slowly, stubbornly, fighting desperately with their fruitless weapons at every turn and twist of the battle. Again and again they rushed forward to thrust the invaders from the sacred city, finally to waver and fall back as the American rifles were solidly turned on them, not only by Carson's men but by Claiborne's entire army, every column of which was now pressing into the town. Still the Indians rallied and resisted the foe. As the Americans pressed them backward a sure aim from a soldier in the ranks toppled over a richly arrayed prophet wildly leading a charge. Here and there, these gorgeously robed creatures with arms upraised in frantic gestures were suddenly swept to the earth by American gunmen.

As the Creeks advanced with a last sudden fury, Carson let his men go and soon all that was left of the pomp and glory of the haughty Red Sticks vanished and they turned and wildly fled, Claiborne's army pursuing and driving them through the town and out by the river.

Weatherford was the last of the defeated host to quit the battle field. While his warriors were fleeing in confusion, seeking the canebrake and deep woods, he lingered to proudly cast a look of scorn at his assailants, then instantly mounted his fleet-footed "Arrow" and disappeared from their view. For the sake of its color and action we give here Major Dreisback's glowing picture rather than Woodward's skeptical account of Weatherford's leap into the Alabama on his faithful warhorse as he left the invaded and reduced Creek capital whose temples had been cast down and whose streets were red, as we view it, with the blood merely of heathen prophets. Describing the daring leap, which could well have served for an incident in a thrilling romance of Scott, Dreisback says:

When Weatherford found that most of his warriors had deserted him, he thought of his own safety. Finding himself hedged in above and below on the river, he determined to cross the Alabama. He was mounted on a horse of almost matchless strength and fleetness and with the swiftness of the wind turned down a long hollow that led to the bank of the river; on his arrival he found the bluff about twelve feet high; he took in at a glance the situation and determined to make the leap. He rode back about thirty paces and turned his horse's head towards the bluff, and then, with touch of the spur and the sharp 'ho ya' of his voice, he put the noble animal to the top of his speed and dashed over the bluff full twenty feet into the flashing waters below, which opened its bosom to receive the dauntless hero, who sought its sparkling waves as a barrier between him and the pursuing foe. He did not lose his seat; his horse and the lower part of his own body went entirely under the water, he holding his rifle high above his head. The gallant horse struck out for the opposite shore with his fearless rider upon his back. When he had advanced some thirty yards from the shore, the balls from the guns of the troopers who were above and below him began to spatter around him like hail, but it appeared that the "Great Spirit" watched over him, for not a shot struck either man or horse. As soon as he reached the farther shore he dismounted and took off his saddle and examined his brave and noble horse to see if he had been struck. One shot had cut off a bunch or lock of the horse's mane just in front of the saddle. Finding his noble "Arrow" unhurt, he resaddled him and mounted, and sending back a note of defiance, rode off, to fight again on other ensanguined fields.

When Claiborne had conquered the Holy Ground and had driven out its inhabitants—both prophet and warrior, he occupied it with his soldiers for a few hours during which the Choctaws under Pushmataha were given the privilege of possessing themselves of the victor's spoils, the white soldiery now embittered by memories of Creek atrocities disdaining to appropriate to themselves anything that belonged to the savages. Their passing disdain turned into horror and bitter invective when they discovered in the public square of the Holy City a tall pine pole from which was suspended the scalps of those who had been murdered at Fort Mims. From this gruesome object hung the curly scalp of the infant and its mother's long braids intermingling with the hoary locks of the aged. The letter, too, found in Weatherford's house, in which Governor Manique of Pensacola congratulated him upon the victory of Fort Mims, filled them with renewed purpose to stamp out the Creek Nation.

After ordering the torch to be applied to the town and reducing it to ashes, Claiborne with his army swept the whole territory in which the Holy Ground was located, destroying all towns, villages, farms and boats that were to be found.

With Claiborne's forces pursuing and laying waste the country the Indians began losing strength. The fairest possessions of the Nation were now in ruins. But even with their hopes shattered and their imperial strength ebbing, they still, though rarely themselves giving battle, fought heroically in defense of their lives and strongholds. While they continued to the last to fight with spirit and at times with the greatest valor, their champion, Weatherford, must have realized that he was the leader of a lost cause since, according to some of the best authorities, he never after the destruction of the Holy Ground appeared on the battle field.

Writing of the victory J. F. H. Claiborne says:

> The moral effect of this bold movement into the heart of the nation upon ground held sacred and impregnable, was great. It taught the savages that they were neither inaccessible nor invulnerable; it destroyed their confidence in their prophets, and it proved what volunteers, even without shoes, clothing, blankets, or provisions would do for their country.

The news of the fall of the capital of the Creek Nation instantly spread all over the country, from house to house and town to town, and everywhere on the frontiers in camp and in assembly halls, Claiborne's victory was applauded and celebrated, bonfires flaming along the whole eastern frontier and far into the interior of the Mississippi Territory. Not even the great Jackson had won so distinctive a victory, nor had he, as yet, met Weatherford anywhere on the battlefield. The signal victory of Holy Ground, however, was not to be without its sacrifice. The men were returning to Camp Vernon in a pitiable condition, half naked, bare-footed and hungry, to face a failure of crops on arriving home. On Christmas Day they with their beloved General had dined on parched corn and boiled acorns. He was returning with them broken in health from exposure, and suffering from wounds from which he never recovered. On January 14, 1814, he had written from Camp Mount Vernon.

> My volunteers are returning to their homes with eight months' pay due them and almost literally naked. They have served the last three months of inclement winter weather without shoes or blankets, almost without shirts, but are still devoted to their country and properly impressed with the justice and the necessity of the war.

But notwithstanding the gloomy side of the picture, the fact that the capital of the Creek Nation had been conquered and razed allayed all fears for the present. It is a question, after the destruction of Holy Ground, whether the Indians would have left their own country to make further open war on the whites or whether what has been called the decisive battle of Horseshoe Bend was necessary to draw from them a surrender. It is very certain, however, that they would have continued to give aid to the British.

Larger dangers than the trouble with the Indians were now looming up before the young American Republic, and Jackson's last expedition against them was only a foreword to his coast campaign against Great Britain whose fleet and army had been hovering near to encourage and aid the Creeks as a preliminary of their own design. Viewed from any standpoint Jackson's presence in the Mississippi Territory seems providential at this crisis of the American government. Had New Orleans been captured by the British, which would have been certain had he not been present, the entire Southern Coast, irrespective of any treaty, would have temporarily become a British possession.

After the battle of Holy Ground had been fought by Claiborne, General Jackson, having to his own credit a number of brilliant exploits during the autumn, with a small army remained on the battlefront and continued to make war on the Indians.[38] Many of his troops had returned home, some had mutinied outright, and for the time being the skies looked dark, but the shrewd and indomitable hero holding steadily to his main purpose continued to clear his path of all obstacles. He pursued and harried the Creeks through forest and over water, in nearly every encounter overwhelming and punishing them severely. The various collisions and skirmishes that occurred between the Americans and Weatherford's party after Jackson invaded their country in the Spring of 1814 have been briefly sketched not that they bear on or answer any main question involved, but simply in order to follow the path of war to Pensacola where the British, with a great naval force gathered in the South Seas, were anxiously watching the Creek uprising. Following the hard fighting near Amukfau Creek, where the Indians made an all day but vain attack on the invading American forces, and the fierce encounter at the Hillabee village of Enitachopoco, where they continued their efforts to drive Jackson and his army out of the Creek country, both sides prepared for what proved to be the final battle between the two warring nations. The Enitachopoco fight must have elated and given

---

[38] It was at this time, when his men had nearly all returned home, that he employed in his service a number of Cherokees, also a large party of Creeks who had opposed the war.

the Indians great satisfaction since it was here that they proudly boasted that they "ran Captain Jackson into the Coosa River," a dilemma virtually admitted by the Americans. The conclusive battle of Tohopeka, or Horseshoe Bend, which occurred March 27, 1814, had yet to be fought, some authorities think, before the proud Weatherford would replace the red plume in his head-dress with a white one. Slight victories in the Callabee swamps and especially the victory over Floyd during the month of January had heartened the Indians, and with high hope of driving the Americans out of their country they gathered in full force to meet Jackson on the Tallapoosa. The Tennessee troops, as has been stated, had been constantly returning home and Jackson during the winter had been left at times with a straggling army with which to meet the foe. In February he was amply reinforced by fresh troops from Tennessee and many volunteers from the Mississippi Territory seeking adventure under the famous Indian fighter, who had set himself a task in the accomplishment of which the Creek Indians must be practically exterminated.

The Coosa River was the scene of stirring military action throughout the month of March, a large number of troops camping on or near its banks. When drilling and especially when on parade, clad in white trousers and dark blue coats, the army made an imposing spectacle in the heart of the bare, gray wilderness. It was about this time that still another force from Tennessee made its way to the Mississippi Territory for the purpose of aiding Jackson in his last effort to break the remaining strength of the Red Sticks, whose late stubborn resistance and brilliant exploits had surprised and embarrassed the Americans. Nettled by the Indians' triumphant boasts, Jackson's army was daily augmented by volunteer troops and he soon found himself at the head of a large force well supplied and ready to go against not only the Creeks but to move at any time on the British lurking about Pensacola.

For their last stand the Creeks had chosen a place they called "Tohopeka" which occupied a peninsula containing about one hundred acres in the bend of the lovely Tallapoosa. It was also called in their own wild, sweet tongue "Cholocco Litabixbee"—the Horseshoe—on account of its shape. The stronghold was prepared and defended in such a manner that, when no longer secure, it could be easily evacuated and, as Pickett observes, "was admirably adapted by Nature for security if well guarded but equally for destruction if not well defended." Safe within their peninsula fastness, which had been fortified by a strong breastwork constructed of heavy logs across the neck of land connecting it with the mainland, they determined to defend it at every cost, and if failing, to escape by way of the river where hundreds of large canoes had been moored for that purpose near the town proper. It was blustering March weather but the trees though still skeletons, were slightly budding, and a variety of early spring flowers were in bloom in the Tallapoosa Bend when Jackson appeared before the town. The Indians were ready for his approach. The Hillabee warriors led the defense and were bitter in retaliation for the cruel manner in which Generals Cocke and White had ignored their proposals of surrender, a misunderstanding for which Jackson was now suffering. With the Hillabees were the warriors of the following towns: Ocfuske, Oakchoie, New Yanca, the Fish Pond, Hickory Ground and Eufaulahatche, numbering about one thousand. Weatherford was not present, yet it cannot be doubted that his faithful warriors and prophets had been fully instructed by him as to the course to pursue.

With the exception of the massive breastwork erected with both British and Spanish aid General Jackson regarded the Muscogee defenses, though artfully planned from the standpoint of the Creeks, as little better than the work of children, and on examining them exclaimed regretfully, "They have penned themselves up for slaughter!" Conscious of the fate that awaited them he immediately sent a flag of truce toward the town but the proud Hillabees with an outburst of scornful hoots and yells fired upon it. The Americans then, without hesitating, prepared for battle. General Coffee, now a well-known figure in the war with the Creeks, crossed the Tallapoosa and stationed his troops so as to have a full sweep at the peninsula, an astute design well executed that the Red Sticks were not expecting. With Coffee's troops in position, Jackson pressed hard against the breastworks and with two pieces of cannon began to fiercely bombard the Creek fortress. But it was only after a number of fierce advances and pounding of guns that he began to weaken the fortifications. For several hours he stormed the breastworks to be repulsed again and again, and more than once Jackson, Coffee, Russell, Morgan and many others commanding the American forces recoiled at the furious charge of the enemy before the town was taken. In vain for a while did Jackson's riflemen approach the port-holes while his cannon belabored the works with renewed energy. The gallant Tennesseans mounted and strove upon the breastworks to finally dye them with American blood as a number of the advance guard led by the brave Major Montgomery and Lieutenants Moulton and Somerville, who fell in the attempt, gained an entrance into the town. In a last effort to go over the breastworks and enter the town, Ensign Sam Houston of Tennessee, who years later became governor of Texas, though wounded, led the way. In the meantime General Coffee had destroyed the canoes on the river and set fire to the town which was soon a sheet of flame. Seeing the pitiable plight of the Indians, wedged in between his own forces and Coffee's with the town each moment becoming a furnace, Jackson again dispatched a messenger to assure them of American favor if they would surrender. Once more the proud Muscogees disdained his overtures and amid yells of derision and a discharge of fire-arms proclaimed that they had no faith in the pale faces who had broken faith with them. The Indians, though sorely beset on all sides, asked for no quarter but went to their death with as sublime heroism as was ever shown by the Caucasian on any battlefield where life was the price to be paid for liberty. When once the Americans had gained an entrance into the city both sides fought like wild beasts, the bayonet in the white man's hand in the end proving too much for the gallant bowmen who, too proud to sue for quarter and in many instances wounded for life, scattered in confusion, fleeing in every direction through the swamps, over sloughs and bayous and across the river, leaving only a trail of blood to mark the course of their flight. The peninsula was literally strewn with their dead bodies; the rifle and bayonet had done their worst; but it took, says Brewer, "the combined power of the whites, the Cherokees, Chickasaws and Choctaws, assisted by a large party of their own people, to subjugate them." It was now that the haughty spirit of the Muscogee was crushed and subdued if not wholly extinguished; but not until Valkyrie had borne to the happy hunting-ground some brave Manowa who, to all dwellers there, would embody the spirit of the Creek, did this powerful Indian nation yield to its fate.

The evening shadows had enveloped the land when the battle of

Tallapoosa Bend came to a close and the flames that destroyed the citadel had died down to embers. The Horseshoe was a heap of ashes; the mighty Red Sticks were no more; and their last fortress had become their burial ground, not more than twenty, says Jackson, having escaped. Now ready to surrender on any terms, they crept from hiding-place and covert throughout the nation and bent their proud necks to the dominion of the white race whose civilization had proved too strong for theirs. And though they continued foemen, it was with but few exceptions that they gave further practical aid to their old allies the British.

Some historians denounce this last battle as a massacre—a riot of butchery equal to Fort Mims. Whether this be true or not, it is evident that Jackson, though humane himself in victory, was on this occasion unable to restrain his troops. These, forgetting that a brave people had died for the sake of their homes and country and while recoiling in horror and disgust from the savage practice of scalping a foe overcome by hate and revenge, had no hesitancy in cutting the noses from the faces of the dead warriors as they covered, like a winding-sheet, the sacred soil of their fathers.

In the defense of Horsehoe Bend the Creeks numbered about 1000. Historians disagree about the number that escaped and also about the number engaged in battle. Pickett thinks that not more than 200 escaped while he places the army's strength at 1000. The Indians, in nearly every instance, had proved to be poor marksmen and Jackson lost only 32 men, 99 having been wounded. Among the dead were several brave spirits who had been close to their fiery-hearted and devoted commander and it was in keeping with his fervent and loyal nature to pour out his grief in passionate lament over the loss of the heroic young Virginian, Major L. P. Montgomery, of the 39th Regiment, who was the first to mount the breastworks at Tallapoosa Bend to fall with sword in hand while urging his men to take the stronghold. His dead body drew from the stern soldier the tribute of tears as he, with romantic fervor that calls to mind King Arthur, pronounced him "the flower" of all his brave army.[39]

---

[39] Major Lemuel Purnell Montgomery was a native of Wythe County, Virginia, and was descended from patriotic Revolutionary ancestors. His biographer states that the county of Montgomery, Alabama, was named in honor of him while the capital of the State preserves in its name the memory of his father General Montgomery who fell at the storming of Quebec.

The bloody battle of the Horseshoe having become a thing of yesterday, General Jackson left the Tallapoosa and placed his army in line of march and on April 2 found himself at Fort Williams, a fort that he had erected on his march thither.

Jackson's army moved forward with such provisions as the men could carry, the constant rains making it impossible to transport heavy supplies through the rough wilderness. The terrified Creeks fled before his march in every direction, many stopping on the roadside to surrender, while others made their way to Pensacola to join the British, and some going into Florida. Jackson in victory was neither revengeful nor vindictive and the Indians found in their adversary one who, while he had slight faith in their integrity, was ready in every instance to sympathize with them in misfortune. Their appeals for succor and aid now touched him, and their wretched condition was relieved in every possible manner. He was pardonably elated over his success in reducing the Creek Nation and was profuse in praise of his troops. If the jealousy and lack of co-operation evinced by Colonel Milton commanding the eastern troops with several Carolina companies at Decatur across the Tallapoosa annoyed him, and General Cocke's attitude had given him much concern, his victory fully compensated for any want of appreciation or petty clashes incident to his campaign. His fame as an Indian fighter was secure. Tennessee regarded him as her most renowned soldier and eagerly set about to furnish troops for his future expeditions. Governor Holmes of the Mississippi Territory and General Ferdinand L. Claiborne always regarded him with every expression of esteem and confidence and their admiration for him as a soldier was no less ardent than that which characterized the entire soldiery of the Mississippi Territory who were now ready to follow him to any point designated to meet the British. By the Creek Indians whom he had conquered and almost destroyed as a nation he was regarded as some strange and great being endowed with supernatural power.

Not only Jackson but his entire army won fame in the Creek war and Governor Holmes in a letter to Governor Blount generously wrote as follows respecting the aid of the Tennessee troops:

The conduct of the State of Tennessee upon every occasion when our Territory has been menaced by an enemy, entitles that member of the Union to our peculiar gratitude; but the patriotism evinced by their statesmen, soldiers, and citizens, upon the late occasion of the disasters which happened on the Eastern frontier, exhibited a magnanimity of character and a national sensibility, worthy of being emulated by all who justly estimate that pride of Country so essential to the maintenance of those rights which the constitution of the United States was intended to secure and to perpetuate.

From their armies now acting against the enemy, we have every thing to expect that distinguished talents, courage, a love of country and a laudable desire for fame and honor can promise.

The British still hoped to enlist the Creeks in their service and did to some extent use them as land forces, but the peace party in the Creek Nation was greatly strengthened by Jackson's victory, many of them becoming open adherents of the American cause. Whether his invasion of the Creek Nation was necessary or not in perfecting a treaty with them after General Claiborne's victory at Holy Ground, it should be again noted that as a preliminary for the coast operations against the British it was a valuable factor in shaping and strengthening that campaign. Jackson was not willing to take any chances and felt that the only way to prevent the Indians from giving aid to the British was to completely break their strength and render them helpless. He foresaw the storm gathering on the Southern Coast and not as long as the British hovered about Pensacola and Mobile did he believe that the American Republic in this section was safe.

Before leaving the Tallapoosa country which had now become historic, General Jackson who, though usually of a practical enough cast of mind, possessed a deep undercurrent of the finest and richest sentiment, displayed his strong patriotism and nationalism in a pleasing manner. On striking camp he took occasion to plant the American colors on the spot where a century before under the orders of Cadillac had been erected Fort Toulouse[40] when the French were in possession of the country. The old French garrison became the site of new fort manned with a strong block-house and outer walls. The fort received the name Jackson, and it was here that large deputations of Creek warriors constantly came to make formal surrender. The daring and utterly fearless Weatherford, dark, sinewy and tall, shrewd and eloquent and handsome after the manner of the half-breed, was the most conspicuous figure, next to Jackson, at the fort. Though a Creek in every instinct and aspiration, he affected little of the manners and customs of his people. His dress, of the pioneer variety and fashion, had none of the barbaric adornment characteris-

---

[40] This fort was on the Coosa four miles above its junction with the Tallapoosa near Wetumpka.

tic of the Indian civilization. But no warrior among them, not even a prophet, though he could in their sight perform miracles, could sway the heart of the Red Sticks so completely as the tall Red Eagle whose haughty bearing, set off with a wild, free grace, and shrewd and eloquent speech, held for them a charm acknowledged for few others. With a daring inconceivable he suddenly appeared at the fort on a splendid charger, a deer killed on the way swung across his saddle. General Jackson, while regarding him as the evil genius of the war and having ordered his capture on sight, in the end, was completely charmed with his romantic appearance and magnetic personality. Though furious at this bold appearance before his very *marquée*, the American General, whose whole life reveals the fact that he was not without a keen appreciation of the pure romanticism of all high exploit and adventure, could but acknowledge the superb courage of the splendid creature whose scorn of risk and danger or shrewd dissembling, whichever it may have been, won for him a soldier's protection. Many of the more peaceful, or as the case might be, timorous, Creek warriors feared and hated the haughty half-breed, and it was with a spirit of childish exultation and revenge that Big Warrior,[41] high in the graces of General Jackson as he now thought himself, forecast the doom of the Red Eagle. "We've got you now, Bill Weatherford!" coming from such a source stung the haughty half breed as no word of condemnation from Jackson could have done. However, concerned with weightier matters, after anathematizing the source of the insult, he cast a look of scorn upon the traitor, as he termed him, and turned to confront his conqueror. Eye-witnesses aver that he faced Jackson with perfect composure, proudly calling himself a Creek warrior and telling him that if it were possible he would continue to make war upon him. His speech was full of fair-spoken words and worthy appeals. He asked for naught for himself but what they chose to deal him, but for the helpless Creek women and children he craved assistance and protection. Having thus touched Jackson's heart for a worthy object, he received the benefit that is often conferred on the espouser of noble aims and purposes even though he be insincere in his purpose. The chord he struck in the great Jackson's heart was always keenly alive. It was with secret elation that the shrewd Weatherford perceived the stern features of his adversary relax,

---

[41] The chieftain who refused to unite with Tecumseh to aid the British.

feeling that, though the rank and file clamored for his instant death, he had charmed his great foe whose remarkable ability for hardheartedness and soft-heartedness had always been equally characteristic. The presentation by Weatherford of the deer he had slain, and a glass of brandy by Jackson concluded the hospitality of the fort, and it was with a look of "By the Eternal!" darkening his worn, sallow face that he signified that none present should harm a hair of Weatherford's head.[42] In this manner the terms of surrender proceeded.

---

[42] The following story, concerning William Weatherford, by Prof. H. S. Halbert, a leading authority on the Indians of Mississippi, will prove interesting to the reader. It is now on file in the Claiborne Papers in the custody of the Mississippi State Historical Department.

"A few years before the Creek War of 1813, William Weatherford married and established himself on a plantation on the Alabama River, in what is now Lowndes County, Alabama. Here he dispensed a profuse hospitality, and his home became the resort of the dissipated young Creek warriors, over whom Weatherford exercised an unbounded influence. As the plantation of Weatherford lay upon a route leading through the Creek nation to Mobile, travelers going in that direction, often claimed the hospitality of his mansion. However much Weatherford may have embittered the whites against him in after years as the leader of the Creeks in their disastrous war, he was a man possessing many noble traits of character. In early life, wild, reckless and dissipated, he was, nevertheless, ever of an honorable and generous nature and extremely hospitable. Being a half-breed planter, he adhered to many of the customs of the whites, always dressing in their costume.

"Whilst Weatherford was living at the above-mentioned plantation, one summer's evening, a white traveler stopped before his door, and claimed the hospitalities of the day. The traveler was a notorious character from Georgia, known among his acquaintances as Wild Bill Thurman. He was a desperate gambler and horse-racer, addicted to rude sports and practical jokes, which gave him a notoriety far and near, but withal possessing much native goodness of heart.

"A day or so before arriving at Weatherford's house, Thurman was seized with a whim to have some sport out of the Indian chief, though in what manner he should have the sport, he left to circumstances. He accordingly sold his horse and bought a miserable broken-down hack, that could with difficulty drag one foot after the other, and in this plight, presented himself at the house of the Creek warrior. Weatherford, meanwhile, soon found out from other guests who were present, what kind of character Thurman was, and the object he had in view, and resolved to checkmate him.

"As the guests were sitting in the bar-room after partaking of a bountiful supper, Weatherford sent for his negro fiddler to entertain the company. Whilst the fiddler was discoursing his liveliest music, and the enjoyment of all was at its height, Weatherford suddenly drew a pistol and ordered Thurman to dance. Thurman, astonished but taking in the situation at a glance, and knowing that remonstrance was useless, went to work with heel and toe. For a long time he danced, the pistol of Weatherford steadily cocked upon him, and the assembled guests looking on. He began to grow weary, streams of perspiration flowed from his face, but still on he danced for dear life, the deadly pistol ever threatening him. Finally Weatherford relented; told him that would do, that he might now rest, and they would take a drink together. To this Thurman gladly assented. Whilst the two were refreshing the inner man Thurman all at once, with the speed of lightning jerked up the pistol which Weatherford had laid aside, and levelled it full upon the breast of the chief. 'Now, Bill Weatherford,' said he, 'it is your time to dance. Now you dance until I tell you to stop, or I will drive a ball through you instantly.' Turning then to the negro fiddler, he told him if he valued his life, to play that fiddle until he was told to stop. Weatherford, brave as he was, saw at once that the tables were turned upon him, and knowing that Thurman possessed a nature as reckless as his own, he submitted with the best grace possible. For nearly an hour the chief was compelled to play the same role which he had enforced on Thurman. No one white man or Indian dared interfere, as they knew Thurman too well.

"At last, Thurman, satisfied with his revenge, lowered his weapon, told Weatherford that he had danced enough, and that both were now even. Weatherford accepted the situation; and after some general conversation, all parties retired for the night. However, before retiring, Weatherford secretly ordered a party of Indian's to take Thurman's horse out into the woods and kill him; which was done forthwith.

"Weatherford arose the next morning by no means satisfied with the night's experience. As he excelled in all the athletic sports of his people, he hoped yet to get the upper hand of Thurman. Accordingly, after breakfast, the chief challenged Thurman to a wrestling match, which the latter accepted. They wrestled several times, but in every encounter, Weatherford was worsted and was mortified at the result. He next challenged Thurman to a boxing match, or rather to a rough fist fight. The agreement was that no one was to interfere, until one or the other cried out, 'enough.' After a long and violent struggle, Weatherford, at last had to yield to the superior prowess of the white man. Both parties then shook hands, and pledged a mutual friendship. Weatherford began to conceive a strange liking for his antagonist. Although the idol of the Creek warriors, and the best ball-player in the nation, he felt no chagrin at his defeat, but regarded his antagonist with favor and admiration. Thurman spent several days with Weatherford, who treated him with marked kindness, and entertained him with all the sports and amusements peculiar to the Indians.

"At last, one morning, Thurman expressing a desire to resume his journey, Weatherford sent a servant to bring the finest horse out of his stable, which, equipped with elegant bridle and saddle, he presented to his astonished guest, at the same time, handing over to him a hundred dollars in silver. 'Here, Thurman,' said he, 'take this horse, and never again ride such a horse as the one you rode here, and which I had killed for humanity's sake, but always ride a horse that is fit for a gentleman to ride. And whenever you pass along this way, be sure and come to see me, and make my house your home.' Thurman was forced to yield to the strange generosity of the chief. The two, with many expressions of good will, then separated devoted friends. They often met afterwards, and the friendship thus strangely formed, lasted during all of Weatherford's eventful career until his death in 1826.

"The above story illustrating the early life of William Weatherford, we received from an aged citizen of Alabama, a soldier of the War of 1812, who vouches for its authenticity."

Another story preserved by Halbert runs as follows, though he later, as has been stated, in his history of the Creek War asserted with emphasis that Weatherford never appeared in any battle except that of the Holy Ground:

"As is well known, at the battle of Caleebe, Weatherford made a furious night assault upon Floyd's army. In the confusion incident to the attack Floyd was heard with a loud voice encouraging his troops. 'Cheer up, boys, we'll give them hell when daylight comes.' Instantly from the ranks of the Creeks came back the voice of Weatherford in reply. 'Yes, d—n you, and we will give *you* hell *before* daylight comes.' And well did Weatherford make good his retort, killing and wounding over one hundred of Floyd's men before the break of day, and displaying in every respect, a generalship equal to that of the American commander.

"After the war Weatherford settled in Monroe County, Alabama, and became a permanent citizen. Notwithstanding the wildness of his early life, all reports agree in stating that after the war, Weatherford lived a sober and industrious life, and died a useful citizen."

Since the aggressor must always bear the indemnities that accrue from failure, the lovely lands of the Coosa and Warrior which now form a part of northern Alabama passed into the hands of the American government. A short while after Jackson concluded his treaty with the Indians at Fort Jackson, General Pinckney of the United States Army arrived and gave his approval of what had transpired.

On April 21, 1814, General Jackson discharged the West Tennessee troops at Camp Blount near Fayetteville with a stirring address full of praise of their loyalty, devotion and prowess. His language possessed a vital quality that charmed men and in times of stress moved them to action. His praise of them, now, was extremely pleasing. Highly spectacular in his manner and methods he was at the same time singularly sincere in all his purposes, and his knowledge of human nature and genius for leading or, as the necessity demanded, driving men evinced a sagacity that at times savored of craft. Every spirit about him caught his enthusiasm and had faith in his purpose.

Everything now being quiet on the Southern border, so far as the Indians were concerned, Jackson, leaving the gallant and vigilant Major Blue to quell any local disturbance that might arise during his absence, retired for a short while to the "Hermitage." The Indians in all probablity would have retired to their own towns thoroughly subdued but for their British and Spanish sympathizers on the coast. While the British could expect little in the way of assistance in the future from the Creek Nation it continued to be their policy to keep hostilities alive between the Indians and the Americans and more than once, as has been stated, they uniformed and equipped them as field forces in their coast campaign against the American Republic.[43] Appeals of runners sent into the Creek Nation led many destitute and starving Red Sticks to join the British with the hope of receiving protection and assistance. The Indians were in a pitiable condition throughout the Nation and besides the assistance afforded them by the British, Americans at several places were feeding as many as 5000 at a time.

---

[43] Gayarre says of the Creeks at Pensacola, that they "openly wore the British uniform in the streets in violation of the laws of neutrality which Spain was bound to observe." They were promised a reward of ten dollars for every scalp taken irrespective of age or sex.

While resting from his arduous campaign against the Indians, General Jackson was promoted major-general of the army and empowered to conclude a treaty of peace with the Indians by the Federal Government. Having repaired to Fort Jackson with a small escort, he immediately assumed command of the Southern army. In peaceful surroundings his health had slightly improved but it continued poor throughout his Southern campaign.

During the treaty making the Indians, despite Big Warrior's protestations of friendship and his liberality in bestowing certain small gifts of land to all distinguished persons present, manifested their usual opposition to surrendering their native lands, an opposition led by Big Warrior himself when large areas were demanded. After much inveigling the Indians were finally induced to sign the treaty. Among the distinguished personages present besides Jackson were Colonel Hawkins[44] and Colonel Arthur P. Hayne.[45]

It was an auspicious day in the governmental affairs of the American Republic but it had another significance more far reaching. Where the wayside shrine—a cross or a blue and red symbol of the Christ and the Mother, had been set in hope by the Jesuit among the sun worshipers, American patriots were preparing to erect the Protestant churches of England.

In connection with affairs in the South about the time of the treaty Woodward in his reminiscences has said:

> The treaty of Ghent, which declared peace between Great Britain and the United States, was signed December 25, 1814, but as the treaty of Fort Jackson did not actually terminate the war with the Creeks, so neither did this European treaty actually terminate the "War of 1812" of which the Creek War became a part. Pensacola had first to be captured and New Orleans to be defended.

In unison with this view an English officer writing of the failure of the British to take possession of the coast country deplored the loss of such rich possessions to England and enumerated the many advantages had victory crowned their arms.

Returning to the affairs and military operations of the Mississippi

---

[44] See sketch of Col. Hawkins in this narrative.
[45] Colonel Hayne was a native of Charleston, South Carolina and was descended from a family distinguished in the Revolutionary War. He was for a while with the army in the North during the War of 1812 and was noted for his gallantry and patriotic ardor. He was one of General Jackson's most trusted officers and during the battle of New Orleans rendered service of the most valuable nature.

Territory, it was to Colonel Thomas Hinds that Jackson now looked for active support in the campaign against the British at Pensacola. The physical condition of General Claiborne, at present an invalid confined to his home facing a speedy death in his early prime, precluded any possible thought of his longer performing military service of any nature, though his connection with the military organizations still continued as the following formations for 1814 show, the roster having been taken from the *Natchez Almanac*:

Ferdinand Leigh Claiborne, Brigadier-General; Andrew Marschalk, Adjutant-General; Aides-de-Camp to Governor Holmes, Joseph Sessions, Thomas Percy, John Haines, Charles K. Blanchard; John Wood, Aide-de-Camp to General Claiborne; Lieutenant-Colonels Commandant: David Neilson, 1st Regiment, Amite County; Samuel Stocket, 2d Regiment, Wilkinson County; David Fleming, 3d Regiment, Adams County; David Carradine, 4th Regiment, Jefferson County; Raymond Robinson, 5th Regiment, Claiborne County; James Caller, 6th Regiment, Washington County, now Alabama; Peter Perkins, 7th Regiment, Madison County now Alabama; James Powell, 8th Regiment, Baldwin County, now Alabama; James Patton, 9th Regiment, Wayne County; Henry Manadere, 10th Regiment, Warren County; Robert Witherspoon, 11th Regiment, Franklin County; Josiah Skinner, 12th Regiment, Greene County; George H. Nixon, 13th Regiment, Marion County; John Hinson, 14th Regiment, Mobile County, now Alabama; Reuben Saffold, 15th Regiment, Clarke County, now Alabama; Charles Burris, 16th Regiment, Madison County, now Alabama; William Bates, 17th Regiment, Jackson County; Jordan Morgan, 18th Regiment, Hancock County.

From these regiments which conformed very nearly to the organization of 1813, had been drawn the infantry and the Mississippi cavalry. All were engaged in active and effective service of various kinds throughout the Creek uprising and the campaign along the coast against the British. Sometimes in local companies and even in small bands and knots or as volunteers and recruits in the regular army, they rendered effective service in the defense of the Territory and Republic. Many hundreds of Mississippi soldiers whose names have never appeared as volunteers from the Mississippi Territory assisted Jackson in his Southern campaign.

It was during hostilities, as we have seen, with the Creek Indians that Major Hinds began to realize some of his ambitions as a soldier. His capacity as an officer of unusual ability was instantly acknowledged by Jackson, nor was the superior character of the Dragoons, culled from the best population of the State, lost to his observing eye. When the Mississippi Territory faced a more serious trouble than she had experienced with the Creeks, this famous troop of horse once more sprang into action and eagerly followed Jackson's fortunes.

Jackson was scarcely through arranging his treaty with the Creeks concluded August 9, 1814, when designs on the part of Great Britain and Spain to keep alive their slumbering animosities toward the Americans became so patent that he was no longer in doubt as to the course to pursue. Persistent rumors of military assistance and encouragement given the Indians by both the British and Spanish at Pensacola aroused his indignation. In addition he had discovered that the closest communication had been opened up between the Spanish and British; that the latter from the brig *Orpheus* had landed arms at Apalachicola. His correspondence with Governor Claiborne at New Orleans confirmed all of his suspicions and he lost no time in reporting the situation to the Government at Washington. All orders from the War Department were delayed and from the very nature of things authorities there were so out of touch with the situation that he, unwilling to risk failure, assumed the initiative in moving against the Spanish capital.

The prime motive that actuated Jackson in his expedition against Pensacola where the British for many months had been very active was the defense of the American Republic. Any impartial study of the records reveals this fact beyond question.[46] Previous to the appearance of the British he had given evidence of a desire to raise the American flag along the whole coast of the Gulf of Mexico. But, it

---

[46] Extracts similar to the ones quoted in this note from Jackson's war reports and letters can be numerously cited showing that the defense of New Orleans was in his mind at all times during the summer and fall of 1814.

General Jackson from his headquarters at Mobile wrote to Governor Claiborne on August 22, 1814:

"I have no power to stipulate with any particular corps, as to particular or local service but it is not to be presumed at present that the troops of Louisiana will have to extend their services beyond the limits of their own state. Yet circumstances might arise which would make it necessary they should be called to face an invading enemy beyond the boundary of the state to stop his entry into their territory."

Again in a letter to Governor Claiborne, dated headquarters, 7th Military district, Fort Jackson, July 21, 1814, he says:

"This morning I was presented with a new British musket given to a friendly Indian by those at Appalachicola Bay. Information has been received by this fellow tending to confirm the rumour of a considerable force having landed there with a large quantity of arms and other munitions of war, and with intention to strike a decisive blow against the lower country. Mobile and Orleans are of such importance as to hold out strong inducements to them, at such a crisis: I must look to the constitutional authorities of the State of Louisiana for such support as will be effective in any emergency, and I trust this support will be afforded with promptitude whenever required."

must be acknowledged by all discerning and impartial historians that this thought was in his mind at present only as it related to his main purpose of driving the British from the Gulf Coast. The alliance or affiliation of the Spanish with the British presented a situation that made it necessary for him to attack the former at Pensacola in order to dislodge the latter. With this purpose he began his campaign with enthusiastic energy, an energy that continued forcible and potent to the end though his poor health and the hot climate were sufficient to have deterred him.

The statement of Henry Adams[47] that Jackson intended to attack Florida through Pensacola is based entirely on a false conception. When Jackson went to Pensacola with his army it is clearly evident from a close study of his whole campaign that he had planned a movement against the British that involved New Orleans. Furthermore he was fully aware that he had been contending with the British throughout the Creek war. While engaged in conquering the Creeks he had requested the Government at Washington to send a large quantity of military supplies to New Orleans. Also on September 5, 1814, he wrote to Governor Claiborne to hold all Louisiana militia in readiness for active service. Accordingly, Fortier says:

Major General Villeré was ordered to organize companies in New Orleans on September 10, 1814, and Major General Philemon Thomas at Baton Rouge on or about October 1st.

The Governor said:

Major General Jackson commanding the Seventh Military District invites me to lose no time in preparing for the defense of the state. This gallant commander is now near or at Mobile watching the movements of the enemy and making the necessary preparation to cover and defend this section of the Union. He will in due time receive reinforcements from the other states on the Mississippi. He calculates, also, on the zealous support of the Louisianians and must not be disappointed.

Pending the expedition then to Pensacola, Jackson with a sagacity hardly surpassed by Napoleon, suspended all designs against the Spanish that did not directly relate to the British. To give ample opportunity for the expression of Spanish neutrality, three flags of truce were sent, and great pressure was brought to bear on the governor of Pensacola, before Jackson proceeded to attack the city. It

---

[47] Volume VIII, *History of United States*, p. 318.

Mississippi Territory in War of 1812—Rowland.   93

seems even more than carping criticism for Adams to say Jackson was contemplating a move against East Florida (West Florida already was a part of the Mississippi Territory). However, after forcing the Spanish to clearly define their position as the acknowledged and active sympathizers of Great Britain he henceforth regarded and treated them from that standpoint. He decided that either way the die was cast it would suit his purpose. But had the Spanish governor signified in sincerity his willingness to drive the British out of Pensacola it is hardly possible that Jackson would have refused to tender his aid in the accomplishment of this end, nor is it thinkable, admitting that he cherished a desire to see them ultimately quit the Gulf coast, that he would have refused their assistance at Pensacola along the coast of the Mississippi Territory and in the defense of New Orleans.

Though commanding but a small force Jackson was ready for action when the British sloop with several smaller vessels appeared at Pensacola. It proved to be the van of a large naval force already in the Gulf waters. The Spanish made no objection to Colonel Edward Nichols, when landing troops and gathering about him the hostile refugee Creeks. The alliance between the Spanish and British became more evident hourly and none could question it when the Cross of St. George was hoisted over one of the forts of the Spanish town.

Secret messengers had been sent through the country to the Seminoles and Creeks inviting them to come to Pensacola and join the British service. About one thousand of these deluded people, still sore from their recent defeat, came in answer to the call. These were immediately armed, clothed in the British uniform and instructed as to the service expected of them.

To the French, who had settled along the Gulf coast as a survival of French occupancy, inflammatory appeals were sent with the hope of alienating them from the American government, no effort being spared to render the inhabitants of the entire coast region false in their allegiance to the Americans. Colonel Nichols in extending his appeal to the people of every race and creed throughout the coast country promised that a victory on the part of the British would be the means of breaking the chains of the American government that were being forged about them. To the Spaniards especially he was urgent to the point of entreaty.

With the Spanish known to be in league with the British, Jackson recognized the opportunity at this juncture of ridding the country ultimately of both British and Spanish dominion and it can be readily believed that he now waged war looking to that end. In addition to the Tennessee troops brought with him, as has been observed he had a large aggregation of volunteer Mississippi troops collected in regular and irregular manner. On these he relied for the most exacting service, since it concerned the Mississippi Territory so vitally, and the troops knew the country and its people better than did any forces at that time in his service. The Territory was thoroughly aroused and we gather from the message of Governor Holmes of November, 1814, that in conformance with a requisition made by President Madison upon the governors of the several States and territories for a corps of 93,500 militia he issued orders immediately for the quota assigned the Mississippi Territory which was 500 infantrymen and a full troop of cavalry. The troops were to be organized and rendezvoused at several points where they could be most conveniently ordered to Mount Vernon (now in Alabama). They were reorganized into five companies conformable to the military organization of the United States. These were ordered immediately to positions assigned them by General Jackson. Governor Holmes in his message further states that in addition to these corps he furnished for service in the United States Army upon the requisition of General Andrew Jackson four full troops of Dragoons subject to the General's orders. Colonel Hinds still commanded the Dragoons and General Jackson stationed them at Washington, Liberty and John Ford's on Pearl River to be ready when summoned to Fort Bowyer, situated on a barren sand-tongue, thirty miles south of Mobile in the Mississippi Territory. Jackson had placed at this point a small garrison of 130 men, protected by 20 pieces of cannon under Major William Lawrence who commanded the fort.[48]

On the morning of September 12, the British landed 600 Indians and Spaniards and 130 marines. Sentinels stationed in the direction

---

[48] Latour in a very elaborate and supposedly scientific description that many historians have vainly attempted to rephrase describes Fort Bowyer at the entrance of Mobile Bay, while a strategical point of much importance, as a redoubt occupying the worst possible place for a fort, commanded by a row of sand hills, and with cannon defectively mounted on makeshift platforms that exposed the whole upper part of a man's body.

of Lake Borgne, also, reported that a number of English sloops of war and two brigs had dropped anchor six miles east of the fort. Major Lawrence lost no time in placing his artillery in position, and though the temporary platforms in a number of instances exposed his men to the enemy's fire, the distribution of the guns, in some respects improperly mounted, was in the main favorable.

On September 13 the British attempted to shell the fort but failing to effect any serious damage fell back into ill-provided sand bank entrenchments from which they were driven by the galling fire from the fort. As the situation grew more momentous Major Lawrence called a council of his officers who, after binding themselves in a sacred pledge to defend their country with every effort and sacrifice possible to men, adopted a resolution not wholly unique in warfare which stipulated that should the fort be blown up by the enemy and the garrison in the main destroyed before the remaining forces capitulated no surrender would be considered that did not give the Americans the full assurance that they would be treated in every respect as prisoners of war, permitted to retain their arms and protected from any outrage by the Indians as to their person or property. They pledged themselves furthermore that these terms should be carried out to the last man.

By the morning of September 15 the enemy with a fleet composed of the sloops *Hermes* and *Caron* and the brigs *Anaconda* and *Sophia* under the command of Commodore Percy, growing impatient at the thought of the easy victory in sight, decided to quit dallying and begin a determined attack on the small garrison. The ships weighed anchor moving under a favorable breeze towards the fort, the *Hermes* commanded by Percy leading the way into the channel and anchoring within musket shot of Fort Bowyer's batteries. Major Lawrence, noting the advance of the squadron and realizing his desperate situation, after again pledging his men to faithful service, with the battle cry of "Don't give up the ship" ringing upon his lips, began his preparation to cope with his powerful enemy in a final struggle for the protection of the fort on Mobile Bay. On the afternoon of September 15 the land forces of the enemy became very active and the cannon from a land battery concentrated a fierce fire on the fort. A brilliant marine and land battle raged for several hours and though assaulted by 92 pieces of artillery and struggling with six times as

many infantry as he himself commanded, the gallant defender of the
fort with a loss of but a few of his men, and only two of his twelve
guns being silenced, repulsed the enemy with severe loss, caused the
destruction of the flagship *Hermes* and drove the remaining vessels
with disheartened and humiliated commanders back to sea filled with
wounded men. The *Sophia* was so disabled that it was with difficulty
that it put to sea.

The following incident taken from Eaton's *Life of General Jackson*
reveals the type of national character taking hold of the people in
the far Southern section:

> It is worthy of remark to show the difference in battle between the two combatants to mark the conduct of British and American officers, under circumstances precisely similar. Whilst the battle raged the flag of the van ship was carried away and at this moment she had ceased to fire. What had caused its disappearance none could tell; no other opinion was or could with propriety be entertained than that it had been hauled down with a view to yield the contest and surrender. Influenced by this belief, Lawrence, with a generosity characteristic of our officers, immediately desisted from further firing. The appearance of a new flag, and a broadside from the ship next the *Hermes* was the first intelligence received that such was not the fact; and the contest again raged with renewed violence. It was but a few minutes, however, before the flag staff of the fort was also carried away; but so far from pursuing the same generous course that had just been witnessed the zeal of the enemy was increased, and the assault more furiously urged. At this moment, Nichols and Woodbine, at the head of their embattled train, perceiving what had happened that our "star spangled banner" had sunk, at once presuming all danger to have subsided made a most courageous sally from their strong hold; and pushing towards their vanquished foes, were already calculating on a rich harvest of blood and plunder; but a well-directed fire checked their progress, dissipated their expectations and drove them back.

Always bitter in his denunciation of ineffectual service Jackson
was equally extravagant in his praise of that well-performed and
Major Lawrence was the recipient of much sincere and oft-repeated
encomium from his enthusiastic superior.

Jackson immediately left his headquarters at Mobile and, taking
every precaution as to supplies and financial needs, even to the extent
of securing loans upon his own liability, assembled his troops near
Fort Montgomery on the Alabama River with a view of meeting the
British at Pensacola to which place they had retired. His forces
consisted of three regiments of United States Infantry, the 3rd Regiment having been heavily recruited from the Mississippi militia, a
company of Tennessee militia and the Mississippi Dragoons under
Colonel Thomas Hinds. General Jackson was deeply impressed with
the fine body of young men who composed the Mississippi cavalry,

a number of whom he had known personally during his residence at "Old Greenville" and on the Bayou Pierre in the Mississippi Territory. So struck was he now with their physical appearance and soldierly bearing that he took time to write to Governor Holmes and thank him for his prompt manner in assembling and organizing his quota of troops, referring to them as fine young men calculated to endure every hardship. In the reorganization of this Cavalry Battalion, which was to become famous as the "Mississippi Dragoons" during the last hostilities of the War of 1812 on the Southern Coast, Major Hinds was again placed in command.

In the expedition to Pensacola General Jackson's small but effective force included much of the best fiber of the young manhood of Tennessee and the Mississippi Territory. It is principally as was stated at the outset of this narrative the province of the author to record the part that the Mississippi Territory took in the struggle for American independence in the Southern section, but it has been and will continue to be the pleasure of the writer to emphasize the heroism of the brave Tennesseeans and that of the troops of all other States in Jackson's service during his campaign against the British.

The various units of the army now assuming shape for the expedition against the British at Pensacola were in training within a few weeks of the assembling of the various corps. Many of the soldiers from the Mississippi and Tennessee commands had seen service together in the terrible battles with the fierce Creek Indians during the fall of 1813. Their spirit was at a high tide of patriotic devotion to the Republic and its cause and they sought further outlets for it under the magnetic Jackson who by this time stood out as the commanding genius of the army in the South. Victory, however, was not to be had without great sacrifice and the facing of every danger. They still had in mind the cruelty of their Creek adversaries at Fort Mims and along the Tombigbee and Alabama. Then, too, the rumors of the horrible acts of the enemy along the Georgia coast and on Cumberland Island were not forgotten. But they were the sons of American patriots many of whom had perished for their rights and liberties. In addition they were hardy frontiersmen wholly unacquainted with fear and eager for that adventure that spurns the credible and is at home only with the improbable.

It was in this mood that the Americans leaving their horses at

Fort Montgomery marched on foot to Pensacola. The Mississippi Dragoons under Colonel Thomas Hinds led the way through the forest. As they approached the Spanish stronghold a small detachment of the Dragoons under Lieutenant Murray were sent forward to reconnoiter. While advancing the brave young Lieutenant was mortally wounded by an Indian, a lamented circumstance that convinced Jackson more strongly of an hostile reception awaiting him. But with a due appreciation of the usages of war, he dispatched another emissary in the person of Major Pierre and though this last went more as an ambassador approaching the city with a flag of truce he, too, was received with open hostility.

Though it was reliably reported that the colors of Spain and Great Britain were flying together over the fort and that Colonel Nichols and his staff were guests of the city, Jackson, still determined to give the Spanish every opportunity of defining their position, sent an ambassador again at midnight to join in a proposition that he should permit the American troops to occupy the forts until the Spanish government could send a sufficient force to maintain neutrality. The Spanish governor rejected the proposition claiming he was unable to resist the invasion of the British. The shrewd frontiersman was now fully assured that the protestations of inability to cope with the British were only pretexts to cover a more sinister motive. He immediately ordered 3000 troops from the encampment to attack the city, disposing them in three columns. Major Woodruff with a detachment of the 39th and 44th Regiments of United States Infantry, with two pieces of artillery composed the center, while the right was composed of the Mississippi Dragoons under Major Hinds and the Tennessee Volunteers under General Coffee, Majors Blue and Kennedy on the left commanding a company of Mississippi and Tennessee militia to which belonged a number of friendly Choctaw Indians. The columns moved against the town eastward along the beach. The old fort had once been a place of great beauty and importance. The splendid evergreen trees, the harbor and the warm southern skies making a brilliant setting for the little city on the Escambia. Though church bells still proclaimed the coming of an old world civilization the place had changed and the streets of later years the rendezvous of pirate, smuggler and Indian trader, presented an uninviting appearance; still many Spanish families and quaint Spanish houses remained as lonely survivors of colonial dignity. When Jackson attacked the town the inhabitants, including men, women and children, heroically joined in its defense. The Mississippi Dragoons led the army into the place their blue uniforms faced with scarlet and sabres slung within white belts giving cheerful color to the scene. The entrance of the Americans was stoutly resisted by a two-gun battery erected in the principal street which poured volley after volley on the brave Major Laval[49] and his men as they strove to take it, while from every house-top and window an avalanche of bullets, rocks and missiles of every description rained down upon the invaders. The defense as furious and fierce as any recorded in history was still as but the efforts of children. The sturdy columns of Jackson stormed the city with one fierce onslaught, carrying the Spanish battery at the point of the bayonet, after which a flag of truce was sent out by the worsted Spanish. When the hand to hand conflict ceased and the smoke cleared from the streets of the old Spanish town, the victory belonged to the Americans who had conducted the capture of the city with the form and order belonging to the best military sieges. The loss of eight brave men killed and eleven wounded robbed Jackson of several gallant officers. Consternation reigned among the inhabitants of the town. The governor of Pensacola under a flag of truce agreed to give the Americans possession of forts St. Michael and Barancas, and after some insubordinate conduct on the part of the Spanish commandant of Fort St. Michael had been punished, the American garrison occupied the forts.

The people of the Mississippi Territory, so near the scene of trouble after the fall of Pensacola, felt more secure. The territorial population was intensely devoted to the American cause and though sparse throughout its broad expanse had furnished Jackson besides the famous battalion under Major Thomas Hinds 500 infantry. "Mississippi," Parton has stated, "was now sending all her forces to Mobile."

---

[49] Major William Laval was a native of Charleston, South Carolina. He was the son of a French officer who was attached to the legion of the Duke of Lauzon who assisted the Americans in their struggle for liberty. When the Creek War broke out Major Laval was promoted to the post of captain and marched with the Regiment to which his company belonged to Fort Claiborne and from thence to the Holy Ground where he participated in the battle. From the wound which he received upon the occasion of the siege of Pensacola, he was a severe sufferer for two years and was rendered a cripple for life.

The British were greatly astonished at the sudden successful attack upon Pensacola and forgetting their alliance with the Spanish fled hastily from the scene of battle, blowing up Fort Barancas which was six miles below the town. General Jackson enjoyed the chagrin of the Spanish on their desertion by the British and the abject manner in which the Creeks now acknowledged his superiority was extremely serio-comic. The news of Major Lawrence's defense of Fort Bowyer and Jackson's victory at Pensacola immediately spread along the Gulf coast and wherever there was a French colony its allegiance was greatly strengthened. These recognized that the American general had struck a vital blow at Pensacola in driving the British from the place, punishing the Spaniards for their perfidy, and demoralizing the belligerent remnant of the Creek Indians. This last was a work that the gallant Major Blue[50] of the 39th Regiment continued to perform with the utmost success while Jackson was busy with preparations for the defense of New Orleans.

Jackson had managed his campaign with great genius and strategy and, with an eye to the future, his garrison was not suffered to leave Pensacola until every fort was destroyed and it was rendered useless as a harbor for the English navy. Elated over the success of his campaign so far he withdrew his army from Pensacola and stopped at Mobile. Both officers and men were in the best spirits. The Mississippians and Tennesseans bore themselves with fine and easy grace as they sang and jested their way through the beautiful Southern forest and Jackson now had the satisfaction of witnessing a thoroughly united spirit among his troops.

The defense of Mobile Point and capture of Pensacola were brilliant military feats executed in a masterly manner. In the *Encyclopedia of Mississippi History* the author has observed that the movements of the small army in this campaign and the return to Mobile through a wild and almost pathless wilderness were as well conceived and brilliantly and rapidly executed as anything in the history of Napoleon's marches or in the achievements of Stonewall Jackson or Grant, yet historians have never done the campaign justice, some barely mentioning it, others garbling the story. This is explained

---

[50] The narrative by Major Blue of his war upon the Indians has not been preserved and is thought to be a decided loss to the history of the campaign in the Southern country.

by the fact that American historians have had little access to the records of the South. General Jackson did not believe that the defense of Fort Bowyer or Mobile Point, nor the capture of Pensacola, had put an end to the designs of the British in the lower South. Though at the age of forty-seven, past the exuberance of youth, sick and exhausted by exposure to the winter rain and suffering from malaria, he kept his plan well in hand with a view of being ready at any moment to move to the defense of New Orleans, the place that he believed would be the next point of attack.

The British fleet continued to gather in the Southern waters and Governor Claiborne of Louisiana was filled with the gravest apprehension for the safety of the Louisiana capital. Parton describing the fleet says:

At the western extremity of the Island of Jamaica there are two headlands eight miles apart which inclose Negril Bay and render it a safe and convenient anchorage. If the good Creoles of New Orleans could have surveyed from the summit of one of those headlands the scene which Negril Bay presented on the twenty-fourth of November, 1814, it is questionable if General Jackson could have given them the slightest confidence in his ability to defend their native city. The spectacle would have given pause even to the General himself. It was the rendezvous of the British fleet designed for the capture of New Orleans. The day just named was the one appointed for its final inspection and review, previous to its departure for Lake Borgne. A fleet of fifty armed vessels, many of them of the first magnitude, covered the waters of the bay. There lay the huge *Tonnant* of eighty guns, one of Nelson's prizes at the Battle of the Nile, now exhibiting the pennant of Sir Alexander Cockrane, the admiral in command of the imposing fleet. Rear-Admiral Sir Edward Codrington was also on board the *Tonnant*, a name of renown in the naval history of England. There was the *Royal Oak*, a seventy-four, the ship of Rear-Admiral Malcolm. Four other seventy-fours, the *Norge*, the *Bedford*, the *Asia*, the *Ramilies*, formed part of the fleet; the last-named in command of Sir Thomas Hardy, the beloved of Nelson, to whom the dying hero gasped those immortal words, "Kiss me, Hardy; I die content." There, too, were the *Dictator* of fifty guns; the *Gorgon* of forty-four; the *Annide* of thirty-eight, commanded by Sir Thomas Trowbridge of famous memory; the *Sea-horse* of thirty-five, under Captain James Alexander Gordon, late the terror of the Potomac; the *Belle Poule*, of thirty-eight, a ship of fame. Nine other ships, mounting thirty-eight, thirty-six, and thirty-two guns; five smaller vessels, each carrying sixteen guns; three bomb craft and eleven transports completed the formidable catalogue. Nor were these all the vessels destined to take part in the enterprise. A fleet from Bordeaux was still on the ocean to join the expedition at the entrance of Lake Borgne, where, also, Captain Percy's squadron from Pensacola, with Nichols and the brave Captain Lockyer, were to effect a junction. And yet other vessels, direct from England, with the general appointed to command the army, were expected.

The decks of the ships in Negril Bay were crowded with red-coated soldiers. The four regiments, numbering with their sappers and artillerymen three thousand one hundred men who had fought the Battle of Bladensburg, burnt the public buildings of Washington and lost their general near Baltimore the summer before, were on board the fleet. Four regiments under General Keane had come from England direct to reinforce this army. Two regiments, composed in part of negro troops, supposed to be peculiarly adapted to the climate of New Orleans, had been drawn from the West Indies to join the expedition. The fleet could furnish, if required, a body of fifteen hundred marines. General Keane found himself on his arrival from Plymouth in command of an army of seven thousand four hundred and fifty men, which the marines of the fleet could swell to eight thousand nine hundred and fifty. The number of sailors could scarcely have been less than ten thousand, of whom a large proportion could, and did, assist in the operations contemplated.

Here was a force of nearly twenty thousand men, a fleet of fifty ships, carrying a thousand guns, and perfectly appointed in every particular, commanded by officers some of whom had grown gray in victory. And this great armament was about to be directed against poor, swamp-environed New Orleans, with its ragged, half-armed defenders floating down the Mississippi, or marching wearily along through the mire and flood of the Gulf shores, commanded by a general who had seen fourteen months' service, and caught one glimpse of a civilized foe. The greater part of General Keane's army were fresh from the fields of the Peninsula, and had been led by victorious Wellington into France, to behold and share in that final triumph of British arms. To these Peninsular heroes were added the ninety-third Highlanders, recently from the Cape of Good Hope; one of the "praying regiments" of the British army; as stalwart, as brave, as completely appointed a body of men as had stood in arms since Cromwell's Ironsides gave liberty and greatness to England. Indeed, there was not a regiment of those which had come from England to form this army which had not won brilliant distinction in strongly-contested fields. The *élite* of England's army and navy were afloat in Negril Bay on that bright day of November, when the last review took place.

The scene can be easily imagined—the great fleet of ships spread far and wide over the bay, gay with flags and alive with throngs of red uniforms; boats rowed with the even stroke of men-of-war's-men gliding about among the ships, or going rapidly to and from the shore. On board all was animation and movement. The most incorrigible croaker in the fleet could not, as he looked upon the scene on that bright day of the tropical winter, have felt a doubt that the most easy and complete success awaited the enterprise. As every precaution had been taken to conceal the destination of the expedition, the officers expected to find the city wholly unprepared for defense. To occupy, not to conquer Louisiana, was supposed to be but the preliminary business of the army. From New Orleans, as the basis of operations, they expected to ascend the Mississippi, pushing their conquests to the right and left, and, effecting a junction with the army of Canada, to overawe and hem in the western States. So certain were they of taking New Orleans, that several gentlemen with their families were on board the fleet who had been appointed to civil offices in the city of New Orleans. Among others, a collector for the port, accompanied by his five beautiful daughters. Many wives of officers were on board anticipating a pleasant winter among the gay Creoles of the Crescent City. Music, dancing, dramatic entertainments, and all the diversions of shipboard, were employed to relieve the monotony of the voyage.

On December 2, 1814, General Jackson arrived in the City of New Orleans. The people were greatly relieved, and Governor Claiborne, intensely American and full of patriotic zeal, received him with great joy. The Livingston[51] home was thrown open to him and not only

---

[51] Edward Livingston was a distinguished lawyer of New Orleans. He was an American patriot in every sense of the term. It has been stated that he assisted General Jackson in the preparation of his several addresses to the people of Louisiana. All original documents left by Jackson furnish ample proof that he was capable of having written any paper ascribed to him.

the members of this exclusive family but all guests and friends who visited it felt the charm of General Jackson's personality. Some delightful entertainment was arranged for him by Mrs. Livingston during which the beautiful young women of the city beamed upon him full of admiration for the singular but fascinating soldier who had come to protect their city from an invading foe.

Some historians have charged the people of Louisiana with great indifference to their fate. Henry Adams[52] has represented them as "distrustful" and "volatile;" but careful investigation shows that the Louisiana soldiery as a whole coöperated in the most gallant spirit with Jackson and Claiborne in their heroic efforts to rid the country of the enemy and that, notwithstanding the ill will that had grown up between Jackson and a majority of the legislature, the people of the city were full of patriotic ardor in its defense. The Creoles no less than the American population responded with the truest patriotism. If a small element of the Spanish was despondent this was brought about by local dislike of the French and Americans. The people of the State were fast developing a national spirit and were unaffected by the numerous appeals of the British, though these appeals carried the most extravagant promises. With the exception of a few fishermen not a single instance is recorded where a reputable person of Spanish descent in Louisiana was influenced by the appeals of the British, though the Spanish government at Pensacola was known to be in open and active sympathy with the enemy.

On his arrival in New Orleans Jackson immediately set about a twenty days' preparation for the defense of the city. The Mississippi on which the British in all probability would move against the place now received the most careful attention in the matter of fortifications. Major Latour, who was not only a skilled engineer and a good soldier but a remarkable man in many respects, was called into close consultation by Jackson in his plans for the defense of the city. It was found unfortified and though the British were known to be at this time with their fleet in the Southern seas it had been neglected or overlooked by the government. Jackson had called attention to the importance of supplying New Orleans with some means of defense during September of the previous year, but after having prevented the

---

[52] Adams, p. 346.

British from finding a lodgment at Pensacola and Mobile he had now to face the fact that nothing had been done by the government at Washington to fortify the place. Lying narrowly between the river and the wide stretch of morass, it demanded only that the former should be well fortified, and it did not take the discerning soldier and the talented engineer long to place an adequate defense about the city, building better than the unprotected inhabitants dreamed. As a main part of the defense, two effective batteries mounted with 24-pounders were located on the side of the river opposite Fort St. Philip, one at old Fort Bourbon and the other a half mile below. These were to operate in conjunction with the fire from Fort St. Philip. Another battery was placed at the confluence of the Bayou Sauvage and the Chef-Menteur River. The plans and construction of all fortifications were put in charge of Major Latour who was a few weeks later to take a heroic part in the artillery defense of the city.

In addition to the construction of batteries Jackson sent orders to Governor Claiborne to have the bayous obstructed along the entire coast from Attakapas to Chef-Menteur and Manchac in the Mississippi Territory. The inhabitants of the parishes of Plaquemine, St. Bernard, St. Charles and St. John the Baptist were called on by Governor Claiborne in accordance with a resolution passed by the legislature to assist with their slaves in the erection of fortifications for the defense of the city, and the patriotism, zeal and energy displayed by the Governor is worthy of a more extended notice. His patriotic appeals to the inhabitants throughout the trying period when the city was in danger of falling into the hands of the British were second in fervor only to those of Jackson. Being fully aware of the local jealousies between the American, French and Spanish elements in the State's population, and knowing the attitude of the Spanish at Pensacola, he at times was disposed to be despondent regarding the situation.

While Jackson was busy preparing for the defense of New Orleans the British fleet was known to be approaching from Jamaica. The arrival of sixty vessels, men of war and gunboats, in the Gulf waters with rumors of a larger number expected was sufficient to alarm the small naval force at the New Orleans station. The United States Navy at this point was commanded by Commodore Daniel T. Patterson who had been in command since the inception of the war. A few gunboats carrying in all 23 guns and 182 men was a weak naval defense for a city threatened with invasion by a strong nation, and, indeed, the American navy was insufficient everywhere and the cause of great disaster to the country. Little attempt was made to strengthen it at New Orleans, and both Claiborne and Patterson indignantly protested when the construction of the gun-boat in Lake Pontchartrain, a vessel intended to carry 42 cannon, was suspended. The American Government, however blameless, was unwise in not maintaining a sufficient naval defense at this important outpost, and had it not been for the heroic and spirited manner in which Jackson resisted the enemy New Orleans would have fallen a prey to British invasion and a later construction of the treaty made between Great Britain and America might not have included this far Southern section when disputed territory everywhere in the Western Hemisphere was the order of the day.

The letter apprising Commodore Patterson of the arrival of the British fleet came anonymously from Pensacola and on account of its interesting character is given here in the original:

To commodore Daniel T. Patterson, New Orleans,

Pensacola, 5th December, 1814.

Sir,

"I feel it a duty to apprize you of a very large force of the enemy off this port, and it is generally understood New Orleans is the object of attack. It amounts at present to about eighty vessels, and more than double that number are momentarily looked for, to form a junction, when an immediate commencement of their operations will take place. I am not able to learn, how, when, or where the attack will be made; but I heard that they have vessels of all descriptions, and a large body of troops. Admiral Cochrane commands, and his ship, the *Tonnant*, lies at this moment just outside the bar; they certainly appear to have swept the West Indies of troops, and probably no means will be left untried to obtain their object.—The admiral arrived only yesterday noon.

I am yours, &c.

N———.

Whoever "N" may have been, whether American, French, or friendly Spaniard, Patterson was nevertheless grateful for the information and hastened preparations to meet the enemy at the Mariana and Christiana Passes. He immediately sent five gunboats, one tender and a dispatch boat, to watch the powerful British fleet which on the morning of December 13, was seen shaping its course towards Pass Christian. A few hours later the enemy's flotilla gained the Pass and moved westward towards the American boats under command of Captain Thomas A. P. Catesby Jones.[53] The shallow water of the lake caused by a constant westerly breeze prevented the American boats from floating though every effort was made to remedy the situation by throwing overboard all articles of any weight. At 3:45 of December 13, the enemy dispatched boats to cut off the schooner *Seahorse* which had been sent into the Bay St. Louis by the American officers to assist in the removal of the public stores which had been previously ordered. On finding that it was impossible to remove them they were ordered destroyed for fear of capture by the British. A volley of grape shot from the *Seahorse* caused the three boats attacking to retire out of reach of her guns until joined by four more when the enemy, now in command of seven boats, renewed the attack. Sailing-Master Johnson, commanding the *Seahorse*, took position near the land fortification from which battery two 6-pounders kept up a constant action for half an hour causing a partial loss of one of the enemy's boats and several of the crew. In the afternoon of December 13, the flood tide set in and Captain Jones's small division of the little American fleet moved out of its groundings and sailed for Bay St. Louis; the appearance of the enemy in large numbers caused it to steer towards Petite Coquille which fort stood at the entry of the pass at the Rigolets, Lieutenant Jones having been ordered to make a last desperate stand at this point. Adverse winds caused the boats to ground again in the channel of Malheureux Island. Their situation was discovered early in the morning of December 15, by a British flotilla of barges which moved forward in solid line to attack the helpless gunboats. The perfect calm and swift ebb tide in the pass exposed the American boats to serious danger and Captain Jones, seeing that the only course to pursue was to force the enemy to battle, set about occupying as advantageous position as possible. He immediately called all commanding officers on board of his ship and made them aware of his plans giving each vessel its position and ordering all to "form a close line abreast across the channel anchored by the stern with springs on the cable" (see original report of Captain Thomas A. P. C. Jones). It was in this position that the small American fleet on Lake Borgne in the west end of the passage of Malheureux Island awaited the advancing foe, the

---

[53] Captain Jones' name is spelled differently in many histories. This signature is attached to his original report.

powerful British fleet consisting of 45 launches and barges mounting one cannon each of 12, 18, and 24 caliber. In addition there were two launches mounting each one long brass 12-pounder and three gigs supplied with small arms, the total number of cannon being 43 pieces. The flotilla was manned with 1200 men and officers. It was commanded by Captain Lockyer who received several severe wounds during the engagement. It was with the deepest anxiety, but cool and undaunted courage, that the little fleet received the approach of its powerful enemy. At 9 o'clock on December 15, the attack began. The tender *Alligator* had been grounded two miles to the southeast of Malheureux Island and could not join the gunboats and the enemy spying her sent a small division forward. After a spirited resistance the tender capitulated and the British immediately turned her guns upon the American boats, the entire fleet of 45 barges advancing in line. The fire from the American gunboats temporarily checked the advance and the fleet divided, one division of 15 barges attacking Gunboat 156. Upon this division Captain Jones directed his guns. By 11:00 a.m. the entire British force was attacking the small flotilla. The stubborn resistance made by the Americans is graphically told by Lieutenant Jones in his report to Commodore Patterson which is given in part:

> At 10:30 the enemy weighed forming a line abreast in open order and steering direct for our line, which was unfortunately in some degree broken by the force of the current driving Nos. 156 and 163 about one hundred yards in advance. As soon as the enemy came within reach of our shot a deliberate fire from our long guns was opened upon him but without much effect, the objects being of such small size. At 10 minutes before 11 the enemy opened a fire from the whole of his line when the action became general and destructive on both sides. About 11:49 the advance boats of the enemy, three in number, attempted to board No. 156 but were repulsed with the loss of nearly every officer killed or wounded and two boats sunk. A second attempt to board was then made by four other boats which shared almost a similar fate.

One of the boats that went down before the fire of Gunboat 156 carried 180 men. It was about this time that Captain Jones was severely wounded by a ball in the left shoulder which caused his removal from deck. Master's mate Parker immediately took charge and while gallantly defending the vessel he too was wounded, when the victorious enemy with superior numbers swarmed down on the gallant boat and gained possession of its deck a little after 12 o'clock. The enemy immediately turned the guns of his prize on the struggling gunboats, firing several shots before striking the American colors. The plucky little fleet still continued heroic resistance a half hour longer when it surrendered though not without having nobly defended the honor of the American Navy. Had there been a strong naval force at this point the British would have found it difficult to land close enough to attack New Orleans as far inland as it was situated. The loss of the British in this naval engagement was very great, numbering in killed and wounded about 300 which included many officers.[54] Captain Lockyer who commanded the flotilla which consisted of 1200 men and officers was severely wounded three times during the action. The loss to the American fleet was slight in comparison with that of the British, being near 60 which was one-third of their whole number. The stubborn resistance of the little squadron especially of Gunboat 156, commanded by Captain A. P. Catesby Jones, has been noted by many historians, but the best story is found in his original reports of the affair.

The naval operations of the British being successful in this engagement, their determination to shortly attack New Orleans was evident to General Jackson who knew that since the coast had not afforded a landing place the enemy had determined to concentrate on the capture of this city. Every effort possible must now be made to defend it and the determined, alert, and resourceful Jackson lost not a moment in making preparations to that end. His energy and patriotic zeal were contagious and the people responded with the keenest enthusiasm. In addition to all local measures, which to execute required the most delicate if not crafty diplomacy, and at times the utmost firmness savoring of license, he sent a hurried order to Generals Coffee and Carroll, whom he had stationed at Baton Rouge, informing them of the fate of the American gunboats and directing them to march immediately into camp at New Orleans with their troops. Coast defense was also recommended to General Winchester at Mobile. The Secretary of War was notified of the exposed condition of the city, that the greatest danger was apprehended and that arms should be immediately supplied.[55] The inaccessibility of the coast country

---

[54] Latour, p. 61.
[55] Anyone who has studied Jackson's methods throughout the campaign has seen that it was one of his wiles to underestimate his strength thinking that this would secure the assistance he so greatly needed in the defense of the country.

prevented close coöperation between it and the Government at Washington, the great distance and difficult transportation making it almost impossible for speedy aid to be secured. The lukewarm response and, in some instances, open defiance which the Louisiana legislature gave to General Jackson's calls for assistance were not creditable to a body representing the interests of a people already a part of the American union, a people, too, who were in great peril from a ruthless invasion. But so many racial differences existed, that unanimous action could hardly have been expected.

Notwithstanding the attitude of the legislature, General Jackson continued to make such appeals to the people as could not fail to secure response. His address, delivered when the militia of the city was reviewed, had a telling effect, and treason, if there was any, never thrust its head above the appeal, exceptional for its spirited fervor and eloquence, delivered on Sunday, December 18, to the citizens, the battalion of uniformed companies, all volunteers and the Baratarian pirates.

With the utmost speed and precaution he continued his preparations for the defense of the city, knowing that at such a crisis every hand must be raised against the enemy. As the days passed it became evident that the spirit of the city was in full unison with his own. He now had the satisfaction of seeing all things yield to his powerful purpose. The somewhat ill-natured criticism by Henry Adams that he had done nothing for the defense of New Orleans before the arrival of the British shows a want of accurate information hardly excusable in an historian.[56]

Relative to Jackson's movements before the arrival of the British a lengthy excerpt from Latour,[57] for the purpose of sustaining my contention, is here inserted:

> General Jackson was returning from a tour of observation to the river of Chef-Menteur, when the intelligence of the loss of the gun-boats reached him. He immediately ordered the militia-battalion of men of colour, commanded by Major Lacoste, and the dragoons of Feliciana, to proceed with two pieces of cannon and take post at the confluence of bayou Sauvage and the river of Chef-Menteur, in order to cover the road to the city on that side, and watch the enemy's movements. Major Lacoste was also ordered to erect a close redoubt surrounded with a fosse, according to a plan which I drew agreeably to general Jackson's orders.

---

[56] Adams, p. 339.
[57] Latour's statements are generally accepted as authoritative and have in the main been used by historians much as original records.

On his arrival in town, the general bent his attention to the fortifying of all assailable points, it being impossible to ascertain which the enemy would make choice of, the want of vessels on the lake depriving us of all means of obtaining any certain intelligence of his movements, before he could effect his landing.

Captain Newman of the artillery, who commanded the fort of Petites Coquilles, which stands at the inner entry of the pass of the Rigolets, towards lake Pontchartrain, was positively ordered to defend his post to the last extremity, and in case of his not being able to hold out, to spike the guns, blow up the fort, and evacuate the post of Chef-Menteur.

Captain P. Jugeant was authorized to levy and form into companies all the Chactaw[68] Indians he could collect.

On the 15th the commander-in-chief informed generals Coffee, Carrol and Thomas of the taking of the gun-boats, by letters sent by express, urging them to use all possible speed in marching to New Orleans with the troops under their command.

General Winchester commanding at Mobile, was also informed of the loss of our naval force, and it was earnestly recommended to him to use the greatest vigilance in protecting the vicinity of that town, as the enemy might endeavour to make an attack in that quarter.

On the 16th general Jackson wrote to the secretary of war, apprizing him of the capture of the gunboats; he expressed to him his concern for the consequences that might attend that event, which he apprehended might happen, when he wrote to government suggesting the propriety of giving the necessary orders for finishing the block-ship building at Tchifonte, and when he gave orders for supplying forts Strother, Williams and Jackson, with six months provisions. The general apprehended lest the interruption of our communications by water with Mobile, might be attended with consequences fatal to the safety of the country. He however assured the secretary of war that, should the enemy effect a landing, he would, with the help of God, do all he could to repel him. He also informed the secretary that neither the Tennessee troops nor those of Kentucky had yet arrived, but that they were daily expected, and that in the meanwhile he was putting the river below the city in the best possible state of defence. He acquainted him with the taking of the post of the Belize, with all the pilots, and a detachment of troops that was there stationed, but he informed him at the same time of the establishment of martial law, and of the rising of the militia in mass. "The country," said the general, "shall be defended, if in the power of the physical force it contains, with the auxiliary force ordered. We have no arms here—will the government order a supply? If it will, let it be speedily. Without arms, a defence cannot be made."

During the summer, while yet among the Creeks, general Jackson had made a requisition of a quantity of arms, ammunition, heavy cannon, balls, bombs, &c. to be sent to New Orleans; but such was the fatality that appeared to be attached to all the measures adopted for our defense, that it was not till the middle of January, 1815, that a very small proportion of what had been ordered, arrived at New Orleans.

A special law of the state had, some time before, authorized the formation of a battalion of free men of colour; and we have seen that it had already taken the field under the command of major Lacoste, and had been stationed at Chef-Menteur. Colonel Michael Fortier, senior, a respectable and worthy citizen of New Orleans, having the superior command of all the corps of men of colour, presided over the levying of a new battalion of the same description, formed by the exertions and under the direction of the gallant captain Savary,who had acquired an honourable and distinguished reputation in the wars of St. Domingo. It was chiefly with refugees from that island, that colonel Savary formed that battalion,

---

[68] Choctaw.

whose officers were immediately commissioned by the governor of the state; and its command was confided to major Daquin of the 2d regiment of militia. We shall hereafter see in the relation of the different engagements, that that brave corps realized, by a brilliant display of valor, the hopes that had been conceived of it.

The capture of the gun-boats was announced to the senate and house of representatives of the state, by a message from the governor: "I lay before you," said he, " a letter addressed to me by commodore Patterson, announcing the capture of five of the United States gun-boats of the New Orleans station, by a vastly superior force of the enemy. The length of the combat is a proof of the valour and firmness with which our gallant tars maintained the unequal contest, and leaves no doubt that, although compelled ultimately to strike, their conduct has been such as to reflect honour upon the American name and navy. The ascendancy which the enemy has now acquired on the coast of the lake, increases the necessity of enlarging our measures of defence."

Commodore Patterson addressed a second letter to the governor, in which he complained of the want of seamen to man the armed vessels then at New Orleans, and requested the support and assistance of the state authorities. This letter was laid by the governor before the legislature, who, on the —— day of December, passed a resolution giving a bounty of twenty-four dollars to each seaman who would enter the service of the United States for three months, and to this end placed at the disposition of the governor six thousand dollars. The governor forthwith issued his proclamation (see Appendix No. 19). Between seventy and eighty sailors received the bounty of the state, and were of the number of those brave tars who, by their incessant fire from the ship Louisiana and the schooner Carolina, so annoyed the enemy in all his movements, and so particularly harassed him on the night of the 23d of December, as will be seen hereafter.

On the 18th of December, general Jackson reviewed the New Orleans militia, the first and second regiments, the battalion of uniform companies under the command of major Plauché, and part of the free men of colour. Addresses were read to them, and answered with acclamations of applause. My voice is too weak to speak of these addresses in adequate terms; I leave the reader to form an idea of the effect they must have produced on the minds of the militia, from the impression that the mere perusal of them will make on himself. (See Appendix, No. 20.) These corps had two days before entered upon actual service, and did regular duty like troops of the line. On the 18th, Plauché's battalion was sent to bayou St. John, and the major took the command of that post.

A general order of this day enjoined all officers commanding detachments, outposts, and pickets, on the approach of the enemy, to remove out of his reach every kind of stock, horses, &c. and provisions; and directed them upon their responsibility to oppose the invaders at every point, and harass them by all possible means. It concluded with this animating sentence:

"The major-general anticipating that the enemy will penetrate into this district in a few days, requests of the people of Louisiana to do their duty cheerfully, and bear the fatigues incident to a state of war, as becomes a great people, anticipating from the ardour pervading, and the present help at hand, to make an easy conquest of them, and teach them in future to respect the rights of liberty and the property of freemen."

The garrison of fort St. John, on lake Pontchartrain, had been reinforced by the volunteer company of light artillery, under the command of lieutenant Wagner.

By an order of the day of the 19th, the commander-in-chief ordered several persons confined in the different military prisons, for having violated the laws of the country, to be set at liberty, on their offering to take up arms in defence of the country.

But that favour was restricted to such persons as were within two months of completing the term of imprisonment to which they had been condemned. These and all others not under sentence were, in pursuance of that order, set at liberty by the commanding officer at fort St. Charles, the barracks, and the powder magazines.

The country being now in imminent danger, it became necessary to adopt the most vigorous measures to prevent all communications with the enemy; and in order that such persons as might be apprehended for having given the British information as to the situation of the country, its means of defense in troops, artillery, fortifications, etc. might not escape punishment, general Jackson wrote to the governor, suggesting to him the propriety of his recommending to the legislature to suspend the writ of *habeas corpus*. As the danger was daily increasing, the general could not, without exposing the safety of the country, whose defence was committed to him, wait till the dilatory forms of deliberation should empower him to take steps necessary for saving it. Nor did it escape his penetration that the legislature was not disposed to second his views, by that energetic measure. The hour of combat drew near, that of discussing, deliberating, and referring to committees, had gone by. The time called for action and promptitude; and accordingly General Jackson proclaimed martial law, (see Appendix, No. 21), and from that moment his means became more commensurate with the weight of responsibility he had to sustain. The object of his commission was to save the country; and this, he was sensible, could never be effected by half-measures. It was necessary that all the forces, all orders, all means of opposition to be directed against the enemy, should receive their impulse from the centre of the circumference they occupied. They ought to be radii, diverging from one and the same point, and not entangling chords intersecting that circumference and each other. From the moment martial law was proclaimed, every thing proceeded with order and regularity, nor did any of our means prove abortive. Every individual was stationed at his proper post. The guard of the city was committed to the corps of veterans and fire-engine men, who were to occupy the barracks, hospitals, and other posts, as soon as the troops of the line and the militia should be commanded on service out of town.

The privateers of Barataria,[59] and all persons arrested for, or accused of, any infraction of the revenue laws, sent to tender their services to general Jackson. Mr. J. Lafitte, adhering to the line of conduct he had marked out for himself, and from which he had never deviated from the beginning of September, when the

---

[59] Of these smugglers or pirates Gayarre writes: " . . . . John and Pierre Lafitte, who were originally from Bordeaux, or, according to other reports, from Bayonne, but who, emigrating from their native country, had settled in New Orleans as blacksmiths. Tempted by the hope of making a speedier fortune than by continuing to hammer on the anvil, they abandoned the honest trade they were engaged in for one of a more dangerous character, but promising a life of excitement, which was probably more congenial to their temperament, and which held out to them ample compensation for the perils they were to encounter. They began with being the agents of the Baratarian buccaneers in New Orleans, and ended with being their leaders, and being proclaimed outlaws by the country where they resorted for illicit purposes.

"On the coast of Louisiana, west of the mouth of the Mississippi, there is an island called Grande Terre, which is six miles in length and from two to three miles in breadth, running parallel with the coast. Behind that island, about six miles from the open sea, there is a secure harbor which is reached by the great pass of Barataria, in which there are from nine to ten feet of water. This harbor communicated with a number of lakes, lagoons, bayous, sea-outlets, and canals, leading to the Mississippi, and which, skirted by swampy forests, and forming a labyrinth of waters, offered a tempting field of operation to the Robin Hoods of the sea. These men pretended to be privateers cruising with letters of marque issued by France and the new Republic of Carthagena, to prey upon the commerce of Spain; but the world called them pirates, and accused them of capturing vessels belonging to all nations, without excepting those of the United States,

British officers made him proposals, waited on the commander-in-chief, who, in consideration of the eventful crisis, had obtained for him a safe conduct from judge Hall, and from the marshal of the district.

Mr. Lafitte solicited for himself and for all the Baratarians, the honour of serving under our banners, that they might have an opportunity of proving that if they had infringed the revenue laws, yet none were more ready than they to defend the country and combat its enemies.

Persuaded that the assistance of these men could not fail of being very useful, the general accepted their offers. Some days after, a certain number of them formed a corps under the command of captains Dominique and Beluche, and were employed during the whole campaign at the lines, where, with distinguished skill, they served two twenty-four pounders, batteries Nos. 3 and 4. Others enlisted in one or other of the three companies of mariners, raised by captains Songis, Lagaud, and Colson. The first of these companies was sent to the fort of Petites Coquilles, the second to that of St. Philip, and the third to bayou St. John.

All classes of society were now animated with the most ardent zeal. The young, the old, women, children, all breathed defiance to the enemy, firmly resolved to oppose to the utmost the threatened invasion. General Jackson had electrified all hearts; all were sensible of the approaching danger, but they awaited its presence undismayed. They knew that in a few days they must come to action with the enemy, yet calm and unalarmed they pursued their usual occupations interrupted only when they tranquilly left their homes to perform military duty at the posts assigned them. It was known that the enemy was on our coast within a few hours sail of the city with a presumed force of between nine and ten thousand men, whilst all the forces we had yet to oppose him amounted to no more than one thousand regulars and from four to five thousand militia.

These circumstances were publicly known nor could any one disguise to himself or to others the dangers with which we were threatened. Yet such was the universal confidence inspired by the activity and decision of the commander-in-chief, added to the detestation in which the enemy was held and the desire to punish his audacity should he presume to land, that not a single warehouse or shop was shut nor were any goods or valuable effects removed from the city. At that period New Orleans presented a very affecting picture to the eyes of the patriot and of all those whose bosoms glow with the feelings of national honour which raise the mind far above the vulgar apprehensions of personal danger. The citizens were preparing for battle as cheerfully as if it had been a party of pleasure each in his vernacular tongue singing songs of victory. The streets resounded with *Yankee Doodle, the Marseillaise Hymn, the Chant du Depart* and other martial airs while those who had been long unaccustomed to military duty were furbishing their arms and accoutrements. Beauty applauded valour and promised with her smiles to reward the toils of the brave. Though inhabiting an open town not above ten leagues from the enemy and never till now exposed to war's alarms, the fair sex of New Orleans were animated with the ardour of their defenders and with

---

within whose territory they brought their prizes in violation of law. Many horrible tales were related of them, but were stoutly denied by their friends, who were numerous and influential.

"The Government of the United States had attempted several expeditions against them, but of so feeble a character as to be necessarily abortive. Whenever any attack was meditated against the buccaneers, they seemed to be mysteriously informed of the coming danger, and in time to avoid it. On such occasions, they would break up their settlement and carry it to some unknown part of the coast; should the new quarters be discovered and threatened, they were transported elsewhere; and the buccaneers would invariably return to the places formerly occupied by them, as soon as evacuated by their foes. It was even rumored, and believed by many, that the pursuers never had any serious intention of capturing the pursued."

cheerful serenity at the sound of the drum presented themselves at the windows and balconies to applaud the troops going through their evolutions and to encourage their husbands, sons, fathers and brothers to protect them from the insults of our ferocious enemies and prevent a repetition of the horrors of Hampton.

The several corps of militia were constantly exercising from morning till evening, and at all hours was heard the sound of drums, and of military bands of music. New Orleans wore the appearance of a camp; and the greatest cheerfulness and concord prevailed amongst all ranks and conditions of people. All countenances expressed a wish to come to an engagement with the enemy, and announced a foretaste of victory.

Commodore Patterson sent gun-boat No. 65 to fort St. Philip. Lieutenant Cunningham who commanded it had orders to send an armed boat to the Balize, for the purpose of bringing up the custom-house officer, and of ascertaining, if possible, the enemy's force. He was further directed to give to the commanding officer at Plaquemine all the assistance in his power. The commodore ordered captain W. B. Carroll, the officer who had the command of the navy-yard at Tchifonte, to cause the brig Aetna to ascend the bayou, and take a station opposite the unfinished block-ship, for the defence of the latter, in case of the approach of the enemy. Captain Carroll was further ordered not to suffer any boat to leave Tchifonte for the bayou St. John, without a passport, and in the event of the enemy's entering lake Pontchartrain, not to let the mail-boat pass.

While New Orleans was making preparation for a stubborn defense the British, after sweeping away the slight naval resistance from the Gulf shore, proceeded with much nonchalance to find a landing place for their troops. Their inhospitable reception of the bearers of the flag of truce sent by Commodore Patterson to gain information relative to the officer and members of the crew who had been made prisoners on the gunboats was indicative of an over-strict military spirit that incensed the Americans though the wounded themselves were found to be well and kindly treated.

The British having anchored their fleet near the Isle aux Pois transferred their troops to barges and continued to advance through Lake Borgne, Bayou Bienvenu and Bayou Masant and effected a landing at the mouth of Villere's Canal. A small and straggling colony of Spanish and Portuguese fisherman who used the waters of Lake Borgne and the bayous emptying into it as a fishing ground secretly assisted them in disembarking their troops, also in piloting them over safe pathways. These, furthermore, acted as spies and in connection with a disguised British soldier gathered much valuable information for the enemy, making it clear to him that his best advance after landing would be by Villeré's Canal, the ground along the canal affording a firm footing. Only ten of these creatures, however, could be named by Latour in his execration.

While the enemy's first barges were approaching, their appearance brought on a dramatic scene in the great dark Louisiana Delta whose silence at night was usually broken only by the cry of the panther or the ta hoo of the owl. An American sentinel reported a different noise; for moving quietly up the bayou through the bare midwinter forest could be seen by the pale rays of the moon five barges filled with men and several pieces of artillery. The little American detachment guarding the far outpost, deeming it imprudent to fire on account of the great disparity of numbers, concealed itself behind a log cabin. When the barges had passed the sentinels at this point determined to give notification of the arrival of the enemy. A number of these were discovered and captured by the first detachment of the enemy while landing; others made their escape and wandered in the tall grass of the low marshes for a whole day to finally become captives of the British, one alone having escaped to the American lines on the road leading from Gentilly to Chef-Menteur where Jackson had placed Claiborne with a part of his forces to guard the city. The treatment of their prisoners by the British was not in accordance with the best military customs. A serio-comic phase of the situation developed when one of the Spanish fishermen captured with the American party was detained as a prisoner. Who can be adjudged better than his company?

Another exciting incident connected with the landing of the enemy has been preserved by historians. While the British were arriving about noon of December 23, in the strip of forest on the River and running along the Villeré Canal, the advance guard entered a beautiful orange grove and came upon the fine plantation house of General Villeré which they captured, making prisoners of Major Villeré and a small company of the 3d Regiment of militia stationed there as a guard. This feat was not to be accomplished without a stout resistance from Major Villeré, the General's son, who later broke from his confinement and escaped through a window pursued by a shower of bullets.

While the brave young soldier, in a remarkable experience filled with hazard and adventure, was making his way from the right bank of the River a kindred spirit, Colonel Denis de la Ronde, commanding the 3rd Louisiana Militia, also made his escape from the enemy and reached the American lines from the other bank. I do not vouch for the many stories told of Major Villeré in his escape but I do for the fact that it was in no volatile spirit such as has been ascribed to them by Adams that these brave young Frenchmen determined to carry in person the news of the enemy's approach to General Jackson.

Furthermore the the true story of General Jackson's first reception of the news of the landing of the British is not presented by Henry Adams.[60] According to Latour's own account, Colonel La Ronde who commanded the Louisiana detachment of militia at the Villeré house sent on the evening of December 22 a courier to apprise Jackson of the appearance of several sail in the three bayous behind Terre aux Boeufs. Latour claims that he was sent the next day to verify this report but admits that he met several persons "flying" towards town who told him that the British had landed, were in possession of Villeré's house and had taken prisoner General Villeré's son. On receiving this news Major Tatum was sent back to the American camp to help confirm the story while Latour proceeded to reconnoiter the British. If the people who were "flying" towards town did not stop in their flight they were the first to apprise Jackson that the enemy had landed, a fact that was becoming very generally known through many sources.

That Jackson was prepared to meet the British is shown by the fact that he attacked them immediately on landing. He had now about 4000 troops gathered from Mississippi, Tennessee, Kentucky and Louisiana, an untrained but heroic band that thrilled with the spirit of high adventure was destined to conquer an army hitherto invincible though tested in many hard fought European campaigns.

With special reference to troops from the Mississippi Territory it may be noted that there was a large number of Mississippi volunteers scattered through the various commands. The 3rd United States Regiment had again been recruited at Cantonment Washington by Mississippi volunteers, the 44th Regiment contained Mississippi riflemen and the infantry which had been with Jackson throughout the Coast Campaign. Many were to be found in General Coffee's Brigade, while volunteers were daily arriving from the Mississippi Territory to be formed into companies with Louisiana troops or placed in other commands. The Mississippi Dragoons, composed of four troops of horse, were at all times present during the conflict to perform the many arduous duties required of them. We have seen that every man in the Mississippi Territory within military requirements had, so far, taken part in the defense of the country since the inception of the Creek War and had borne the brunt of the hostilities in

---

[60] Adams, p. 343.

camp and at home. These were now ready with the same zeal and spirit to assist in the defense of New Orleans.

The Mississippi Dragoons, under Thomas Hinds, after a march over muddy roads for four days arrived in New Orleans on the afternoon of December 23 and halted at what is at present Lafayette Square.[61] On arriving, amid a storm of cheers from both sexes who lined the streets, they were immediately confronted with an order from General Jackson to reconnoiter the British camp. With 100 of his gallant troopers and Colonel Hayne, Inspector-General of the Army, Major Hinds galloped out of the city, neared the enemy's position and dashed into his pickets, throwing him into such a state of confusion that Colonel Hayne was enabled to make an estimate of his strength immediately reporting it to Jackson to be about 2000. During this hazardous service one of the dragoons was seriously wounded and several horses were killed.

Jackson, though brandishing a thirsty lance, was not quite ready, as he expressed it, "to meet the enemy." It was a crisis where chances could not be taken, and not until the right moment would he give the signal for his army to advance upon the British whom he determined to attack that night in their first stronghold. It was ready to move at a moment's notice and consisted of many of his best troops. In his report, in enumerating his forces with which he intended to attack the enemy, which did not exceed in all 1500, he placed Major Hinds' Dragoons first in the list, the fact being noted here to show his reliance on the cavalry.

The British had little difficulty in landing their troops and while confident of success were led, through sagacious American prisoners and also through Mr. Shields, a purser in the United States Navy, and Dr. Murrel who had been the bearers to them of the flag of truce in behalf of the prisoners taken in the naval engagement, into the error of believing that a force of 18,000 men would confront them in battle when they moved against the city. After casting about for several hours, a hesitating that proved fatal to success, they somewhat leisurely began preparations for battle. The English colors had been hoisted on the treetops immediately on their arrival and the strains

---

[61] On this forced march Major Hinds and his command rode two hundred and sixty miles in four days, the road lying partly through the forest and in places obliterated by the winter rains.

of "God Save the King" now floated out on the midnight air. The house of General Villeré was occupied as headquarters while the open lands around it were rapidly filling up with red-coats numbering fully half of General Keane's division, the other half arriving during the midnight battle. Sir Edward Packenham, Commander-in-Chief, had not yet arrived. The first division disembarking numbered the light brigade of Colonel Thornton comprised of various large regiments, detachments of sappers and miners and the rocket-brigade. The second disembarkation landed the famous 21st, 44th, and 93rd Regiments of the Royal North Britain Fusileers, besides which numerous artillery-men amounting in all to over 4980.

Great excitement prevailed in the city so soon to become the object of defense. Small parties were constantly making their way towards the American camp to inform General Jackson of the arrival of the enemy in large numbers, and old men, women and children lingered anxiously in the streets and on door-steps to hear the comment of each passer-by. Proclamations posted along the fences and on farm houses everywhere near the British camp, signed by Admiral Cochrane and General Keane, contained many strong inducements to the people to withdraw their allegiance from the American government. The large element of foreign population here and the spirit of secession manifested throughout New England gave them the impression that the people of the new State of Louisiana would prove disloyal to the Republic.

Among the many stories afloat news had spread everywhere that Major Villeré and Colonel Denis de la Ronde with the 3rd Louisiana Militia stationed at the Villeré house had been captured and were held as prisoners. This and many other statements filled the people with the gravest apprehension. But every heart now trusted in the great Jackson who, like the bald eagle beating its wings against Appalachian peaks, seemed to revel in the thought of the unequal contest awaiting him. As much a votary of freedom as Patrick Henry his genius and emotions were in full play at this pinnacle of human endeavor. Communicating his rough exuberance of spirit to his small army and stirring it with such appeals as rarely fail to arouse in men a high tide of ardor he now had the satisfaction of seeing it eager for the most daring exploits. None knew better than he the numerical weakness and lack of training of the raw soldiery that was to be pitted against the trained legions of the British army, and his fixed resolve revealed in his burning avowal to "die in the last ditch" rather than see the enemy victorious might have easily been construed as meaning that he intended to lay the city in ashes rather than surrender it to the foe. Always dramatic he readily shifted from an intensely composed manner to one highly gesticulative. It was in the last mood that he now gave orders to his army.

About five o'clock in the afternoon of December 23 he began moving his forces out of camp to attack the enemy.

The intelligence of the activity of the British communicated to him continually served to deepen the terror of his voice as he fiercely proclaimed that he would drive the invaders out of the country. His heated declaration, "By the Eternal they shall not sleep on our soil," soon became the slogan of his army.

It has already been seen that Governor Claiborne for fear of a double attack had been stationed with the 1st, 2nd and 4th Regiments of Louisiana militia and the Volunteer Company of Horse under Captain Chauveau in the Gentilly plain to protect the city on the side of Chef-Menteur. Major Plauché's battalion was stationed at Bayou St. John. General Coffee, in command of the left of Jackson's army, with his Tennessee Brigade, the Mississippi Dragoons and mounted riflemen under Major Thomas Hinds lead Jackson's forces, piloted by the gallant Colonel de La Ronde who was now a member of Beale's company. In addition to Hinds', Coffee's and Carroll's troops, the defense on the night of December 23 was composed of the 7th Regiment under Major Pierre and the 44th Regiment commanded by Captain Baker, the latter having been recruited by Mississippians. Other forces included the uniformed company of militia under Major Plauché, 18 Choctaw Indians under Captain Pierre Jugeant, 200 San Domingo negro troops under Major Daquin and a detachment of artillery directed by Colonel McRea with two 6-pounders under command of Lieutenant Spotts, also a detachment of marines stationed at the right wing of the army. The left wing of the army, commanded by General Coffee, also contained the Orleans Rifle Company under Captain Beale. The whole number engaged in this first battle in defense of the city did not exceed 2000, many of them being raw recruits and poorly armed for actual battle against near 5000 well-armed, trained and seasoned British soldiery. With this small but determined force Jackson moved nearer the enemy about seven o'clock and immediately began disposing his troops for action. The schooner *Carolina* with Captain Henley was ordered to drop down and take position across from the enemy. Commodore Patterson boarded her and remained throughout the battle. Latour says:

> About nightfall the left entered on La Ronde's plantation and took position in the back of it on its boundary with Lacoste's. The right formed on a line almost perpendicular to the river stretching from the levee to the garden of La Ronde's plantation and on its principal avenue. The artillery occupied the high road supported by a detachment of marines. On the left of the artillery were stationed the Seventh and Forty-fourth of the line, Plauché's and Daquin's battalions and the eighteen Choctaw Indians commanded by Captains Jugeant and Allard form'ng the extremity of the right wing towards the woods. The superior command of the battalions of militia was given to Colonel Ross.

The British without opposition having reached the Mississippi at a point about nine miles out from the city were known to be very confident, and the small American force felt that the first encounter would be a desperate one staged as it was at night and on a low ground cut up with canals and ditches. But with their commander's fiery appeals ringing in their ears, they awaited with impatience the signal from the schooner *Carolina* which the British had supposed to be an ordinary river boat. At half past seven the *Carolina*, now commanded by Commodore Patterson, dropped down the river and opened upon the British camp a galling and unexpected fire. Extinguishing the fires in their camp the British replied to the *Carolina* with a volley of musketry followed by Congreve rockets but without especial effect. The schooner with her guns at full play for a half hour was so destructive that the enemy was compelled to abandon his camp.

General Coffee, who had been ordered to turn the enemy's right, while General Jackson himself with the remaining force would attack his strongest position on the left, now advanced from the back of the La Ronde plantation. Leaving his horses he ordered the division forward so as to fall on the British flank and rear. He was closely followed by Beale's company. His division in an extended line was now drawn up between the Lacoste and Villeré plantations with Major Hinds and his cavalry stationed near the middle of the latter plantation ready for any use that cavalry could perform at night. When the order to advance and fire upon the enemy was given Coffee's whole line promptly and with perfect precision moved forward and emptied their rifles, the division advancing rapidly and driving the enemy before it. The entire company under Captain Beale taking the foe completely by surprise dashed into his camp, a number of his brave men having been captured in the daring feat. General Jackson in a fierce charge at the same time advanced from the right against the British lines posted on the levee, the enemy contending more stubbornly at this point. The heavy enfilading fire from the schooner *Carolina* in the face of a five-gun battery of the enemy was now incessant and delivered at the very nick of time. Confusion soon spread in the ranks of the British and all organization was lost as the American forces concentrated their fire from the infantry with the guns of the *Carolina*. Encircled by a galling fire, blinded in the night by smoke and flame, their outposts battered to pieces, their camp swept with shot, and confusion reigning all along their lines, the British were driven back towards the river and though reinforced by two fresh regiments from Lake Borgne made no further advance.

The quiet almost silent manner in which the Americans began the attack and the precision with which they obeyed orders at night while facing a strong foe would have reflected credit on the best trained troops. The British commanded by Major-General Keane resistedthe attack with 4980 men composed of part of the 85th Regiment, part of the 95th Rifle Corps, a detachment of the Rocket Brigade, the 4th Regiment, the 21st Regiment of Royal North Britain Fusileers, the 44th and 23rd Regiments, besides numerous sappers, miners and artillerymen.[62]

This splendid army met the swift onrush of the American forces with a spirit equally as eager for battle, but surrounded and outmatched by Jackson's daring and strategy they were forced to give way at every town, both armies fiercely contending, often in hand to hand conflicts. The British finally abandoned the struggle about 10 o'clock. They had suffered much during the fierce combat and vexed and chagrined fell back to their camp to spend the night resting on their arms.

The heavy smoke and fog that gathered over the battle ground in the night, obscuring the position of the various corps, caused General Jackson to await further attack until morning. His small force of 2131 men rested on the cold and muddy field for a few hours and at four in the morning assumed a stronger position near the city. Major

---

[62] Latour, p. 104.

Hinds with his dragoons was placed on guard between the two armies throughout the night.[63]

In this action the 7th Regiment, commanded by Major Pierre, conducted itself with great gallantry and very naturally receives from Latour the warmest praise. The 44th Regiment, also, in which were many volunteers from the Mississippi Territory, distinguished itself under the command of Captain Baker. This, with General Coffee's gallant Tennessee brigade and all other troops in action, received the highest commendation from General Jackson. Major Hinds with the Mississippi Dragoons had conducted the force to the point of attack and during the battle remained drawn up in sight ready at any moment to use his cavalry. Before the battle he had constantly reconnoitered the enemy's position rendering Jackson the most valuable aid. Among the brave officers who were especially commended by the commander, along with Colonels Butler and Piatt, was Major Chotard of the Mississippi Territory. Their intrepidity, he claimed, saved the artillery. Tennessee and the Mississippi Territory suffered a loss in Colonel Lauderdale[64] of General Coffee's brigade who fell while heroically repulsing the enemy.

---

[63] The following extract taken from a letter written by an eye-witness gives an interesting account of the devotion and faithfulness of the Mississippi Dragoons in the defense of the country and of the City of New Orleans throughout the Christmas season:

"Our squadron," the author says, "was not in action on the 23d but were on the ground in the rear. since from the darkness of the night the cavalry was unable to act. Our duty since then has been very hard, as we have not unsaddled our horses since, but lay at their feet every night on our arms and without fires. After the battle our squadron was stationed between the two armies as picket guards, and lay three days within four hundred yards of the enemy's chain of sentinels and in the morning of the fourth day (December 28th) were compelled to retire to the main army, the enemy under cover of the night having erected batteries on the levee, and in the morning opened upon us, but did no execution except one horse killed and as we retreated they followed and made three attempts to charge our breastworks, but were as often repulsed, and were again compelled to retire, with a loss of about one hundred and fifty killed. On our part, the number in killed and wounded did not exceed twenty. To-day we have been endeavoring to draw them out, but without success, for which purpose our noble commander, Major Hinds, drew his squadron within two hundred yards of their lines, which drew their fire pretty heavy, and wounded three men and two horses. . . . . We were kept there for one hour and a half by our major, who put us through a number of evolutions in the face of the enemy, to the astonishment of all the army, and when we returned to camp were met by three cheers from the army, and General Jackson's compliments, presented to us through one of his staff, Colonel Hayne, who said to us, 'Gentlemen, your undaunted courage this day has excited the admiration of the whole army.'"

[64] Colonel Lauderdale at this time was a resident of the Mississippi Territory. Mississippi and Alabama each later named a county in his honor.

Brigadier-General David Morgan, who commanded a detachment of Louisiana drafted militia in cantonments at the English Turn, hearing of the arrival of the enemy on Villeré's plantation, finding it difficult to withstand the solicitation and impatient entreaty of his troops, though without orders, marched against the British. Latour, an eye-witness, in his *Historical Memoirs* gives a highly creditable account of the part taken in the affair of December 23 by General Morgan and his troops whose conduct under the circumstances was all that could have been expected.

During the first battle with the British, General Jackson's personal bearing was beyond criticism. His strategy, firmness, composure and disregard of personal danger in the face of a fierce charge by a powerful enemy and his skill and ardor in directing and urging his troops forward amid the fury of the battle, called forth an outburst of praise from all who witnessed the engagement. He had now become the idol of his army, his strong and singular personality possessing a charm for nearly all with whom he came in contact.

The successful attack on the British by the Americans on the night of December 23 is thought by many to have made possible the easy victory of January 8. The blow delivered the English troops so soon after disembarkation was such as to disconcert their plan for an immediate attack on the city, which might have been carried out had they not received this decided check. Protected in all by barely 5000 men, many of whom were inexperienced backwoodsmen not even acquainted with the use of the bayonet, General Jackson knew that the city would without the greatest strategy and resistance fall a helpless prey to the enemy. His little army was astir by four o'clock in the morning. A force composed of the Mississippi and the Feliciana Dragoons with the 7th Regiment commanded by Major Hinds was left near La Ronde's place to keep an eye on the movements of the enemy, the Dragoons being posted as sentinels from the levee to the swamp close to the British lines where they remained until daylight. Through the gray dawn the faithful sentinels saw a field covered with the enemy's dead and wounded which were being silently cared for.

On the morning of December 24 scouting parties of the Jefferson Troop of the Mississippi Dragoons reported that the British had formed into position between the levees three hundred yards from La Ronde's boundary with the evident purpose of giving battle. A little later their lines broke and they returned to camp deeming themselves unready for an engagement with a foe that had given them such a warm reception the night before. For the first few days they busied themselves in disembarking more troops and supplies at Isle aux Pois and transporting them to the river. Colonel Hinds, on whom Jackson now depended for knowledge of the enemy's movements, soon discovered that Lacoste's plantation was literally overrun with red coat and tartan while their sentries were posted as far out on the roads as discretion permitted.

To the small American army, constructing with might and main along Rodriguez' Canal what was to become one of the most famous breastworks[65] of history and mounting cannon along its rugged front, the invaders seemed, indeed, a formidable foe. Large companies of British troops were massing everywhere in the open plantations and the ditches were rapidly filling up with infantry. A sagacious order of General Jackson to cut the levee and flood the foreground of the Chalmette plantation in front of his lines unfortunately failed on account of the low water on that day which was unusual for the season. Every strategy possible was resorted to by the Commander-in-Chief for he knew that supreme efforts would have to be made for the protection of the city from invasion and that by an army that the Duke of Wellington believed strong enough to capture any city in America.

Not less ardent and enthusiastic in the defense of the city was Governor Claiborne whose nationalism and devotion to the American government had always been very pronounced and was now at white heat. As the second governor of the Mississippi Territory he began a period of service that would have easily ushered him into a great national career had death not cut him short at the age of forty-two. In the present crisis he manifested a spirit of freedom and patriotism not surpassed by his Revolutionary ancestors.

---

[65] The breastwork which could not have been constructed with any hope of success before the British landed and selected their line of battle was built of every conceivable material including fence rails, staves and rafters and in some parts even of cotton bales. The latter after a time were discarded on account of being easily set on fire. In the construction of the breastworks the canal was deepened and widened, the Americans working in mud and water knee deep and using every available help in the city, the entire population responding in the most spirited manner.

The British though recruited by fresh regiments and thoroughly equipped for fighting continued cautious throughout December 24. The *Carolina* and *Louisiana* kept up such a constant fire that they could scarcely move from cover, both companies and single parties seeking coverts everywhere to escape the accurate aim of the guns from these two vessels. The cavalry under the fearless Hinds reconnoitered their lines constantly through the day, displaying in full view several times, but they offered no resistance to the daring and fearless Mississippians who, led on by their brilliant commander, exhibited a courage that astonished and kept the enemy in continual alarm. The author of *Jackson and New Orleans* gives this vivid description of the operations of the cavalry of the American army during the defense of the city:

Prominent among the bands which kept the British in perpetual alarm was the command of the indefatigable Major Hinds, whose troopers from Mississippi and Louisiana were ever hovering about the English outposts, charging to the very mouths of their cannon, and driving in their pickets. Unfortunately for the British, so at least they thought, they were unable to mount their dragoons for field or fighting service; and Hinds, having none of his own arm to try his mettle on, was compelled to satisfy his impatient valor in unequal and ineffectual but dangerous, and to the British vexatious, charges on their redoubts and outposts. Hinds was of very great use to Jackson in executing reconnoissances, which he always did with brilliant daring and success. As soon as the British would throw up a redoubt or commence planting a battery in any new position, Jackson had only to say, "Major Hinds, report to me the number and caliber of the guns they are establishing there." Immediately the stalwart trooper would form his dragoons, and advancing in an easy trot until he had arrived within a few hundred yards of the object of the reconnoissance, would order a charge, and, leading himself, would dash full speed at the enemy's position, as near as was necessary to ascertain their strength and situation, and then wheeling under their fire and shower of rockets, would gallop back to headquarters and report to Jackson all the information he possessed.

In such incessant scouting parties and volunteer operations as we have described a majority of Jackson's command were engaged during the greater part of the night. So daring were these attacks that on more than one occasion the six-pounders were advanced from the lines and drawn within cannon shot of the outposts, when they would be discharged at the sentinels or any living object, generally with some effect, and always with great terror to the British camp, causing a general apprehension that the Americans were advancing to attack them in full force.

On December 25 Villeré's plantation was filled with British troops scattered in various positions, the bright hue of their uniforms making brilliant splashes of color amid the live oak, magnolia and bare, gray cottonwood groves along the river. Their enthusiasm greatly increased on the arrival of the gallant young commander, Sir Edward Packenham who was already distinguished in military circles. Closely connected by marriage with the great Wellington and a soldier by instinct and training, he represented the very bloom of the English army, that was later to overcome and send into permanent exile the great Napoleon. Lessons of daring and fortitude learned perhaps in these western wilds and borne across the seas served to animate the heroic spirits that won the field at Waterloo.

Immediately upon his arrival, General Packenham took command of his troops and an army seemingly never faced a more conspicuous fortune. It was on Christmas Day that he found himself in command of a force that by the first week in January had swelled to 8000 splendid troops with more constantly arriving. Beyond a handful of raw, half-trained, poorly armed regiments and a line of rude fortifications lay the rich prize, the fair city of New Orleans that was even then fast becoming the city of Bienville's dream. It had been rumored that the American general commanded a strong force in his defense of the city but nothing in its appearance now substantiated the rumor and it was with light hearts that the British made preparations as the days passed, the weakness of Jackson's defense becoming more apparent to them each day.

Very little transpired for several days after the night of December 23, though the restless Dragoons continued to harass the enemy, often drawing close enough at times to his lines to exchange shots, during which feats there was an occasional loss of a brave Mississippian.

A report that the British had landed at Chef Menteur and were engaged in active operations spread alarm among the troops guarding the Gentilly plain and caused General Jackson to send Major Latour with a detachment of two hundred men from General Coffee's brigade to take entire command of that point. In this manner he narrowly watched the approach towards the city deploying his small force so as to guard all possible entrance.

While ready to march against the American lines, Packenham, who had been greatly annoyed by the *Carolina* and *Louisiana* on the Mississippi determined to use first his artillery against them. This he had brought in considerable numbers from his vessels and on December 27 at seven o'clock in the morning his battery of several 12- and 18-pounders and a howitzer began firing on the *Carolina* and after a most strenuous effort succeeded in destroying the plucky little ship. The *Louisiana* would have suffered the same fate had it not been towed up out of reach of the enemy's guns.

It was on the day previous that General Morgan on receiving orders left the English Turn, sent the artillery to Fort St. Leon, and took position on the right bank of the river opposite Camp Jackson. He was the recipient of an unfortunate instruction about the same time. An order from Jackson had caused him to cut the levee near Jumonville's plantation and the flooded canals afforded the British ample water to float up their heaviest artillery, but not enough to render the ground unfit for camping. The Americans were now watching every movement of the enemy but still the British had made no move to march. On the evening of December 27, however, they moved forward and drove in the advanced guard of the Americans. Pressing forward in heavy columns they took position on the rich plantations of Bienvenu and Chalmette, ground that was to become famous in the history of the world.

The night saw great batteries looming up on the river and early on the morning of December 28 a number of splendid colors could be seen displayed, the infantry advancing and pressing still further back the advanced guard of the little American army which had itself fallen back from La Ronde's plantation. The cavalry under Major Hinds continued in the very face of the overwhelming foe to reconnoiter his lines, the troops sustaining the heavy fire of all his outposts. It was in one of those desperate, close encounters with the enemy that three heroic Mississippi cavalrymen lost their lives while several were mortally wounded. The 7th Regiment acted with Major Hinds on the occasion and the advanced sentries and pickets fell so rapidly before their fire that General Packenham sent a flag to the American commander complaining of the shooting of sentinels as barbaric, compared with European warfare. General Jackson, however, saw in the present hostilities nothing more than a cruel war of invasion and made it very plain to the British officers that sentinels of the opposing armies would be running great risks to drink out of the same stream.

As the dawn threw its silver light through the thickly draped folds of gray fog the enemy continued to advance against the American lines preceded by heavy artillery which divided its fire between the *Louisiana* and Jackson's lines. The British, hardened Peninsular veterans, both tartan and redcoat, were in gay, good spirits, their hearts beating high with expectation of victory. As Subaltern very naïvely admits, when not charged by Hinds' Dragoons they regarded their passage into the city something in the light of a royal entrance. It was about this time that Jackson ordered the blowing up of all the buildings on the Chalmette plantation which protected the enemy.[66] The same fate was intended for the house on the Bienvenu place but its execution failed. The British made much of their artillery as they confidently advanced, their guns cheerily playing upon the *Louisiana*. They little dreamed that as soon as they came within proper range the modest-looking vessel would return a most destructive fire. In a few moments more the deep columns pressing upon Jackson's lines with such enthusiasm and confidence were losing position and Packenham was destined to witness many of his bravest men fall, his guns silenced and confusion prevail in his ranks. Throughout the destructive flanking fire from the *Louisiana* which wrought such havoc among the British, a terrific fire from Humphrey's battery and Latrobe's 24-pounder was kept up incessantly. Commodore Patterson vividly describes the action in his report to the Secretary of the Navy in the following words:

U. S. Ship Louisiana, 4 miles below New Orleans.
29th December, 1814.
SIR,
I have the honour to inform you that on the morning of the 28th instant at about half past seven I perceived our advanced guard retreating toward our lines—the enemy pursuing; fired shot, shell and rockets, from field artillery with which they advanced on the road behind the levee; sprung the ship to bring the starboard guns to bear upon the enemy; at 25 minutes past 8 A. M. the enemy opened their fire upon the ship with shells, hot shot and rockets which was instantly returned with great spirit and much apparent effect and continued without intermission till one P. M. when the enemy slackened their fire and retreated with a part of their artillery from each of their batteries evidently with great loss. Two

---

[66] The manner in which the Chalmette buildings were blown up is interestingly told by the English historian Subaltern: "That the Americans are excellent marksmen," says this author, "as well with artillery as with rifles we have frequent cause to acknowledge; but, perhaps, on no occasion did they assert their claim to the title of good artillerymen more effectually than on the present. Scarce a ball passed over or fell short of its mark but all striking full into the midst of our ranks occasioned terrible havoc. The shrieks of the wounded, therefore, the crash of firelocks, and the fall of such as were killed, caused at first some little confusion; and what added to the panic was, that from the houses beside which we stood bright flames suddenly burst out. The Americans, expecting this attack, had filled them with combustibles for the purpose, and, directing against them one or two guns, loaded with red-hot shot, in an instant set them on fire. The scene was altogether very sublime. A tremendous cannonade mowed down our ranks and deafened us with its roar, whilst two large chateaux and their out-buildings almost scorched us with the flames and blinded us with the smoke which they emitted."

attempts were made to screen one heavy piece of ordnance mounted behind the levee with which they threw hot shot at the ship and which had been a long time abandoned before they succeeded in recovering it and then it must have been with very great loss as I distinctly saw, with the aid of my glass, several shot strike in the midst of the men (seamen) who were employed in dragging it away. At 3 P. M. the enemy were silenced; at 4 P. M. ceased firing from the ship, the enemy having retired beyond the range of her guns. Many of their shots passed over the ship and their shells burst over her decks which were strewn with their fragments; yet, after an incessant cannonading of upwards of seven hours, during which time eight hundred shots were fired from the ship, one man only was wounded slightly by the piece of a shell and one shot passed between the bow-sprit and heel of the jib-boom.

The enemy drew up his whole force, evidently with an intention of assaulting General Jackson's lines, under cover of his heavy cannon; but his cannonading being so warmly returned from the lines and the ship Louisiana caused him, I presume, to abandon his project as he retired without making the attempt. You will have learned by my former letters that the crew of the Louisiana is composed of men of all nations (English excepted), taken from the streets of New Orleans not a fortnight before the battle; yet I never knew guns better served or a more animated fire than was supported from her.

Lieutenant C. C. B. Thompson deserves great credit for the discipline to which in so short a time he had brought such men, two-thirds of whom do not understand English.

General Jackson having applied for officers and seamen to work the heavy cannon on his lines furnished by me, Lieutenants Norris and Crawley of the late schooner Carolina instantly volunteered and with the greater part of her crew were sent to those cannon which they served during the action herein detailed. The enemy must have suffered a great loss in that day's action by the heavy fire from this ship and general Jackson's lines where the cannon was of heavy caliber and served with great spirit.

I have the honour to be with great consideration and respect your obedient servant,

DANIEL T. PATTERSON.

During the encounter of December 28 Jackson's land forces were equally as daring and successful in repulsing the enemy. Throughout the whole engagement the British without cessation threw shrieking Congrieve rockets into General Carroll's troops who occupied a part of Rodriguez' Canal, but, though exposed on account of insufficient protection by their thin breastworks, the Americans suffered only a slight loss from the noisy shells that were meant to strike terror to their hearts. In this engagement the 1st Regiment of Louisiana Militia remained on duty during the whole of the action. Captain Dominique and Lieutenant Crawley commanding Batteries 3 and 4 rendered good service during the battle and served their pieces with the utmost skill and precision and it was the great destruction the artillery dealt the enemy that caused the death rate in his columns. The loss of the Americans in the affair of December 28 was very slight, numbering in all seventeen killed and wounded, Colonel Henderson of the Tennessee Division commanded by the chivalrous General Carroll being among the killed, a lamentable occurrence caused by his misinterpreting orders and carrying his gallant force into the face of a galling fire from the enemy. The British loss was considerable, being estimated between 150 and 200. Victory still crowned the Americans and the rejoicings in the army and in the city filled the air with notes that broke into a jubilate.

If the engagement of December 23 had not convinced Packenham of Jackson's determination to resist his advance, the affair of December 28 showed plainly that the Americans were not to be daunted and awed by the sight of heavy advancing columns nor the shriek of high explosives whose misdirected fire had come to be a subject of comment and amusement.

Moment by moment unheeding the cold rains and mud and water Jackson continued to strengthen his position both breastworks and batteries, and day by day through the heavy fogs that veiled the battle lines the fortifications rose up like huge spectres which faded as the sun each day advanced up the horizon, the clear morning light revealing the stern defenses of the city. And though the British still doubted the Americans' ability to cope with them in a serious engagement, before their eyes everywhere it seemed that American batteries were looming up. Supported by the *Louisiana* they constituted a formidable defense not yet wholly acknowledged by the enemy. Conspicuous among them were two 12-pounders and a 24-pounder which formed the famous Marine Battery.[67] Commodore Patterson armed a battery established behind the levee with these heavy guns from the *Louisiana* to protect Jackson's front. A galling fire from this battery caused the British to retire from the Chalmette and Bienvenu houses and remove his camp to the back of the plantations. In vain they strove to keep the outposts sentineled but the brave Tennessee riflemen picked them off at such a rapid rate that any successful attempt along the river at reconnoissance was in vain. The persistency, too, of the cavalry in the face of heavy guns was the

---

[67] The pieces of this battery which rendered such valuable and heroic service in the defense of the City of New Orleans were served by sailors from the Louisiana who had been gathered from the streets of the city and pressed into service after the capture of the American gun boats. Few of them spoke the same language and it was largely due to Lieutenant Thompson's care in training them that they rendered such efficient service.

cause of great surprise and annoyance to the British but of much gratification to Jackson who knew the value of daring cavalry in moments of danger in heartening a small, poorly equipped army facing a large body of well organized troops. It was about this time that the adventure of the ditch occurred, an adventure that has been preserved in original narrative by an eye witness of the feat. Trimble, a member of the Jefferson Troop of which Isaac Dunbar was captain, says:

> Colonel Hinds reported at headquarters that his pickets had detected a strong party of the British creeping up a wide and deep ditch traversing the field before us. Some doubt being expressed, he obtained permission to make an immediate reconnoissance. He formed the battalion and said, "Boys, you see that big ditch! It is full of red coats. I am going over it. Whoever wishes may follow me; whoever chooses to stay here may stay." He galloped away at full speed with every man close behind him. They leaped the ditch which was crowded with British soldiers, made a circuit in front of the British lines, and charged over the ditch returning, each dragoon, as he bounded over, firing his pistol at the astonished red coats. But they recovered in time to give us a general volley which wounded several of our troop and a number of horses. L. C. Harris and Charles H. Jonisdon each got a bullet in the right shoulder.

It was this close encounter with the enemy that caused Jackson to exclaim of the Mississippi Dragoons in such extravagant language, "They are the pride of one army and the admiration of the other." It was such high courage and almost reckless daring, too, that put spirit into the whole army and won for the gallant commander of the Mississippi Cavalry the sobriquet of "Old Pine Top," a name not only suggested by his residence in the great pine forests of Mississippi, but because of the pine and all kindred species of that evergreen being emblematical of endurance in the clutches of storm and blast.

In the face of great annoyance from the cavalry the British on December 31 cast up a strong redoubt near the swamp and opened up a terrific fire on the left of Jackson. During the following night the entire army moved forward and when only a few hundred yards of the American lines began throwing up entrenchments upon which they planted heavy siege guns. Their fortifications began to assume a formidable appearance. Within only six hundred yards of the American breastworks they erected three half moon batteries, right, center and left. Thirty pieces of heavy ordnance were mounted upon these and all manner of picked guns brought from the ships. On January 1, a thick fog usual to the section wrapped the entire plain, hiding every vestige of preparation from view. Secure in the belief that their cannon would sweep away the defenses of the straggling American army, they began opening up a sharp and well ordered fire. But the American fortifications, to Packenham's utter astonishment, resisted the fierce attack. Though the British guns roared and flamed pouring salvo after salvo upon the air, and missiles from the rocketeers fell in showers within their fortifications damaging to some extent both batteries and guns, the brave defenders of New Orleans met it with the imperturbable coolness of trained veterans. The heavy guns of Jackson made haste to reply with deadly aim to the confident enemy. Humphreys leading, the plucky Baratarians and Flangeac with his volunteer patriots immediately followed, and opened up a deafening thunder along the American lines. The British recoiled an instant under the terrific storm but came forward immediately with an attempt to turn the American left at the swamp. To their chagrin, they were met by a perfect rainstorm of missiles from Coffee and his riflemen. Noon found the half moon batteries of the enemy's fortifications broken, all the defenses along the levee destroyed, the cypress swamps and laurel groves trampled and torn and the wreckage of battle strewn everywhere. The dismayed British soldiers sought the entrenchments for protection during the remainder of the day and during the night retreated to their camp, many of their cannon left in the mud and mire and the entire army suffering not only from the wet and cold but from hunger and loss of sleep. While the New Year dawning on the Southern capital found the Americans confident and joyful, to the discomfited British there was little in the day that relieved their minds of their recent defeat, and humiliation was visible on every countenance. Sixty hours they had been with but little sleep, and on account of their position cut off from food and closely engaged in a terrific battle with an enemy that fought desperately. Memories of New Year's Day and the warm, well ordered firesides of Old England came no doubt to their minds during the bitter experience. But they were English soldiery and there was not the faintest trace of cowardice in the souls of the men who had been with Wellington in his famous campaigns. Though news that the American army was hourly increasing reached Packenham, knowing the mettle of his troops he determined to put his army in order again and with one swift onslaught storm Jackson's lines on both sides of the river, General Morgan being in command of the right bank.

Mississippi Territory in War of 1812—Rowland.   133

General Jackson shrewdly discovered the enemy's plans. His own forces had been augmented by the arrival of 2000 drafted men from Kentucky under General John Thomas, 700 of whom were sent to the front under General Adair. Poorly clad and armed they excited the sympathy of the city and the legislature. The citizens of the State immediately took steps to relieve their pitiable condition. The women of New Orleans sewed all day and far into the night until uniforms were provided for all. The tardiness of the national government in supplying arms and clothing brought about grave complications at times during the defense of the city.

We have seen that the batteries were mainly in charge of Humphreys, the Baratarians and the veteran Garrigues Flaugeac. On January 6 and 7, Jackson began disposing his land forces between the batteries with a view of meeting the concerted and general attack of the British. His artillery commanding an advantageous position played an important part in the defense of the city. His lines, five miles out from the city, were now being given daily inspection. Taking Latour, the principal engineer, for authority we give here the following distribution of the artillery as it assisted Jackson on January 8: Battery 1, stationed seventy feet from the river was commanded by Captain Humphreys. The enfilading fire of this battery and the fierce fire of the center batteries were very effective. Battery 2 was commanded by Lieutenant Norris; Battery 3 by Captains Dominique and Bluche; Battery 4 by Lieutenant Crawley; Battery 5 by Colonel Perry; Battery 6 by General Garrigues Flaugeac; Battery 7 by Lieutenants Spotts and Chauveau; Battery 8 placed near the elbow of the line that passed into the wood was in such condition as made it impossible for it to render good service. The artillery here was served by militia of General Carroll's command. The line from this battery through the wood and to its extremity was a sheet of mud and water in which Jackson's troops stood in places knee deep. The breastworks though hardly sufficient at one point to withstand concentrated attack heretofore had been strengthened each day so that by January 7 and 8 they were proof against the cannon of the British. Behind them the American army waited on the night of January 7 for the approach of the enemy, the low ground at places compelling them to stand in ooze and water as they listened to the scathing fire of the enemy throughout the night.

The British, though they had pushed forward, had not yet passed out of the Bienvenu and Chalmette plantations where they were busy in constructing fascines and scaling ladders, and making final preparations for battle. The Chalmette plains on the 7th, presented a brilliant and imposing scene. Staff officers in bright uniforms were riding about everywhere giving orders while large parties of troops were moving heavy artillery forward. All through the night of January 7, the noise of many hammers could be heard in the construction of batteries.

The disposition of Jackson's forces on the morning of January 8 was practically as follows: A company of the 7th Regiment commanded by Lieutenant Ross guarded the redoubt on the river; a detachment of the 44th Regiment, which was also in the corps of Colonel Ross, under the command of Lieutenant Mazant served the artillery. The New Orleans volunteer company of riflemen was stationed between the river and Battery 1 on the extreme right. The 7th Regiment came next extending past Battery 3 to the powder magazine which last along with Battery 2 commanded by Lieutenant Norris had been constructed since January 1. The 7th Regiment was commanded by Major Pierre and numbered 430 troops. Lieutenant Crawley[68] commanded the battery here and the space between that battery and Battery 4 was held by Major Plauché's battalion of volunteer uniformed companies of Louisianians who had flocked to the defense of the city and Major Lacoste's Louisiana men of color both numbering about 600 troops. Between Batteries 4 and 5 Major Daquin's battalion of St. Domingo men of color occupied the line consisting of 150 troops; next in order come the 44th Regiment composed of 240 troops commanded by Captain Baker. The entire line from the 7th to the 44th Regiments was under command of Colonel Ross.

Major-General Carroll commanded two-thirds of the length of the remaining line. Beyond on the right of Battery 7, commanded by Lieutenants Spotts and Chauveau, were stationed 50 marines under command of Lieutenant Bellevue. General Adair with 600 Kentucky

---

[68] The name of Crawley is at present prominent in the State of Mississippi. In connection with this, it is an interesting fact that numbers of soldiers from other states who served in the Coast Campaign against the British settled in Mississippi and Louisiana, a Tennessee colony having made a settlement in what is now the State of Alabama.

troops strengthened that part of the line and General Coffee's troops, 500 in number, occupied the rest of the line, also that part that ran towards and into the woods. In addition to Colonel Thomas Hinds' Mississippi Dragoons and Captain Ogden's company of cavalry, the Attakapas Dragoons were stationed ready for use. Colonel Hinds was placed in command of all of Jackson's cavalry and held in reserve for any duty demanded of him. Some untrained troops, aggregating several hundred were placed in various positions. Guards occupied the road behind the line of troops and sentinels were posted from the road to the woods to prevent any passing out of the camp.

The above disposition of troops follows mainly original reports. Parton and Latour estimate Jackson's entire force at about 4000 men including "one hundred artillerists who did not belong to the corps." Of this force only about 3200 men took part in the actual fighting. The Mississippi troops attached to the various regiments and corps have not been given mention by historians, perhaps from the fact that they were not commanded, except in a few instances, by Mississippi officers but they were to be found in large numbers scattered throughout Jackson's army in defense of New Orleans. Jackson himself brought Mississippi militia with his Tennesseeans from Pensacola and besides the recruits in the regular army, volunteers flocked to the city from many points and joined various organizations, the 44th and 3rd Regiments being made up partly of Mississippi volunteers.[69] Among these volunteers who came each day, singly and in squads, was the Creek War hero, Sam Dale of the Mississippi Territory, whose participation in the battle of January 8 is told in the following statement from his diary:

Galloping into the city and down the river, I heard the roaring of the artillery. The battle was in full blast. I gave my horse to an orderly and rushed to the entrenchments.

In something of the same manner hundreds of Mississippians had from day to day joined in the defense of the city while the cavalry under Colonel Hinds, all truthful historians must agree, was by far the most heartening influence in Jackson's army. No one better than Jackson himself recognized this and the fact that its

---

[69] In speaking of the daily arrival of Mississippi volunteers, one of Major Hinds' Dragoons in his diary says: "Our friends, Thockmorton, Breedlove and Richardson are here and I expect will join our troop. . . . . William Bullet has become attached to General Coffee's staff; also General Poindexter."

service won from him the most extravagant praise bestowed on any command connected with the battle is proof of the superior service rendered by the troops from the Mississippi Territory in defense of the city. The historian Trimble, who was an eye-witness of the battle, describes the position of the Mississippi cavalry in the following interesting excerpt taken from manuscript sources:

> There was a scathing fire during the night and the note of preparation in the British camp could be distinctly heard. Our troops were in arms and in their proper places at break of day. Our cannon bristled on the breastwork from the levee to the woods behind which was a long line of riflemen. One hundred and fifty yards in the rear sat our grim old Colonel on his charger with the whole of the cavalry. We were placed there to cover our army in the event of its being compelled to fall back to the second position.

It must have been difficult for one of Colonel Hinds' temperament to have restrained himself. At a time when men were unused to military discipline one would have expected little better of the impetuous commander of the cavalry than to have plunged recklessly into the battle without orders from his superior, but having become a seasoned soldier he knew the value of what Kipling in modern times has styled "everlasting team-work." Always exacting obedience from his subordinates, he was careful of the slightest command of his great superior for whom his romantic nature was fast entertaining heroworship. Between himself and General Jackson there had always existed a deep friendship since "Old Greenville" days when the former was training the Jefferson Troop for service as a part of the Mississippi Dragoons, an organization that was to achieve fame not only in defense of the City of New Orleans, but of the American Republic. On the memorable January 8, we find him in charge of Jackson's whole cavalry, watchful and eager yet superb in self-restraint, giving full proof of the assertion made by Governor W. C. C. Claiborne that he had discovered in him all the talents and requisites of a good soldier.

Little more than a general account of the battle of January 8, will be given here and without minute details in reference to the further position of the troops since their position has already been noted. When the day dawned, cold and foggy, it found Jackson's forces with grim determined faces awaiting the splendid British army drawn up for action. Commanded by the hero of Salamanca, its regiments, brigades and divisions in gleaming battalia awaited his direction with a proud and confident spirit.

A Congrieve rocket speeding skyward from the British lines near the woods answered instantly by a shot from one of the American batteries being regarded as the signal for attack the two armies came together in fierce combat, both artillery and infantry breaking into a heavy rolling fire that shook the ground and wrapped the early morning skies in solid sheets of flame. Instantaneously the heavy guns from Batteries 6, 7 and 8 opened a terrific fire on the enemy's advancing columns and soon the terrible battle that has been regarded as one of the most famous in history burst into full blast. All across Chalmette's wet and miry plains the British lines were drawn and from the glittering rows of embattled steel company after company and regiment after regiment, were constantly advancing. The troops moved steadily forward, not with the light insouciance that charterized their first movements, but with rigid forms and lowering brows, braced to meet the rain of lead that swept their ranks amid wild cheers from the American batteries. The first fierce volleys coming in rapid succession from Batteries 6, 4 and 8 made large gaps in the uniformed ranks advancing in stiff, heavy columns, both Briton and Highlander bearing on their shoulders, beside their muskets, fascines and scaling ladders. These continued to maintain order until Coffee's and Carroll's men and the Kentucky troops under General Adair poured a withering fire of musketry into their ranks, causing them to waver and break.[70] With rattling peals that shook the ground the batteries without a moment's cessation continued to shell the enemy's line. The forces, which composed the right of the British army, were soon losing position and reeled back in the direction of the low morass. In vain were the columns of Gibbs, and Keane's rallied to be instantly repelled by the deadly fire of the American guns.

There was no protection against the blazing artillery that swept the advancing troops; fascines and scaling ladders, which at first were thought to be of use in mounting the breastworks, were forgotten in

---

[70] "The Kentucky and Tennessee troops on the left of Jackson's line," says Latour, "though constantly living and even sleeping in the mud" (from December 24 to January 20), "gave an example of all military virtues."

Of the Kentucky troops under General Adair on the left bank of the river General Jackson says in his general orders: "General Adair, who, owing to the indisposition of General Thomas brought up the Kentucky militia, has shown that troops will always be valiant when their leaders are so. No men ever displayed a more gallant spirit than these did under that most valuable officer. His country is under obligations to him."

the consternation that followed the full play of Jackson's well-served pieces that did not cease action during the battle. Column after column, platoon after platoon, were mowed down to be speedily replaced by splendid, well-disciplined troops who faced the fury of the guns unflinchingly.

Gathering his well trained legions about him, Packenham now came against Jackson's lines where they were weakest. Veteran troops of Wellington, they knew what battle meant and with upright forms and firm tread pressed forward over the dead bodies of their comrades which were beginning to pile up beneath their feet. As they neared the American lines a darker fortune awaited them still, but without a backward glance, with grim, set faces, they went to meet their fate in a blind, stolid fashion typical of their unfearing race. Falling everywhere, they were at once replaced by other columns that instantly went down before the heavy fire of the American guns. With a constant flame Jackson's batteries continued to rake the new-made lines. In the face of hissing shot and shrieking shells and half blinded by the gun glare a company of brave red-coats reached the American entrenchments, but another belch and peal of the cannon, accompanied by a heavy rain of lead from the Tennessee sharp-shooters, and the column struggling in the slippery mud and mire wavered and lost position, then broke and fled to any shelter that could be found. The assaulting party retired to position four hundred yards from Jackson's first line but not without having striven upon his very ramparts. Secreting themselves in a ditch where they crouched wounded and bleeding, they responded with blanching faces to a call for a second attack. But their hesitation was not long. Discarding their heavy knapsacks they sternly came once more into line, recruited in weak places by fresh troops. Wildly cheering each other the Americans eagerly awaited the enemy's advance, the shrill blast of their voices echoing over the plains and along the vast river. The thin, gaunt figure of General Jackson mounted on a foaming charger could be seen through the smoke and glare of the battle, and wherever the tall gray steed appeared with its grim rider, enthusiasm reached its height, shouts of "Old Hickory! Old Hickory!" rending the air.

When the British column came forward for a second attack both musketry and artillery swept it again with a fire that wrought almost total destruction in its ranks. Following the quick flaming of cannon, heavy veils of smoke wreathed the battle ground where the dimly outlined columns of Packenham were seen now advancing, now wavering and retreating in disorderly fashion. The atmosphere seemed on fire and the discomfited enemy could not discern through the smoke enveloping the plains from which point came the hottest attack, nor the strength of the force that led it. Everywhere Packenham was dashing along the front of his lines shouting and animating the drooping spirits of his shattered army. A stinging sensation, and his left arm fell powerless by his side; his steed reared, plunged forward and fell dead, leaving the heroic commander barely time to leap from his back. With the deafening scream of the batteries smiting his ears, a lurid stream of shot and shell raining about him and his men falling everywhere, he instantly mounted another horse and with his right hand urged it forward, while in fierce, rapid commands he rallied his broken squadrons. Animated by his presence in their midst they rushed forward in the face of a galling fire and again reached the American breastworks. But their victory was short-lived. The forces of Jackson were too well organized to yield. Swept on by his shrill, familiar voice the Americans, wildly cheering, continued to hurl back the invaders of their country. A belch of flame from their batteries with an enfilading fire almost completely wiped out the supporting columns of General Keane.

Across the field the sturdy English soldiery moved to be mowed down like grass before the scythe. Their leaders' fortitude and valor stirred at times the entire line and following the quick, sharp commands coming to them through the blinding smoke and glare they made another heroic effort to storm the American defenses. The heavy fire from Jackson's artillery and infantry coming together made open roads through their ranks. The battle was at its height; the tempest scorching and withering everything in its hot breath. Dead and wounded lay everywhere when the final catastrophe came to quench all hope in the breast of the proud English army. The valiant Packenham riding in the midst of the fury with cheers on his burning lips swayed in his saddle; his right arm grew limp, his horse went down under him and with a last stern command ringing on the smoking air he fell forward in the arms of an aide. Loving hands bore him out of the blare and death-rattle to a quiet spot beneath the ancient live oaks standing along the battle's boundary lines, where, doubtlessly, forgetting in the great adventure the alien atmosphere that chilled to death his mortal frame and dreaming of soft English skies, he yielded up his life, breathing his last in the arms of his faithful aide, McDougall. His untimely end cast a gloom over the English army both at home and abroad. Nor was his death the only loss that England sustained that day. Officers of the highest rank had fallen either mortally wounded or killed outright. In the second charge which had proved even more calamitous than the first, General Keane had been shot in the side, while General Gibbs was taken from the field with a mortal wound. Major Wilkinson lost his life on the summits of Jackson's breastworks.

The British made a feeble effort, bringing even the wounded into line to rally the right of their wrecked army, but broken and decimated it went utterly to pieces and pursued by screaming volleys of shot and shell staggered back across the smoke-wreathed valley a bewildered mass of tortured, agonizing life. Nor could General Lambert now in command lead it to a third general charge.

The Americans, sheltered by their fortifications, suffered little from the enemy, the estimate being only thirteen killed and wounded on the left bank of the river. The fate of the right of Packenham's army was not more dire than that of the left. Here the brave and beloved Renee had pressed toward the river with his 1000 troops, swept away the American pickets and stormed the right of Jackson's army, entering, during a fierce hand-to-hand conflict, a half-completed redoubt to remain but a short while. The batteries of Humphreys and Norris and the 7th Regiment commanded this point and the charge had been a fearless one in the face of a galling fire from the American batteries. But none could be more sure of victory than the fearless leader, who gained the parapet of the redoubt with an exultant shout to his men to follow. In another instant he fell dead pierced by a shot from one of Beale's gallant volunteer riflemen. This command defended the extreme end of the line with a valor and patriotism that reflected new honors on its service. The British columns driven out of the redoubt reeled back in disorder through the red tide of battle leaving their dead strewn along the levee and the river. The last reserve under General Lambert could do no more than cover their retreat.

From the field everywhere shattered and depleted regiments were now retreating in disorder. The proud British army was vanquished; its bugles were silent; its colors trampled in the earth; its guns had ceased to reply. The Chalmette Plains, covered with nearly 3000 of England's valiant dead, was soaked in blood. Its orange and live oak groves, in which no bird sang for days, were riddled with shot and shell, and the wreckage of battle was strewn in soiled heaps over the landscape. Beyond, the cold, gray forest outlined the river. The bare limbs of the trees draped in long Spanish moss bedraggled by wind and rain, added a dreary touch to the disconsolate scene.

After the terrible battle that had lasted only a little more than an hour, the dead, the dying and the wounded lay strewn over the plains, along the levee and bayous and within the ditches throughout the forenoon and part of the afternoon, a bleeding, disfigured mass that filled the beholder with horror and dismay.

Never in the history of warfare has there been such rare execution of plans as marked Jackson's defense of the city, nor such inability and helplessness on the part of an adversary to avert catastrophe. Out of raw militia Jackson had created a strong, well-disciplined army and the American rifleman, cool and collected, proved to be not only a good marksman—a skill gained from much practice as a huntsman in the forests and wilds of the undeveloped country, but in every respect the best type of soldier. And the battle! Many historians have tried to describe it, yet none have painted it in its true color and only a Hugo could give it in immortal pictorialization. The story is told here not with the hope of adding anything new but as the climax of the long drawn out struggle for freedom on the Southern Coast of the young American government. In its recital the growth of nationalism can be traced in this section of the Republic.

When the American commanders were assured of victory, in Jackson's lines, cheers and rejoicings rent the air. The news was speedily conveyed to the city—both women and children crowding into the streets to receive it. The New Orleans and Plauché's bands that had played with heroic efforts throughout the battle continued to peal forth strains of martial music, strains that must have fallen strangely on the ears of the wounded and dying of the fleeing remnants of Packenham's defeated army.

Mingling with the bitter realization of defeat was amazement and wonder. That a handful of untrained, raw recruits had contended victoriously and without loss of numbers with a well-equipped, carefully trained army of many times its strength, the mettle of the soldiers composing it having been tested upon a hundred battle fields of Europe was a fact difficult to credit. Who could believe what the eye witnessed!

Some slight sign of victory had perched upon the British spear across the river, the evil fortune of the American commanders there causing the wildest alarm for a few moments among the victorious regiments with Jackson. Though their failure has been the subject of bitter controversy among historians a number of eye-witnesses and students of the battle have expressed themselves in terms of exoneration of all parties concerned. With a mild objection to General Morgan's choice of a line of defense Latour has little condemnation of this General's failure to defend his lines on the right bank of the river.

The forces at this point of attack were known to be poorly armed and also starved and physically exhausted before they went into battle. The defense of the line at several places was so meager as to be scarcely discernible. These conditions, it cannot be denied, contributed largely to the disaster that overtook Morgan's forces on that day.

A more definite summary of the situation on the right bank of the river shows on January 4 General Morgan in command of the Louisiana militia. Colonel Cavelier with the 2nd Louisiana Militia was in camp on an old Spanish plantation. His regiment composed of only 176 men, in no wise equipped to go into battle, on January 5 took a further position on Raguet's Canal. Colonel Dijean left the Piernas Canal and joined the 2nd Regiment on its left and occupied the end of the line touching on the river. A detachment of the 6th Louisiana Militia with a poorly supplied force of 110 men joined this regiment, half of the men bearing no arms at all. The breastworks begun here had been abandoned and the line of defense 200 yards covered but a small length of the great canal that ran two miles into the woods. With a scanty force of 800 half-armed troops and no protection but a ditch, one can easily understand the odds against the Kentuckians when pitted against Thornton's fresh, well-clothed, well-armed brigades. The reinforcements rushed to General Morgan's relief were, says

Smith in defense of the Kentucky troops in his history of the battle of New Orleans, "Poorly armed, and had been without food and sleep for twenty-four hours. Their arms, a mongrel lot . . . . old muskets and hunting pieces some without flints and others too small for the cartridges—how could men be expected to fight with a lot of miscellaneous old guns"? As reported by both General Jackson and Commodore Patterson the British in the attack made on the right bank of the river lost 120 men killed and wounded, the American loss being only one man killed and five wounded.

Returning to the main action, which though of short duration was attended by one of the most tragic consequences recorded in the history of warfare, the Chalmette Plains became the next day after the battle a great burying ground to remain evermore one of the historic spots of the world.

Under a flag of truce, sent with the strictest military ceremony a little after mid-day on January 9, the work of burying the dead began on the left bank of the river. The cause of the delay rested in the fact that the action on the right of the river had not yet been concluded and Jackson refused to recognize the first flag sent forward immediately after the battle. No sooner than General Lambert had ordered Colonel Gubbins, who had succeeded Thornton—now wounded, to abandon his position, the truce was recognized with the utmost military courtesy. The conduct of the Americans upon this occasion deserves the highest praise. Jackson, stern and unrelenting in the defense of the city exhibited a spirit toward the conquered foe well worthy of example in all warfare. A strong detachment of his troops was sent forward immediately after the armistice had been arranged to assist in burying the dead and General Kerr, Surgeon-General of the American Army, was ordered to care for the wounded. The British loss was heavy and included officers of every rank. The body of Colonel Renee found with two other officers where all had been killed during the famous charge on the American redoubt drew from the English soldiers the tribute of tears.

The truth was hard to believe when it was ascertained that upon all the bloody field, where nearly 3000 of England's best soldiery were thickly piled, only eight dead American soldiers could be found. The number of wounded was also, surprisingly small. An eyewitness in the British army was historian enough to understand the significance of the disparity in the number lost by the two armies, and with deep humiliation remarked on the painful fact. General Jackson after viewing the British camp with a company of his officers went in person to see the wounded English officers and assured them that they would receive every attention and care while confined to the hospital. The citizens of New Orleans, both men and women, assisted nobly in the task of caring for the wounded on the battlefield. They were tenderly conveyed by steamboat to the barracks in the city, the hospitals there being full of sick American soldiers. Later a special hospital was provided for the 400 wounded British soldiers who were attended by their own surgeons. The prisoners, also, received the kindest attention, and every possible comfort was provided them. The fact that the two armies spoke the same language and were in the main of a kindred race was not lost on the Americans. In victory the latter bore themselves worthily. Heroism and adventure had had their hour and with every right this far boundary of the young nation took its place beside the older States in defense of American freedom.

Jackson was careful to make his victory complete, and no sooner than the dead had been consigned to Mother Earth, who knows no difference among men and welcomes back to her bosom all her weary children, the guns that had wrought such havoc in Packenham's army renewed their attack. Throughout the following days the American batteries continued to harass the enemy to his great discomfort. Partially destroyed, the British army made no further effort to attack the city. The expedition had failed and its commanders were forced to leave the Mississippi. Jackson, eager to be rid of the enemy, lost no opportunity in hastening their departure. This the British conducted in a prompt and somewhat clandestine manner. Colonel Thomas Hinds supported by Colonels La Ronde and Kemper,[71] on the night after the battle and for several successive days were sent to watch the movements of the disorganized army, the cavalry advancing

---

[71] Reuben Kemper, one of three brothers, was a native of Fauquier County, Virginia. The brothers were frontiersmen of the type that made the Indian fighters and territory conquerors of America. They removed when very young to Pickneyville in the Mississippi Territory and were the leaders in an insurrection known as the Kemper Rebellion which finally culminated in the annexation of the Biloxi and Mobile Country to the Mississippi Territory.

at times within rifle shot of their camp near the banks of the Bienvenu and on several occasions taking prisoners. During the final retirement of the enemy, General Jackson, notwithstanding his conference with General Lambert, still fearing some sinister design on the part of the British, ordered Colonel Hinds with his whole cavalry, General Humbert and the Latrobe engineers to again reconnoiter their position. In this expedition the cavalry lost one man and had several wounded.

Jackson had placed Governor Claiborne in command of the right bank of the river to move against the enemy should he renew the attack. General Morgan also had orders to advance with a strong body of men to harrass the enemy's retreat.

During the entire retreat the British did not show any disposition to renew the struggle on land. At any moment the powerful force could have easily returned for another assault on the American army, but its Commander-in-Chief had the satisfaction of witnessing Packenham's shattered divisions retire cautiously if not stealthily, harassed to the last moment by Thomas Hinds and his dragoons as they laboriously made their way over bayous, marsh lands and prairies. The British on several occasions during their occupation of the country expressed their astonishment at the feats of Jackson's cavalry, and later attributed some of their failure to the fact that they could not make use of their dragoons.

Though the enemy had withdrawn their infantry from the Mississippi, they still were in possession of a powerful fleet and in a spirit of uncertainty as to what course to pursue continued to bombard the American forts, principally Fort St. Philip at Plaquemine, seventy-five miles below the city. "From three o'clock on the 9th," says one who witnessed it, "until the morning of the 18th, the bombardment, one of the fiercest of the campaign, continued without intermission." The amount of shells, powder, round shot and grape expended was enormous causing fear that the enemy might still have designs on the city. Failure, however, continued to mark the last feeble efforts of the invaders, but General Jackson was aware that they still held Bayou Bienvenu and Lake Borgne and continued his efforts to fortify every weak place in the defense of the country. Numerous small companies of Mississippi riflemen had gathered on orders of General Holmes at every vulnerable point on the coast as far down as Mobile to meet the English who failing to pass Fort St. Philip decided to return to their first position and invade the country at a weaker point of defense. The troops in the vicinity of New Orleans had been reinforced on January 8, by Colonel Wilkins and Colonel David Neilson's regiments of volunteers from the Mississippi Territory. Kentucky and other States offered to send Jackson reinforcements. He was now getting his army ready to again meet the foe. But beyond a second successful attack on Fort Bowyer with the hope of commanding the entrance of Mobile Bay the British made no further effort to invade the South, waiting at this point the outcome of the turn affairs had taken between the two nations.[72] Their Southern campaign covering many months and even years had ended disastrously. And now after inciting the Indians through Tecumseh to hostilities, after the bloody Creek War, after the attack on Fort Bowyer or Mobile Point, after the attempt to occupy Pensacola, after the vain effort to capture the City of New Orleans and after a second attack on Fort Bowyer in the Mississippi Territory the British fleet put to sea again passing out between Ship and Cat Islands.

The news of the termination of the war between the two countries made the British eager to quit the Gulf Coast. But it was not without a keen sense of loss that they did so. Touching on this point in his narrative of the campaign the English historian Gleig wrote:

> That our failure is to be lamented no one will deny since the conquest of New Orleans would have been beyond all comparison the most valuable acquisition that could be made to the British dominion throughout the whole western hemisphere. In possession of that post, we should have kept the entire southern trade of the United States in check and furnished means of commerce to our own merchants of incalculable value.

In connection with this it may be noted that Jefferson and other prominent Americans believed that the British would have retained New Orleans had they captured it.

On January 21 General Jackson directed an address to be read to all the corps composing the line below New Orleans in which he reviewed the campaign in a terse summary.

In announcing the victory over the British at New Orleans to Governor Holmes, Jackson in a characteristic letter written in haste

---

[72] Immediately after receiving the official confirmation of the ratification of the treaty of peace, General Jackson communicated the fact to General Lambert at Fort Bowyer who soon arranged for the restoration of that post and all others in possession of the British.

Head Quarters
7. M. District
Camp 4 miles below N. Orleans
18: Jan: 1815

Sir

The repulse which the enemy met with on the 8th has I believe proved fatal to their hopes. Their loss on that day, was prodigious — exceeding according to their own accounts as well as to ours, 2600. Amongst their killed were Genl Packenham the commander in chief, & Major General Gibbs who died the day after the action. Major general Keane was wounded, but still lives. Their army is, at present, conducted by Major general Lambert, who, if I mistake not, finds himself in a very great perplexity. To advance he cannot — to retreat is shameful. Reduced to this unhappy dilemma, I believe he is disposed to encounter disgrace rather than ruin, & will, as soon as his arrangements for this purpose are effected, return to his shipping. This, at any rate, is the design to which many symptoms seem to point. Probably, when it is attempted to be put in execution I shall accompany him a short distance.

Fac-simile copy of an original letter in the possession of the Mississippi Department of Archives and History from General Andrew Jackson to Governor David Holmes announcing the victory over the British at New Orleans.

If ever there was an occasion in which providence interfered, immediately, in the affairs of men it seems to have been on this. What but such an interposition could have saved this Country? — Let us mingle our joys & our thanksgivings together.

At a moment when my feelings are thus alive I should do violence to them if I did not hasten to offer you my thanks, as well for the good dispositions you have manifested, as for the important services you have rendered.

With the highest respect I have the honor to be
Sir
Y. very Obt St.
Andrew Jackson
Major Genl. comdg.

P.S. I must again entreat that when the vessel with the arms shall arrive at Natchez you will use your best means to have them hastened to this point with the utmost despatch — having the man who had been entrusted with the transportation of them arrested & sent to me in confinement. A. J —

from his headquarters expressed his deep appreciation of the service that the Governor had rendered in the defense of the city. This letter and all other documentary reports and letters of Jackson, as has been observed, indicate a higher degree of scholarship than some historians have attributed to him. An original, virile style is noticeable throughout his addresses, letters and reports, many of which were hastily composed in moments of great excitement and anxiety.

The news of Jackson's victory, celebrated in the City of New Orleans with the gladdest acclaim both in church and public building, was carried across the country to President Madison by the Mississippi Creek War hero, Sam Dale, who out of the trenches where he had fought at times hand to hand with the enemy knew the dread story by heart. From the city of Natchez and the little capital of Washington in the Mississippi Territory which had become posts for the care of British prisoners the news of the victory spread throughout the Territory and the people who had borne the brunt of the war since the fierce Creek uprising spent their time in various forms of rejoicing. Joy also reigned in the hearts of the proud and patriotic Louisiana Creoles who bore the British deeper hatred than that the Americans felt as a whole for the people of the Mother country. That the victory in which they shared so gloriously left the people of Louisiana as a mass truer patriots than when Jackson found them cannot be disputed. While it cannot be ignored that a small element of its population but for Jackson's strict espionage would have at least remained neutral, once enlisted the soldiery whether of Spanish, French or English descent evinced a courage and patriotism that compare favorably with any troops in the field.

At General Jackson's request the Reverend Abbé Dubourg apostolic prefect of Louisiana appointed January 23, as a day of prayer and thanksgiving for, as Jackson so often averred in varied phrasing, the interposition of Providence in granting the blessing of victory to the American arms. The following vivid and charming account of the impressive event is given from Latour; who was a participant in the interesting ceremonies:

> Every preparation was made to make the festival worthy of the occasion. The temporary triumphal arch was erected in the middle of the grand square, opposite the principal entrance of the cathedral. The different uniformed companies of Plauché's battalion lined both sides of the way, from the entrance of the square towards the river, to the church. The balconies and windows

of the city hall, the parsonage house, and all the adjacent buildings were filled with spectators. The whole square, and the streets leading to it, were thronged with people. The triumphal arch was supported by six columns. Amongst those on the right was a young lady representing Justice and on the left another representing Liberty. Under the arch were two young children, each on a pedestal, holding a crown of laurel. From the arch in the middle of the square to the church, at proper intervals were arranged young ladies, representing the different States and Territories composing the American Union all dressed in white covered with transparent veils, and wearing a silver star on their foreheads. Each of these young ladies held in her right hand a flag inscribed with the name of the State she represented, and in her left a basket trimmed with blue ribands, and full of flowers. Behind each was a shield suspended on a lance stuck in the ground inscribed with the name of the State or Territory. The intervals had been so calculated, that the shields, linked together with verdant festoons, occupied the distance from the triumphal arch to the church.

General Jackson, accompanied by the officers of his staff, arrived at the entrance of the square, where he was requested to proceed to the church by the walk prepared for him. As he passed under the arch, he received the crowns of laurel from the two children, and was congratulated in an address spoken by Miss Kerr who represented the State of Louisiana. The General then proceeded to the church, amidst the salutations of the young ladies representing the different States, who strewed the passage with flowers. At the entrance of the church he was received by the Abbé Dubourge, who addressed him in a speech suitable to the occasion, and conducted him to a seat prepared for him near the altar. Te Deum was chaunted with impressive solemnity, and soon after a guard of honor attended the General to his quarters, and in the evening the town, with its suburbs, was splendidly illuminated.

The address of the reverend Abbé Dubourg and the reply of General Jackson delivered during the impressive thanksgiving ceremonies conducted in the old St. Louis Cathedral are given in full in a note since they better interpret the occasion and the prevailing sentiments than historians have been able to do.[73]

---

[73] On the arrival of General Jackson in the cathedral accompanied by his staff and all officers the Abbe Dubourg made the following address:

"General, whilst the State of Louisiana in the joyful transports of her gratitude, hails you as her deliverer, and the asserter of her menaced liberties—whilst grateful America so lately wrapped up in anxious suspense on the fate of this important city, the emporium of the wealth of one half of her territory and the true bulwark of its independence, is now re-echoing from shore to shore your splendid achievements, and preparing to inscribe your name on her immortal rolls, among those of her Washingtons—whilst history, poetry, and the monumental arts will vie in consigning to the admiration of the latest posterity, a triumph perhaps unparalleled in their records—whilst thus raised by universal acclamation to the very pinnacle of fame and ascending clouds of incense, how easy it had been for you, General, to forget the prime mover of your wonderful successes, to assume to yourself a praise which must essentially return to that exalted source whence every sort of merit is derived. But better acquainted with the nature of true glory, and justly placing the summit of your ambition in approving yourself the worthy instrument of Heaven's merciful designs, the first impulse of your religious heart was to acknowledge the signal interposition of Providence—your first step is a solemn display of your humble sense of His favors.

"Still agitated at the remembrance of those dreadful agonies from which we have been so miraculously rescued, it is our pride, also, to acknowledge that the Almighty has truly had the principal hand in our deliverance, and to follow you, General, in attributing to His infinite goodness the homage of our unfeigned gratitude. Let the infatuated votary of a blind chance deride our credulous simplicity; let the cold-hearted atheist look up for the explanation of such important events to the mere concatenation of human causes; to us, the whole universe is loud in proclaiming a supreme Ruler, who as He holds the hearts of man in his hand, holds also the thread of all contingent occurrences. 'Whatever be His intermediate agents,' says an illustrious prelate, 'still on the secret orders of His all-ruling providence, depends the rise and prosperity, as well as the decline and downfall of empire. From His lofty throne above He moves every scene below, now curbing, now letting loose the passions of men, now enfusing His own wisdom into the leaders of Nations, now confounding their boasted prudence, and spreading upon their councils a spirit of intoxication, and thus executing his uncontrollable judgments on men, sons of men, according to the dictates of His own unerring justice.

"To Him, therefore, our most fervent thanks are due for our late unexpected rescue, and it is Him we chiefly intend to praise, when considering you, General, as the man of His right hand, whom He has taken pains to fit out for the important commission of our defense; we extol the fecundity of genius, by which, in an instant of the most discouraging distress, you created unforeseen resources raised as it were, from the ground, hosts of intrepid warriors and provided every vulnerable point with ample means of defense. To Him we trace that instinctive superiority of your mind, which at once rallied around you universal confidence; impressed one irresistible movement to all the jarring elements of which this political machine is composed; aroused their slumbering spirits, and diffused through every rank that noble ardor which glowed in your own bosom. To Him, in fine we address our acknowledgments for that consummate prudence which defeated all the combinations of a sagacious enemy, and tangled him in the very snares which he had spread before us, and succeeded in effecting his utter destruction, without once exposing the lives of our citizens. Immortal thanks be to His supreme majesty, for sending us such an instrument of His bountiful designs! A gift of that value is the best token of the continuance of His protection—the most solid encouragement to us to sue for new favors. The first which it emboldens us humbly to supplicate as it is the nearer to our throbbing heart is that you may long enjoy, General, the honor of your grateful country, of which you will permit us to present you a pledge in this wreath of laurel, the prize of victory, the symbol of immortality. The next is a speedy and honorable termination of the bloody contest in which we are engaged. No one has so efficaciously laboured as you, General, for the acceleration of that blissful period; may we soon reap that sweetest fruit of your splendid and uninterrupted victories."

To which General Jackson replied: "Reverend Sir, I receive with gratitude and pleasure the symbolical crown which piety has prepared. I receive it in the name of the brave men who have so effectually seconded my exertions for the preservation of their country—they well deserve the laurels which their country will bestow.

"For myself, to have been instrumental in the deliverance of such a country is the greatest blessing that Heaven could confer. That it has been effected with so little loss—that so few tears should cloud the smiles of our triumph, and not a cypress leaf be interwoven in the wreath which you present, is a source of the most exquisite enjoyment.

"I thank you reverend sir, most sincerely for the prayers which you offer up for my happiness. May those your patriotism dictates for our beloved country be first heard. And may mine for your individual prosperity as well as that of the congregation committed to your care, be favourably received—the prosperity, the wealth, the happiness of this city, will then be commensurate with the courage and other qualities of its inhabitants."

General Jackson, though he had been quite high-handed in measures taken for the defense of the city, reducing both man and beast to a state of martial law, withal had been very tactful in his praise and commendation of the doubtful elements among its population. His reports abound in warm praise for all troops from the State of Louisiana. In quite a contrast was this spirit with that manifested by the State legislature towards the saviour of the city. While Governor Claiborne, the people of the city and the devoted soldiery indulged in effusive praise of him, that body which had as a whole refused to coöperate with him in the defense of the city added a further proof of their disfavor by refusing to mention him in the resolution of thanks voted on February 2 to the troops of Tennessee, Kentucky and the Mississippi Territory and their commanders. Quite a number of the members of the legislature, says Eaton, "Sought the trenches and took part in the defense of New Orleans." The majority, however, could not forget that Jackson had ordered the doors of the capital closed against them and while priestly hands were presenting the hero a wreath of laurel and patriotic voices were singing "Hail to the Chief," this Assembly with ruffled dignity remained sullen and unresponsive. Latour is non-critical of the whole situation, and seems disposed to make out a case for all parties concerned. His praise of Jackson throughout is warm and sincere and his memoir of the campaign will continue to be regarded as a dependable source of information.

The Government at Washington was deeply impressed with Jackson's military leadership and no battle fought during the war attracted as much attention in European Courts as did the closing battle of the Coast Campaign. The political forecasters, who are ever watchful for new recruits to their ranks having great faith in their ability in this particular sky to distinguish stars from nebulae, began quietly but persistently pointing to the man in the saddle, a man who had become a popular hero and an idol of the Southern people who were dominant in the governmental affairs of the young Republic at that period.

The following proceedings of the legislature of the State of Mississippi in welcoming General Jackson years later to the State whose new capital had been named in his honor will be read with interest. From Jackson's acceptance one can gather a true impression of the spirit of the Territory during the War of 1812.

Mr. HARRIS, from the Joint-Committee appointed to meet General Andrew Jackson, and welcome him within the borders of this State, Reported——That they had performed that duty, by delivering him an Address, in the following words, to wit:

GENERAL ANDREW JACKSON:

In pursuance of a Joint-Resolution of both Houses of the General Assembly of this State, now convened, in a place bearing your name, we have the honor to address you, as their Committee; and to assure you of a cordial welcome by them within the borders of this State. This manifestation of their pleasure, is founded in the most grateful feelings the many high and important services you have rendered your country, and particularly the State of Mississippi, which are not confined to your Military achievements, more than your civic services.

We remember with gratitude, when the predatory and savage warfare harrassed us, you were foremost to lay aside domestic ease, and brave the hardships and hazards of war incident to inclement seasons, and the deprivations of a wilderness, to protect our homes and families from savage cruelties.

When we were engaged in a conflict with one of the most powerful Nations of Europe, and they seemed to combine their powers for the extermination of Freedom—it was you, who allayed the asperity of petty parties, and inspired our citizen-soldiers with a confidence which secured the repulsion of an invading foe from the possession and rapine of the great Emporium of our whole Western Commerce, and closed the war with a Halo of Glory which surrounds our Country.

By your counsels have been obtained large and fertile tracts of country—giving homes and comfort to many worthy citizens of this, as well as of our adjoining and sister State, Alabama. This grateful acknowledgment made by so many of your contemporary fellow-citizens, while in the full enjoyment and feeling of their benefits—how pure and extended should be the gratification to a great and virtuous patriot, arising from the reflection, that those benefits will be continued to millions yet unborn, and gratefully acknowledged when you, who have imparted them, shall be mingled with the clods of the valley, and co-extensive with the floating of their commerce on their favorite streams, Mobile, Tennessee, Pearl and Mississippi Rivers?

In conclusion—we assure you of the continuation of our confidence and that our aspirations shall be offered at the Throne, from whence emanates all good, for your future prosperity and happiness.

January 20, 1828.

To which General Jackson replied as follows:

GENTLEMEN:

I have no language to express the gratitude which the kindness of your salutation on the part of both Houses of the Legislature of Mississippi excites in my breast.—While I acknowledge that you set too high a value on, and reward with too liberal a hand, the humble services which Providence enabled me to render my country, I can but admire the generosity of your motives, and hope that it may afford a perpetual and salutary stimulus to public spirit, should future dangers make a demand on the patriotism of our fellow-citizens. When the frontiers of your infant State were pierced and agonized by savage warfare, your Governor and the Legislature I found equally prompt and zealous in the supply of men and means for their defence. When the fairest portion of the Union was invaded by a fierce and ancient foe, 'powerful in the means and habits of war,' your Governor and Legislature, exhaustless in energy and patriotism, poured out the resources of the State, and sent forth her sons to the conflict. The first gave support—the last gave renown to the nation; and their gallant leader[74]—I am proud to see him near me, sharing, as he richly merits, the gratitude and respect of his fellow-

---

[74] General Thomas Hinds, who on his return from New Orleans in the spring of 1815 had been appointed Brigadier-General of the Mississippi Territorial Militia.

citizens. I beg you, gentlemen, to convey to the honorable Bodies from which you emanate, my humble thanks for their kindness, and the assurance of my sincere respects and consideration; and I also pray you to accept for yourselves, the expressions of esteem and regard with which I salute you.
January 20, 1828.

In connection with General Jackson's visit to the State at this period the following invitation, reproduced from the original, to a ball given in his honor by the wealthy and cultured people of Natchez will, as a bit of social life of that period, be found interesting. The record presented to the Historical Department by Mrs. Walter Sillers, Sr., of Rosedale, Mississippi, is an almost square card somewhat yellowed by time. It contains the national coat of arms beneath which appears in printed form, with the exception of the name of the invited guest which is written in long hand, the following formal invitation:

The pleasure of Miss A. Carson's company is requested at a BALL, to be given in honor of GENERAL ANDREW JACKSON, this Evening at the Mississippi Hotel.

R. H. Adams,		G. Winchester,
H. Chotard,		J. A. M'Pheters,
J. Sprague,		R. L. Throckmorton,
R. G. Ellis,	Managers	J. F. Bingaman,
J. Bell,		J. F. H. Claiborne.
R. Archer,		R. M. Gaines.

January 4, 1828

It was in no unfamiliar crowd that Jackson stood at this brilliant reception in his honor. Around him were spirits that had in a large measure made possible the victory by which he had won imperishable fame—spirits that since early manhood had touched his life at many points, had understood him and given him as loyal support as any with whom he ever came in contact. He was on the eve of a great national career and the people of Mississippi vied with those of Tennessee in allegiance and admiration. With the same loyalty and devotion that they had followed his standards in war they now rallied to his support when he sought preferment in peace. They held in the main the same doctrines and faiths, had been bred in the same atmosphere and had grown to be much alike. The author intends no attempt at a detailed character study of Andrew Jackson. In him were to be found many of the great virtues and qualities of George Washington, John Adams and Robert E. Lee. Both the tradition of the Cavalier and Puritan had charmed his fancy. He pos-

Mississippi Territory in War of 1812—Rowland.   153

sessed in a large measure the deep, inward piety and zeal of Jefferson Davis; scarcely a document, speech or conversation of either that did not evince genuine dependence on Divine Providence. But with all he differed widely from any of these for like Abraham Lincoln he had on distant frontiers been cast and shaped by original influences which made him the first great American.

Of the many who took part in the defense of the City of New Orleans, none wielded a more powerful influence with the exception of Jackson than Louisiana's patriotic Governor W. C. C. Claiborne. The second governor of the Mississippi Territory, he had served with distinguished ability and had endeared himself to its people who followed with feelings of commingled pride and affection his appointment later as Governor of Louisiana. Governor Claiborne's entire public service from 1801 to 1816 is contained in six volumes of documentary history which have been published by the Mississippi Historical Department. His service was such as to render him one of the chief influences in the early history of the Southwest and to no public official on its early roster does Mississippi point with more pride. His descendants still help to make up the best element in the State's population.

Governor David Holmes of the Mississippi Territory, from whose original journals and letter-books many of the facts contained in this narrative are drawn, continued to serve the Territory as Governor after its admission into the Union as a State, December 10, 1817. A sketch of his life and public service may be found in the *Encyclopedia of Mississippi History* while the publication of his manuscript journals is in course of preparation by the Mississippi Historical Department. His every public act was inspired by a strong desire for the welfare of the whole country and his spirit burned with patriotic ardor. The confident manner in which he drew on the people of the Mississippi Territory for assistance and support in the defense of the country is evidence enough that the seed of American nationality had been widely sown in the consciousness of its people. That these had flowered and borne fruit during this second struggle for freedom is very apparent.

It has already been stated that General Ferdinand Leigh Claiborne, after a most arduous service in defense of the country, returned from the Creek War broken in health. His death was the result of an incurable wound. His patriotism and zeal in defense of the Territory places his name in its annals with the framers and shapers of its destiny. A brother of Governor W. C. C. Claiborne, there was much in common between the two. In their public service one sees reflected the best ideals of the civilization of their day, while in their patriotism and ardor were to be found a devotion and knightliness as fervent and fascinating as that which had burned the breast of Richard Coeur de Lion.

It is to Colonel Thomas Hinds[75] that we turn for the last figure with which to close this narrative. After his return from New Orleans in the spring of 1815, he was appointed by the President, Brigadier-General of the Mississippi Territorial Militia. The General Assembly of the Territory adopted the following joint resolution, December 18, 1815:

> That the patriotism, bravery and promptitude displayed by Brigadier-General Thomas Hinds, while acting Colonel of Cavalry in the defense of New Orleans, entitle him to our warmest acknowledgments and gratitude; and that a suitable sword be provided at the expense of the Territory and presented under the direction of His Excellency the Governor to the said Brigadier-General as a testimonial of the high sense which the people of this Territory entertain of his services and of his brave companions in arms.

In transmitting the vote of thanks of the Louisiana Legislature, Governor Claiborne wrote that it

> Brings to my recollection the satisfaction I experienced more than twelve years ago on signing the commission which ushered your military talents into light.

Under the first militia law of the State in 1818 he was continued in the highest militia office, that of Major-General, from which he resigned in December, 1819. In 1820 he was joint commissioner with Andrew Jackson to make a treaty with the Choctaws by which a large area of land was granted after two previous failures. In his acceptance he expresses the highest confidence in General Jackson and when notified of his appointment, Jackson wrote: "There is no man I would rather be associated with then General Hinds, nor none in whom I have more confidence." The vast territory that had been acquired was named Hinds in his honor.

---

[75] After being placed in command of all of Jackson's cavalry, Thomas Hinds assumed the rank of Colonel, though historians give him variously the rank of Major and Colonel in their narratives. He bore all through his later life the title of General, having been promoted to this rank by General Holmes.

In 1819 he was a candidate for governor with Daniel Burnet for lieutenant-governor, but his opponent, George Poindexter, was elected.[76] He was a member of the legislature in 1823, was elected to Congress to succeed William Haile and re-elected, serving from December 8, 1828 to March 3, 1831. When Poindexter proposed to defeat the confirmation of President Jackson's nomination of William M. Gwin as United States Marshal for Mississippi in 1833, the President sent in Hinds' name for the place. Poindexter withdrew his opposition to Gwin and the name of Hinds was withdrawn. Afterwards General Hinds was proposed as a candidate for United States Senator in 1835 against Poindexter, but was induced to decline in favor of Robert J. Walker.

General Hinds died at "Old Greenville," Jefferson County, August 23, 1840. During his life he was pre-eminently the military hero of Mississippi. J. F. H. Claiborne described him as "one of the most intrepid men that ever lived." The following estimate is taken from an obituary notice published in *The Mississippian*, of September 4, 1840:

> Although a warm partisan, he enjoyed the unbounded confidence of all parties, and it is believed that he died without leaving a personal enemy. His hospitality was unbounded and few men enjoyed in an equal degree the affectionate regard of all his acquaintances. His wife died many years since and he leaves an only child, a son, to mourn his loss. Many of his soldiers who shared his toil and his glory survive him and still reside in this State—some of them scarred with honorable wounds. Few regiments underwent as many hardships—none covered themselves with more glory.
>
> With deep regret we announce that this esteemed citizen and old soldier is no more. Eulogy upon this truly good and brave man is unnecessary from us. It is well known that he was with Jackson throughout his last campaign against the British and that during the whole of the late war he rendered his country great service and gained for himself distinguished honors. In short, his life was devoted to the common good and all those who revere bravery will mourn his loss. We learn that he died from the rupture of a blood vessel.

The following notice of the death of General Hinds is taken from the *Free Trader* of August, 1840:

> On Saturday, the 29th instant, at 2 o'clock, a large meeting of the citizens of Adams County convened at the court house in Natchez to do honor to the name and memory of Gen. THOMAS HINDS, who died at his residence in Jefferson County on Sunday, the 23rd of August. On motion of Judge George Winchester, Col. James C. Wilkins was called to the chair and on motion of Gen. John A. Quitman,

---

[76] A striking instance of the inconsistencies of political favoritisms is shown in the fact that Poindexter had made a poor reputation as a soldier in the War of 1812 while Thomas Hinds had reflected great honor on the state.

Col. Adam L. Bingaman was appointed Secretary. Col. Wilkins, on taking the chair, read the notice given through the press and explained the object of the meeting.

Gen. Quitman rose and addressed the audience on the life and character of Gen. Hinds and concluded by submitting to the meeting a series of resolutions which were read, and upon motion referred to a committee composed of the following gentlemen: Judge George Winchester, Gen. John A. Quitman, Gen. P. L. Mitchell, Lieut. Thomas S. Munce, Thomas Armat, Esq., and Col. James C. Wilkins. The committee, through their chairman, Judge Winchester, reported the resolutions offered by Gen. Quitman, with one other, which were read and unanimously adopted:

Resolved, That the heroic military deeds of the late lamented General Thomas Hinds, while commanding a corps of Mississippi volunteers in defence of his country during the last war with Great Britain, sheds a lustre upon the arms of this State which should cause its citizen soldiers ever to hold his memory in proud and grateful remembrance.

Resolved, That during a long life of public and private usefulness, amid the storms and conflicts of party excitement, in which his frank, ardent and bold temperament led him to take an active part, the lamented deceased always merited and retained the confidence and affection of his fellow-citizens for his patriotism, his benevolence, his candor and stern integrity.

Resolved, That the name of Gen. Thomas Hinds belongs to Mississippi and will ever be enrolled in bright characters in the pages of her early history and his memory cherished among us, while honor, chivalry and worth are respected and admired.

Resolved, That we deeply sympathize with the family and relatives of the deceased veteran upon this melancholy event and mingle with theirs our tears for the loss which they themselves and our State have sustained.

Resolved, That it be recommended to the several volunteer corps of this regiment at their next parade to appear in military mourning in honor of the deceased.

Resolved, That the chairman cause these resolutions to be published and copies to be sent to the family of the deceased.

JAMES C. WILKINS, Ch'm.

ADAM L. BINGAMAN, Sec'y.

Near the site of "Old Greenville," in a secluded plantation graveyard, the usual type of burial ground in the ante-bellum period, General Thomas Hinds was buried beside his wife, Malinda Marston Green.[77] His deeds are interwoven with the early history of the State.

The heroic assistance that he gave General Andrew Jackson in successfully resisting the British in their attempt to invade the South during the War of 1812 is a story of valor difficult to tell. Not only his deeds have made illustrious our annals in this struggle for freedom but every name on the roster presented here was borne by a pioneer hero whose defense of the Republic at a time when the spirit of nationality had not become uniform nor solidified makes a remarkable chapter in American history.

---

[77] This isolated spot has been recently marked by the people of Jefferson County.

Mississippi Territory in War of 1812—Rowland. 157

ROLLS OF MISSISSIPPI COMMANDS IN THE WAR OF 1812.

HINDS' BATTALION OF CAVALRY, MISSISSIPPI MILITIA

Captain John Doherty's Company
Captain Henry Dunn's Company
Captain Samuel Gerald's Company
Captain James Kempe's Company
Captain John G. Richardson's Company
Captain John J. W. Ross' Company
Captain Jedediah Smith's Company

Alexander, Robert, private
Alford, Robert, private
Alfred (nigger), servant
Allen, — — — —, servant
Allred, John, private
Anderson, Benjamin, corporal
Anderson, John, private
Anderson, William, private
Andrews, Henry, sergeant
Anthony, — — — —, servant
Austin, Ozias, sergeant
Bald, Sampson, private
Barnett, John, private
Baty, Thomas, private
Benjamin (nigger), servant
Benoist, Robert, sergeant
Berry, Thomas, private
Bettis, Richard, Jr., private
Bill, — — — —, servant
Bingaman, Ad, private
Binum, Francis A., sergeant
Bisland, James, dragoon
Bisland, Peter, first lieutenant
Bland, Isaac, private
Blanton, William, private
Boardman, Charles, cornet
Boardman, Francis, private
Boatner, William J., first sergeant
Bob (Captains Boy), private
Bolls, James, private
Boone, John, private
Boone, Joseph H., private
Booth, Joseph, private
Boston, — — — —, servant
Bowie, John F., sergeant major
Bowling, Arthur, private

Bowman, Ira, private
Braden, Joseph, private
Bradford, David, private
Bradford, James M., private
Bradford, Leonard, corporal
Brashears, Nathan, private
Brice, James, private
Bridges, William, private
Brooks, Edward, dragoon
Brophy, John, private
Brown, James, private
Bruin, Preston, private
Brunson, Daniel, private
Bryant, William, private
Buck, William, dragoon
Burch, Washington, private
Burnett, James, private
Burnett, John, private
Burrows, William, corporal
Butler, Aaron, private
Cain, Isaiah, private
Cain, James, private
Calaham, John, private
Caldwell, George, private
Calvett, Saul, private
Calvit, James, private
Calvit, Montfort, dragoon
Calvit, Samuel, first lieutenant and adjutant
Calvit, Tacitus, quartermaster service
Campbell, Allen, private
Campbell, John, private
Carney, Thomas, private
Carpenter, James, sergeant
Carson, William, private
Carter, Parsons, cornet

Cater, John, private
Cater, Josiah, corporal
Chancey, Lewis, private
Charles, — — — —, servant
Christopher, — — — —, servant
Cissna, James, private
Clay, Marston, sergeant-trumpeter
Coates, Austin, private
Coatney, Jonas, private
Cocks, Charles, private
Cocks, Seth, private
Coleman, Isaiah, private
Coleman, Nathaniel, private
Collier, Benjamin S., private
Collins, Parker S., private
Collins, William, corporal
Combs, John P., sergeant
Cook, Edward, private
Cooper, Hugh W., private
Corbell, James H., private
Corbell, Peter, private
Corley, Henry, private
Cotton, Haley, private
Cotton, John, private
Crawford, Alexander, private
Crawford, Henderson, private
Crookes, John, private
Culpepper, John, private
Cuming, David B., dragoon
Curry, Malcolm, private
Dangerfield, William, dragoon
Daniels, Shem, private
Daughtry, Bryant, private
David, David, second lientenant
Davis, Gideon, private
Davis, Green B., corporal
Davis, Isaac W., private
Davis, Joseph E., private
Davis, Samuel, private
Debell, Benjamin H., sergeant
Decell, George J., private
Defrance, Abraham, musician
Derry (nigger), servant
Dick, — — — —, servant
Dickson, Michael, private
Dixon, John, sergeant
Dixon, John, private

Doherty, John, captain
Donahoe, Charles, private
Dortch, David, private
Downing, David, surgeon
Downs, George, private
Dreadin, Jonathin, private
Dromgoole, William A., private
Duck, Ephraim, dragoon
Dubar, Isaac, 2nd lieut.
Dunbar, Roberts, cap.
Dunn, Henry, captain
Edwards, Thomas, private
Elmore, Daniel, private
Erwin, John, private
Erwin, William, corporal
Fair, James, private
Fairbanks, David, private
Fake, Henry, private
Fake, Thomas, private
Ferguson, Augustus, private
Ferguson, John, sergeant
Ferguson, Robert, private
Ferguson, Samuel, private
Findlay, Alexander, private
Finley, Joseph L., private
Fleming, Robert, private
Fletcher, James, private
Flinn, Samuel, private
Flower, James, second lientenant
Foreman, Abraham, private
Fort, John, private
Foster, Shadrach, private
Foster, Zadock S., private
Freeman, George, private
Fretwell, Richard, private
Fristoe, John, private
Fulks, William, private
Funk, John C., private
Fuqua, Drury, private
Gale, Joseph, private
Gardner, Bartholomew, private
Garredee, William, private
Gates, Elisha, private
Gaulden, Zachariah, first lientenant
Gayden, Cadesby, first lieutenant
Gayden, Griffin, musician
Gerald, George, corporal

Mississippi Territory in War of 1812—Rowland. 159

Gerald, Jesse, cornet
Gerald, Samuel, captain
Gibson, Clausius, corporal
Gilbert, James, private
Gilbert, James W., sergeant
Gilbert, Philip A., private
Gilbert, Thomas, dragoon
Gillespie, John F., sergeant
Gilmore, George, private
Ginn, Edmund, private
Ginn, Edwin, private
Girault, John R., private
Given, George W., saddler
Glasscock, Peter R., dragoon
Gober, Cradic, private
Gower, Elisha, private
Grady, John G., sergeant
Grafton, Thomas, private
Graham, Zachariah G., private
Green (negro), servant
Green, Richard M., private
Green, Robert, dragoon
Green, Thomas M., private
Griffin, Mitchel, private
Griffin, Stephen, private
Guest, Samuel, private
Hadly, Joshua, private
Hamilton, John C., dragoon
Hampton, John P., private
Hancock, George, private
Hanson, William, private
Harper, Absolom, sergeant
Harper, Jesse, private
Harper, Samuel, private
Harris, Levi C., private
Harrison, Hay B., corporal-cornet
Harrison, Philip B., sergeant
Harrison, Richard, private
Harrison, Robert L., sergeant
Hatfield, William F., sergeant
Hawkins, Richard, private
Haynes, Charles, private
Haynes, George, private
Hays, Jacob, private
Head, Elbt. G., corporal
Henderson, Alexander, private

Henderson, William, private
Hester, Charles, private
Hewey, James, private
Hinds, Thomas, lieutenant-colonel
Hodge, William, corporal
Hogg, Holland, private ·
Holloman, Kinchen, private
Holloman, Michael, private
Holloway, Reuben, private
Horn, Moses, private
Howard, Thomas, private
Howell, James, private
Huey, Daniel, private
Humes, Robert, dragoon
Hunt, Henry, adjutant
Hunt, Henry, sergeant
Hunter, Pleasant H., first lieutenant
Hunter, William, private
Husbands, Thomas L., corporal
Huston, James, private
Hynum, James, private
Irvin, John L., second lieutenant
Irvin, Reason W., sergeant
Isaac, —————, servant
Ivey, Samuel, second lieutenant
Jackson, Willey, second lieutenant
Jeffry, —————, servant
Jerry, —————, servant
John, —————, servant
Johnson, Charles G., sergeant
Johnson, John, sergeant
Johnson, William A., private
Joice, Absalom, private
Jones, James, private
Jones, Sterling, private
Jones, Zachariah B., private
Joor, John, cornet
Jordan, Charles H., private
Keith, James, private
Keller, George, private
Keller, George, Jr., private
Keller, George, Sr., private
Keller, Jacob, private
Keller, John, private
Keller, Joseph, private
Keller, Thomas, private

Keller, Thomas, private
Kelsey, Thomas, private
Kempe, James, captain
Kemper, Reuben, private
Kemper, Samuel, private
Ker, David, sergeant
Kirkland, Isaac, dragoon
Kitchen, Benjamin F., sergeant
Lambert, Moses, private
Lanehart, Abraham, private
Lape, John, trumpeter
Levis, William P., surgeon
Lewis, Joseph D., dragoon
Linton, Thomas M., private
Lisenby, Henry, private
Love, Charles, private
Love, John J., private
Lowry, Robert, first lieutenant
Madray, William, private
Magruder, Leonard, private
March, ————, servant
Marley, Samuel, private
Martin, John, private
McAllister, Thomas, private
McAlpin, John, sergeant
McCay, Robert, private
McClellan, Walter, first lieutenant
McComas, I. H., Quartermaster
McDermott, Thomas, private
McDonald, Elam H., corporal
McDonald, Thomas O., sergeant
McGuhu, Nath, second lieutenant
McLaughlin, Patrick, trumpeter
McMahan, Jesse, private
McMicken, Chs., Jr., private
Miller, Benjamin, dragoon
Miller, John, private
Miller, Thomas M., private
Moncrief, Sampson, private
Montgomery, Davis, private
Montgomery, Hugh, private
Moor, Ezekiel, private
Moore, John K., corporal
Moore, Joseph, private
Moore, Joseph B., private
Morgan, William, private

Morris, John, dragoon
Mumford, James, private
Murray, Alexander, first lieutenant
Neel, John, private
Neiff, Charles, private
Nesmith, Robert, private
Nettles, Z. B., private
Nicholls, James, private
Noland, Jeremiah, private
Noland, William, private
Norman, Thomas, private
Norman, William, corporal
Norment, William, private
Norris, James L., private
Oats, John, private
Odam, John, private
Ogden, Isaac, private
Oliphant, James, private
Oneal, Edmund, private
Oneal, John, private
Owens, Alexander, private
Owens, Stephen, private
Pannill, A. W., private
Paul, ————, servant
Paxton, John, private
Peck, Patrick, private
Perkin, I. W., dragoon
Peter, ————, servant
Phelps, John, dragoon
Phelps, Samuel, dragoon
Philips, Baker, corporal
Picket, Thomas K., private
Pipes, David, private
Pitchford, Samuel, private
Platner, Henry, private
Pool, Robert, private
Presler, Peter, private
Prince, John, private
Prince, John G. T., dragoon
Prince, William B., private
Raburn, Burrel, private
Rawlings, Thomas, private
Reed, James, private
Reed, Stephen, private
Reed, William, corporal
Richardson, James B., private

Richardson, Jared N., corporal
Richardson, John G., captain
Richardson, Richard, private
Richardson, William A., private
Riley, Isaac, private
Roach, Benjamin, dragoon
Roach, William, dragoon
Roberts, Abner, dragoon
Roberts, William, sergeant
Robertson, Thomas, corporal
Robinson, James, private
Rose, Enoch M., private
Rose, Philip, private
Ross, John J. W., captain
Ruben, ————, sergeant
Ruth, James, private
Ruth, John, private
Samples, Moses, private
Sanders, James, private
Sanders, Joseph, sergeant
Scott, Cason, sergeant
Scott, John, private
Scott, Richard, private
Scott, Thomas, private
Scott, Thomas, private
Scurlock, Thomas M., sergeant
Scurry, Eli, private
Seales, Enoch, private
Seales, James, cornet
Sellers, Silas, private
Selman, Joel, private
Selman, William, dragoon
Semple, James, corporal
Shanks, John H., sergeant
Shaw, Jones, private
Shaw, Malcomb, private
Silcock, John, private
Simmons, John J., corporal
Simmons, Samuel B., private
Simon, ————, servant
Smith, Benjamin, sergeant
Smith, James, private
Smith, Jedediah, captain
Smith, John, private
Smith, Joseph A., private
Smith, Josephus, private

Smith, Reuben, sergeant
Smith, William, dragoon
Smylie, Matthew, private
Snodgrass, John, dragoon
Spain, James, cornet
Spain, Richard, private
Spain, Thomas, private
Steele, Robert, private
Stewart, David B., private
Stoker, Henry, private
Stoker, Matthew, private
Stout, James, sergeant
Straughan, James, private
Straughan, James F., private
Stroud, Dixon, private
Stubblefield, W., private
Sullavan, James, private
Talbert, Lewis, sergeant
Taylor, Robert, private
Terry, James, private
Terry, William, private
Terry, William, private
Thames, Timothy, sergeant
Thomas, William P., private
Thompson, Littleberry, private
Thompson, Roland, sergeant
Tiernan, Peter, first lieutenant and quartermaster
Tomlinson, John, private
Tomlinson, Thomas, private
Tredwell, William, private
Trimble, Michael W., corporal
Truly, James B., sergeant
Truly, John H., private
Tucker, William, private
Vaughan, Thomas C., private
Vaughn, David, private
Vining, Jeptha, private
Watkins, Samuel W., private
Watson, John, private
Watson, Malcom, private
Watt, ————, servant
Weatherby, G. W., saddler
Werden, Robert, sword master
West, Charles, dragoon
West, Thomas, dragoon

Westberry, William, private
Whetstone, Joseph, musician
Whetstone, Josiah, trumpeter
Whitaker, James, private
White, Jacob, private
Whittington, Levi, private
Wilkinson, G. F., corporal
Will, — — — —, servant
Williams, Andrew, private
Williams, James, private
Williams, William, private
Willis, Thomas, private
Wilson, James, private
Wilson, John, private
Wilson, Nathaniel, private
Winston, Samuel L., cornet
Woodruff, Clarke, corporal
Worthy, John, sergeant
Worthy, John, private
Young, Joseph, corporal

LIEUTENANT DRURY M. ALLEN'S COMPANY OF MOUNTED GUNMEN

Allen, Drury M., lieutenant
Box, James, private
Briant, John, private
Brown, Alexander, private
Brown, Thomas G., private
Crage, John, private
Dublin, James, private
Ferrell, David, private
Ice, Thomas, private
Lancaster, Aaron, private
Lancaster, Thomas, private
Landers, Henry, private
Leonax, Nathan, private
Markham, Arthur, private
Morris, Elisha, private
Prude, John, private
Reed, Levi, private
Robinson, Ephraim, corporal
Robinson, Michael, private
Robinson, William, private
Rodgers, George, private
Simmons, Thomas, private
Taylor, Isaac, private
Vernon, Amos, private
Ware, Bennett, private
Wilson, James, private

CAPTAIN BOYLE'S COMPANY OF MOUNTED SPIES

Adcock, John, private
Adcock, Lewis, private
Adcock, Reuben, private
Beckum, Joshua, private
Boyle, Thomas H., captain
Byrne, Thomas, private
Christin, Cary, private
Langham, James, private
Milton, Andrew, private
Mimbs, William, private
Moye, Jason, private
Stedham, Edward, private
Stiggins, George, sergeant
Williams, Thomas, private

CAPTAIN BRADBERRY'S COMPANY OF MOUNTED SPIES

Autry, Alexander, sergeant
Bradberry, James, captain
Davis, Wiley, private
Dodd, Jesse, private
Jackson, Henry, private
Perry, Wilson, private
Walker, Daniel, private
Walker, Mathias, private

CAPTAIN CALVIT'S COMPANY OF MOUNTED INFANTRY

Ardrey, Joseph, private
Byrd, Josiah, private
Calvit, Alexander, captain
Calvit, Montford, private
Castles, Henry H., private
Corbell, John H., private

Mississippi Territory in War of 1812—Rowland.   163

Cox, Henry H., first lieutenant
Ford, John S., private
Ford, Thomas, corporal
Fretwell, John, private
Gibbs, George W., private
Griffin, Thomas, private
Hawley, John, private
Johnson, Jordan, private
Jones, Wilie, sergeant
Lawson, Charles M., private
Lewis, James T., private
Lusk, Amos, private
Madding, Albert, private

Montgomery, Samuel K., private
Neylon, David, private
Powell, Jonathan, private
Powell, Thomas W., sergeant
Selser, Josiah, corporal
Sissions, Boon, private
Sojourner, Hardy, private
Sojourner, William, sergeant
Steele, John, corporal
Whitaker, Isaac, private
Wilborne, Thomas, private
Wilson, Daniel, private

CAPTAIN CASSITY'S COMPANY OF MOUNTED SPIES

Cassity, Hugh, captain
Cole, Armistead, private
Cole, William, private
Curran, John, private

Easly, Edward, private
Easly, Samuel, private
Williams, James, private

CAPTAIN FOSTER'S COMPANY OF MOUNTED INFANTRY

Arnold, Benjamin, private
Blackwell, David, private
Blackwell, James, private
Brashears, Samuel, private
Brewster, James, private
Callier, Robert, Lieutenant
Cobb, James, private
Dassa, James, private
Dean, John, private
Eades, John, private
Foster, Arthur, captain
Foster, William, sergeant
Hamrick, Burrel, private
Hays, Mark, private

Herrald, H., private
Jones, William, private
Laughlin, William, private
Mathews, Samuel, private
Roberts, L., private
Simmons, Elisha, private
Simmons, James, private
Smith, Samuel, private
Stean, Newberry, private
Willson, James, private
Wilson, William, private
Wood, John, sergeant
Woodard, John, private

CAPTAIN WILKINS' RIFLE COMPANY

Alexander, William S., first lieutenant
Anderson, Thomas, corporal
Baillie, Alexander, private
Banks, George D., private
Barland, Adam, private
Barland, William, private
Ben, ————, servant
Benjamin, Adam L., first sergeant

Brice, William, private
Brown, Archibald, private
Burgett, John, private
Bynum, Francis A., private
Bynum, Wade H. T., private
Campbell, Anthony, first lieutenant
Cock, Pleasant B., private
Cook, James K., private

Dunlap, Joseph, private
Durr, Jacob, private
Gloss, William, private
Godiew, Firman, private
Goodwyn, James T., private
Grant, William, private
Hall, Nicholas C., private
Hill, Moses Lloyd, corporal
Hugot, Joseph, private
Jackson, Washington, sergeant
Lehman, William E., private
Mack, ―――, sergeant
McAdams, David, private
McCracken, George, private
McCreary, Hugh, private
McElroy, John, private
McQuiddy, Thomas, sergeant
Metcalf, John, sergeant
Morrison, Joseph, private
Nichols, Philo, private
O'Neal, Anthony W., private
Paimboeuf, Lewis, private
Patterson, Samuel, corporal
Pomett, Joseph, private

Purnell, John M., private
Quiglis, Joseph, private
Reeves, Marmaduke, private
Robinson, J. W., private
Routh, John, private
Rutherford, Joseph H., corporal
Scott, Robert, private
Searcy, Rob, private
Shattuck, Benjamin L., private
Smith, Ralph, private
Smoot, Thomas N., sergeant
Sneed, Jesse, private
Sterne, Peyton, private
Surgett, James, private
Thompson, William, private
Tremoulet, B., private
Vansant, Richard, private
Vidal, Joseph, private
West, G. B., private
Wilkins, James C., captain
Williams, Hugh R., private
Winston, Samuel L., ensign
Woodward, Daniel, private

LIEUTENANT-COLONEL NIXON'S REGIMENT

Aarons, Joshua, private
Adams, Isaac, private
Adams, John, private
Adams, William, private
Adcock, Reuben, private
Alexander, Robert, Ensign
Allen, William, private
Allison, William, private
Anderson, Absalom, private
Anderson, Harriss, corporal
Anderson, John, private
Anderson, Robert, sergeant
Anderson, Samuel, private
Anding, George, private
Anding, John, private
Andrews, Clevers, private
Andrews, Philo, quartermaster
Applewhite, Stephen, corporal
Armstrong, William private
Arnold, James, private

Arthurs, George, corporal
Ashton, Henry, corporal
Ashwell, Solomon, private
Asque, Henry, private
Babcock, Jesse, private
Bagby, John, sergeant
Baker, John, private
Baker, Joseph, private
Baldridge, Francis, private
Baley, James, private
Ball, Sampson E., corporal
Ball, Spencer, private
Ballard, Lewis, private
Ballard, Nathan, private
Bankston, James, private
Barker, David, private
Barksdale, Richard H., private
Barnes, John, private
Barnes, Samuel, private
Barnes, Thomas, private

Mississippi Territory in War of 1812—Rowland. 165

Barnett, Joshua, private
Bass, Robert, private
Batchelder, Samuel, captain
Bates, Elijah, private
Batson, Seth, private
Beauford, Bird, private
Beason, William, private
Beaty, Thomas, corporal
Beck, John, private
Bell, William, private
Bender, Lot, private
Bennett, David, corporal
Bennett, Henry, private
Benson, James, private
Benson, Samuel, private
Berkley, Abraham, private
Bernard, Heslen, private
Berry, John, private
Berry, Middleton, corporal
Berry, Thomas, private
Berry, Young, sergeant
Biggs, David, corporal
Biggs, James, private
Bill, ----, waiter
Binum, Parham T., private
Black, George, private
Blackman, Carrol, private
Blackman, Peter, corporal
Block, George, private
Bond, James, ensign
Bond, John, captain
Bond, Moses, private
Bond, William, private
Booth, John, private
Bossley, William, private
Bostwick, Nathaniel, private
Bowie, John, private
Bowie, John F., adjutant
Bowling, Arthur, sergeant
Bradey, Samuel, private
Bradley, Luther, sergeant
Bradshaw, Richard, private
Brady, William, private
Brandon, Joseph, private
Brazil, Isham, private
Breland, Hilry, private

Brewer, Osborn, private
Brice, James, private
Bridgers, William sergeant
Bridges, John, private
Briley, Job, private
Brimmer, Charles, sergeant
Briscoe, Parmenas, captain
Britton, James, private
Brooks, Charles, private
Brooks, Joseph, private
Brown, George, private
Brown, James, private
Brown, Jesse, corporal
Brown, John, corporal
Brown, John, private
Brown, John A., private
Brown, Moses, private
Brown, Wylie, private
Bucannan, John, private
Buchanan, Hector, private
Buck, John F., private
Buckley, John, private
Buckley, William C., private
Buford, Josiah, private
Bullock, James, private
Burch, William H., private
Burk, James, private
Burk, Martin, private
Burk, William, private
Burnett, John, private
Burney, Joseph, private
Burnham, Gabriel, private
Burns, James, corporal
Burns, John, drummer
Cade, William, private
Cain, William, private
Calcote, James, private
Calvit, Stephen, corporal
Campbell, Silas, private
Carney, Jerry, corporal
Carpenter, Solomon, private
Carroll, William, private
Carson, Samuel M., private
Carson, William, private
Carter, Isaac, private
Carter, Marcus E., private

Carter, Mashak, private
Carter, Moses, private
Case, Joseph, private
Cashin, Lawrence, private
Cassells, Henry, major
Catoo, Wyche, private
Causey, Jonas, private
Causey, Solomon, private
Causey, William, private
Ceaser, Reuben, private
Chambers, Israel, private
Chaney, Ausbon, private
Chapman, George, private
Cheatham, Thomas R., corporal
Cheek, Henry H., Lieutenant
Chestnut, David, private
Chisholm, Cockburn, private
Clark, Lewis, private
Clark, William, private
Clarke, John, private
Clarke, Thomas, private
Clayton, Samuel, private
Clear, John, private
Cobb, Frederick, private
Cockerham, Benjamin, private
Cockerham, David, private
Cockerham, George, private
Coddle, William, private
Coker, Bryant, private
Cole, Mason G., private
Coleman, George, private
Coleman, Levi, private
Coleman, Nathaniel, private
Coleman, Robert, private
Collier, Vines L., ensign
Collins, John, private
Collins, Joshua, private
Collins, William, private
Colvinn, Andrew, private
Conner, Thomas, corporal
Cook, Isaac, private
Cook, Matthew, private
Cook, Tirey, private
Cooper, Jesse, private
Cooper, William, private
Coopper, Hamelton, private

Coopper, John, private
Copeland, Moses, private
Corley, Henry, private
Cotton, Eli, private
Cotton, Willis, private
Coulter, William E., fifer
Courtney, James, private
Coward, Hezekiah, private
Cowen, John, corporal
Cox, Ignatius, private
Cox, Kullin, private
Cozby, William, private
Craven, William, private
Cravens, Michael, private
Crawford, William, private
Crumpton, William, private
Culby, James, drum major
Culwell, Thomas, sergeant
Cup, Michael, private
Currie, Malcome, ensign
Curry, Robert, sergeant
Curtis, Reuben, private
Dadon, Chevalier, private
Daniels, Shem L., private
Darden, Washington, captain
Dagghdrell, John, private
Davis, David, private
Davis, James, private
Davis, John, private
Davis, John, private
Davis, Joseph, private
Davis, Robert P., private
Davis, Samuel, private
Davis, Zacheus, corporal
Dawson, Thomas, ensign
Day, Benjamin B., private
Dean, John, private
DeGraftenreed, Francis, private
Delaney, William, private
Delling, Willis, private
Delvach, Jesse, private
Dennis, George P., private
Dennis, James, private
Denton, James, private
Desha, Benjamin, private
Devine, William, private

Dixon, Shadrack, private
Dodd, John, first lieutenant
Donahoe, John, private
Donley, William, private
Donchoo, Charles, private
Doss, Henry, corporal
Douthill, Jedikial, private
Dowling, John, private
Downs, Jeremiah, captain
Drake, Edmund, sergeant
Drear, Christopher, private
Druyard, Antonio, private
Dukes, Jeptha, private
Dunnum, Robert C., corporal
Durant, Locklin, private
Durdoe, Clement, private
Duvall, John, private
Dyer, Absalom, private
Dyer, Obadiah, private
Eastin, Thomas, first Lieutenant and quartermaster
Edmond, — — — —, waiter
Edwards, Everett, private
Edwards, Jesse, private
Edwards, Matthew, corporal
Elkins, Ralph, private
Elliot, John, private
Elliott, Samuel, private
Ellis, Stephen, private
Ellison, William, private
Ellmore, George, private
Elmore, John, private
Embrey, Elijah, private
Emery, William, private
Eubanks, John, private
Evans, Gideon I., corporal
Evans, Isaac, private
Evans, John, first sergeant
Evans, William, private
Ewell, Reuben, private
Ewell, William, sergeant
Fagan, William, private
Fairman, Benjamin, private
Fake, John, private
Fanner, Joseph D., private
Farchild, John, private

Farley, Elihu, private
Farrar, Dennis B., private
Fatheree, Reading, corporal
Ferguson, Edward, private
Ferguson, William, private
Ferrell, Daniel, sergeant
Ferrell, John, sergeant
Ferry, John, private
Fielder, William, private
Fields, James, private
Finney, John, private
Flemming, William, private
Flowers, James, private
Ford, Absalom, sergeant
Ford, Joseph, private
Fountain, William M., sergeant
Fuller, Oliver W., fife major
Fuller, Richard, corporal
Futch, Onesemus, private
Gardner, William, sergeant
Garlington, Benjamin, musician
Garrada, William, private
Gatling, John, private
German, Prosley, private
Germany, Benjamin, private
Germany, Washington, sergeant
Gibson, Michael, private
Gibson, Reuben, private
Gilbert, Philip, private
Gilbert, William, private
Gilchrist, Malcolm, sergeant major
Gillaspie, Robert, ensign
Gillman, James, private
Gilmore, George, private
Glassburn, Godfrey, captain
Glasscock, Elijah, private
Gold, William, private
Goodson, Benjamin, private
Goodson, James, trumpeter
Gordon, John M., private
Gordon, Sandy, private
Gradey, William, private
Graham, George, private
Graham, James, private
Graham, William, corporal
Graves, Augustus A., private

Gray, David I., private
Gray, George, private
Gray, John, private
Grayson, Robert, private
Green, Ephraim, trumpeter
Green, John, private
Green, Leonard, private
Green, William, private
Greenlee, Elisha, private
Griffen, David, private
Grigg, Hervey, sergeant
Grimes, William, private
Groves, Moses, private
Groves, Richard, private
Guice, Jesse, private
Guice, Jonathan, private
Haddon, Thomas, private
Hale, Thomas, private
Hamberlin, Anthony, private
Hammond, Joshua, private
Handbury, Moses, private
Harden, Abraham, private
Hardin, Jeremiah, corporal
Harkness, Richard, private
Harleston, Solomon, private
Harmon, James, private
Harmon, Joseph, private
Harrill, Edward, private
Harrison, Lewis, private
Harrison, William, private
Harriss, Edward, private
Harry, — — — —, servant
Hartley, Francis, private
Harvey, Lemuel, private
Harvey, Nehemiah, sergeant
Harvey, Richard, private
Hatton, John, private
Havard, David, private
Havens, James, private
Havens, Joseph, private
Hawk, John, private
Haynes, George, private
Hays, Nathaniel, private
Heath, Joseph, sergeant
Hemby, James, private
Henderson, Joseph, private

Henderson, Samuel, sergeant
Henning, Robert, private
Herbert, William, sergeant
Herring, Samuel, private
Hickling, Robert, private
Higgins, Moses, private
Hill, Jacob, sergeant
Hill, William, private
Hilliard, Reuben, corporal
Hilson, Silas, first lieutenant
Hilton, Benjamin, corporal
Hogg, James, private
Hoke, John, private
Hollinger, Alexander, ensign
Holloway, Allen, corporal
Holmes, Drury, private
Holmes, James, private
Holmes, Liberty, private
Holston, King, private
Holt, Isaac, corporal
Honey, Thomas, private
Hood, John, corporal
Hooter, Jacob, private
Hopper, John, private
Houston, John, private
Howell, Joseph, private
Hubbard, James, corporal
Hubert, David, sergeant
Hudnell, Isaiah, private
Huff, Daniel, private
Hull, Miles, private
Humble, John, private
Humphreys, Jonathan, private
Huntsman, John, private
Huston, John, private
Hutchins, Anthony, private
Hutchins, John, musician
Hutchinson, John, private
Isaacs, Samuel, private
Iles, William, sergeant
Isham, — — — —, servant
Jackeway, John, private
Jackson, Andrew, private
Jackson, Davis, private
Jackson, Henry, private
Jacobs, Silas, private

Jenkins, John, private
Jenkins, Nathan, private
Jenkins, William, private
John, ————, servant
Johns, John, private
Johnson, Absalom, private
Johnson, James, private
Johnson, Jesse, corporal
Johnson, John, private
Johnson, Nathaniel, private
Johnson, Simon, sergeant major
Johnson, William, corporal
Johnston, James, private
Johnston, Jesse, private
Johnston, William A., private
Jones, Abraham B., private
Jones, Henry, private
Jones, Matthew, corporal
Jones, Micajah, private
Jones, Samuel W., private
Jones, Sterling, sergeant
Jones, Thomas, private
Jordan, John, corporal
Keen, John, private
Keen, Joseph, private
Keen, Josiah, corporal
Keethly, John, private
Kelly, Thomas, private
Kennedy, Cade L., private
Kennedy, David, private
Kenton, William, corporal
Kimbrall, William, private
King, Thomas, private
King, William, private
Kinnison, Nathaniel, private
Kirkland, Obed, private
Knight, James, private
Knox, Andrew, corporal
Land, Benjamin, private
Landham, Elias, private
Landingham, Malachi, private
Landram, Meredith, private
Landrum, Peter, private
Lane, John T., private
Langly, John H., ensign
Larry, Daniel, private

Laughorn, William, private
Lazarus, Nicholas, private
Leake, Walter, private
Leathlighter, Peter, private
Legrand, Malachi, private
Lewis, David, private
Lewis, John S., captain
Lewis, William, private
Liming, Joel, private
Linder, Daniel, private
Linssey, Isaac, private
Lisenby, David, private
Loflin, James, private
Loflin, William, private
Lofton, Ezekiel, private
Lofton, Thomas, private
Longmire, Robert, sergeant
Lott, Amos, ensign
Lott, Arther, Jr., private
Lott, Arther, Sr., private
Lott, Solomon, private
Lowry, John, captain
Lum, Erastus, private
Mackey, Alexander C., quartermaster service
Magruder, John, sergeant
Manning, James, private
Marshall, Christopher, corporal
Marten, Phillip, private
Martin, Albert, private
Martin, Charles, corporal
Martin, Henry, private
Martin, Richard, private
Martin, Samuel, corporal
Martin, William, private
Mason, Jacob, private
Massey, Drury, private
Maten, Aron, private
Mathis, John, private
Matthews, Lyman, sergeant
May, Ethelridge, private
May, Joseph, private
May, Phillip, private
Mays, John, corporal
McAlister, Archibald, private
McAllister, Benjamin, private

McAnulty, Robert, private
McAnulty, William, private
McCaleb, Daniel, private
McCarty, Jacob, sergeant
McCombs, William M., private
McCook, John, sergeant
McCormack, Samuel, corporal
McCoy, Daniel, corporal
McCoy, Jesse, private
McCrory, John, sergeant
McDaniel, Alexander, private
McDaniel, Benjamin G., private
McDonald, Elam H., private
McDonald, John, private
McDowell, William, private
McDowell, William, private
McDugald, Daniel, private
McGahey, Daniel, captain
McGehee, William, Lieutenant
McGinty, Reuben, private
McGowen, James, Lieutenant
McGowen, Russell, private
McGowen, William, private
McGraw, David, private
McGraw, James, private
McGrew, Robert, private
McGuffee, Alfred, sergeant
McIntire, Dougald, private
McIntire, Hugh, private
McIntosh, John, private
McIntire, Daniel, private
McKahan, John, private
McKenzie, John, private
McKinsey, Alexander, private
McLaughlin, John, private
McLaughlin, Patrick, corporal
McLaughlin, William, private
McLaughlin, William, private
McMellon, Daniel, private
McMillan, Dugald, corporal
McMillan, James, private
McMullin, John, private
McMullin, Robert, corporal
McNamee, John R., sergeant
McNeir, John, private
Melvin, Daniel W., private

Mercer, Eli, fifer
Mercer, Simeon, private
Meriwether, John M., private
Merkinson, John, private
Merrell, Elijah, private
Middlemist, John, private
Middleton, Henry, lieutenant
Middleton, Joseph, private
Miller, Andrew, sergeant
Miller, Cader, private
Miller, George, private
Miller, James, private
Miller, John, private
Milton, Michael, private
Minor, Marshall, private
Mitchel, William, corporal
Mixon, Abed, sergeant
Moke, Andrew, private
Monger, William, private
Montgomery, Alexander, sergeant
Montgomery, Hugh, private
Montgomery, James, private
Montgomery, James S., ensign
Moore, James J., private
Moore, James, 1st, private
Moore, Jefferis H., ensign
Moore, Joseph, corporal
Moore, Samuel, private
Morgan, Elijah, private
Morgan, Thomas, sergeant
Morris, James, private
Morris, John, private
Morrus, William, private
Morton, Hughes, private
Murphy, Jonas, private
Murphy, Morris, sergeant
Murphy, Vincent, private
Murray, John, private
Murray, Joshua, private
Nealy, Parris, private
Ned, — — — —, servant
Need, David, private
Neely, David, second lieutenant-lieutenant
Nelson, James, sergeant
Nelson, Peter, private

Mississippi Territory in War of 1812—Rowland. 171

Nelson, Thomas, private
Nevills, William, private
Newman, Reuben, private
Nicholls, Joseph, first lieutenant and adjutant
Nickols, David, fifer
Nixon, George H., lieutenant-colonel
Noble, Isaac, private
Noble, Levi, private
Nobles, John, private
Nobles, Marke, private
Norman, Presley, private
O'Bannion, Darson, private
Ogden, Elijah, private
Oliphant, James, private
Oliver, Andrew, private
O'Neal, Peter, private
Orr, John, private
Ott, William, private
Owens, Walter, private
Pace, John, private
Page, Jesse, private
Page, John W., ensign
Page, Robert, private
Palmer, Reuben, private
Parish, Hezakiah, sergeant
Parker, Aaron, private
Parker, William, private
Parks, Silas, fife major
Parr, Henry, private
Patton, John, private
Payne, Edward, drum major
Peak, Benjamin, sergeant
Perry, Daniel, private
Perry, James, ensign
Petty, Presley, sergeant
Phillips, Isaac, private
Phillips, Lee Marcus, private
Phinney, John, private
Phipps, William, private
Pitchford, Augustin, sergeant
Pitman, Archibald, private
Plaster, Thomas R., private
Platner, Enoch, private
Platner, William D., private
Plays, Robert W., private

Pollard, John, first corporal
Polatty, Francis, private
Porter, Henry, private
Powell, Ira, private
Powell, William, private
Prescoat, Solomon, private
Prestridge, Robert, private
Price, Ralph, private
Prichard, William, lieutenant
Pritchard, William, private
Ragsdal, Elijah, private
Ragsdale, Edward, private
Ragsdale, William, sergeant
Raines, Stephen, private
Rankins, Frederick, corporal
Rapalje, Isaac, captain
Ratleff, Benjamin, private
Ratliff, James, private
Rayburn, David, private
Rea, Joseph, private
Reagan, John, private
Reaves, Eli, private
Reaves, John, private
Reaves, Thomas, private
Reburn, David, private
Reburn, Mark, corporal
Redman, Jesse, private
Redman, Wilson, private
Reed, James, private
Reeves, William, private
Reynolds, Edward G., surgeon
Rice, Ezekiah, private
Rice, George, private
Richards, Samuel B., lieutenant
Richardson, William, private
Richey, Theodore I. H., sergeant
Richmond, Thomas W., private
Riley, Stephen, private
Ring, Mark, private
Rippy, Jesse, private
Roach, Aaron, private
Roach, Richard, surgeon
Roark, John, private
Robbins, Horace, private
Roberts, George, private
Roberts, Henry, private

Roberts, James, private
Roberts, James P., private
Roberts, John, corporal
Roberts, John, private
Roberts, Phillip, private
Roberts, Raymon, private
Robertson, George, ensign
Robertson, John I., private
Robertson, Thomas, private
Robertson, William, private
Robertson, William H., sergeant
Robins, Horace W., private
Roddy, Peter, private
Rodgers, Evin R., private
Rogers, John, private
Fogers, William, corporal
Rolls, Jabus, ensign
Ross, Samuel, private
Ross, William, private
Rounsoval, William, private
Rowell, Lewis, private
Roycraft, Francis, private
Rude, Abner, private
Rule, William, private
Russell, Alexander, private
Russell, Jacob, private
Rutledge, Dudley, private
Rutledge, Joseph, private
Sandab, Daniel, private
Saucer, Samuel, private
Saucer, William, private
Saunders, Traverse, private
Saval, John, private
Saxton, John, private
Scott, John, private
Scott, Thomas, private
Scott, William, private
Scrivener, Jesse, private
Seals, Eli, private
Seals, Littleton, private
Searcy, Ransome, private
Sedgewick, John, private
Selser, George, private
Selser, Josiah, private
Sermons, Edmond, private
Sermons, Jonathan, private

Sermons, Thomas, private
Sexton, Daniel, private
Shaddock, Isaac, private
Shave, John, private
Shaw, Thompson, private
Shelby, Marquest, sergeant
Sherill, William, private
Shober, William, sergeant
Shuffield, Ishum, private
Sibley, Benjamin, private
Simmons, John, private
Simmons, Richard, private
Simmons, Vincent, private
Simmons, Willis, private
Simolet, Michael, private
Simpson, David B., private
Sims, William G., sergeant
Singleton, Richard, private
Singleton, Washington, private
Six, David, private
Slaughter, David, private
Slaughter, John, private
Slaughter, William, corporal
Slay, Nathan, private
Sluder, Henry, private
Smith, Alexander, private
Smith, Archibald, private
Smith, Carter, private
Smith, Ezechieal, private
Smith, Henry C., private
Smith, James, private
Smith, Jeremiah, sergeant
Smith, Jesse, private
Smith, John, private
Smith, Joseph, private
Smith, Levy, private
Smith, Thomas, private
Smith, William, private
Smoot, Benjamin S., major
Sojourner, Jacob, sergeant
Sojourner, John, lieutenant
Sojourner, William, private
Solomon, — — —, private servant
Sones, Henry, private
Sorrells, Jesse, private
Spencer, William, captain

Mississippi Territory in War of 1812—Rowland. 173

Spradley, William, sergeant
Springer, Solomon, corporal
Sprinkle, John, private
Spurlock, David, private
Stallion, John, private
Stampley, William, private
Stanley, Shadrach, private
Stedham, Jesse, private
Stephenson, Jonathan, private
Stephenson, William, private
Sterns, Peter, private
Stewart, James, sergeant
Stewart, Robert, private
Stiglar, Benjamin, private
Stiglar, George, private
Stoker, Henry, private
Stone, John C., private
Strickland, Simon, private
Stricklin, Henry, private
Stringfellow, James, private
Stroud, Frederick, private
Stroud, Samuel, private
Strouse, Christopher, private
Summerlin, Giles, private
Swan, Thomas T., sergeant
Swearingen, Henry, private
Sweney, John, private
Syx, Benjamin, private
Talbert, Abner, private
Tanner, John, private
Tanner, William, private
Tarver, John, private
Taylor, Brice, corporal
Taylor, James, private
Taylor, Thomas, private
Teek, John, private
Terry, Jeremiah, private
Tervin, Richard, private
Testone, Frederick, private
Thomas, Charles, private
Thomas, Daniel, sergeant
Thomas, David, lieutenant
Thomas, Joseph, Lieutenant
Thomas, Martin, private
Thompson, Archibald, private
Thompson, David, private

Thompson, Felix, private
Thompson, James, captain
Thompson, James, private
Thompson, William, private
Tibbs, William, private
Tidder, Isaac, private
Tidder, Thomas, private
Toler, Elijah, private
Toumbs, William, corporal
Travers, Benjamin, private
Travers, Thomas, private
Travers, William, private
Travis, Prier S., corporal
Trefoe, Michael, private
Troty, Joseph, private
Tucker, John, private
Tucker, William, private
Turvin, Richard, private
Twilley, Robert, captain
Urick, John, private
Usher, William, private
Vancampin, William, private
Vannoy, John, private
Verdiman, Jeremlah, private
Vickory, Charles, private
Vickory, Nathaniel, private
Vincent, Berry, private
Vining, John, private
Wactor, John, sergeant
Wafers, Joel, private
Walker, Felix, private
Wallis, Nazareth, private
Wallis, Oliver, private
Walton, Timothy, private
Ware, Lard, lieutenant
Ware, Nicholas M., private
Ware, William, private
Warner, James, private
Warnuck, Joseph, private
Warren, John, private
Warren, Joseph, private
Warren, Solomon, private
Way, John, sergeant
Way, John, corporal
Wax, John, corporal
Webb, Jesse, private

Weigart, David, corporal
Welch, James, lieutenant
Welch, Nathan, private
Welch, Robert, private
Welch, Young, private
Wells, Edmund, private
Westfall, Samuel, private
Westner, George, private
Westner, Samuel, private
Wetherill, Theophilus, private
Wheat, Joseph, private
White, Isaiah, private
White, James, private
White, Joel, sergeant
White, Joseph, corporal
White, Joseph, private
White, Richard, corporal
White, Thompson, private
White, William, private
Whittington, Elam, private
Whittington, Evan, private
Whittington, Moses, ensign
Wigley, Joab, private
Wigley, Joseph, private
Wilburn, James, private
Wilds, Joseph, private
Wilkinson, Angus, sergeant
Wilkinson, Joseph, private
Wilkinson, William, sergeant
Williams, Benjamin, private
Williams, David, private
Williams, Francis, private
Williams, James, private
Williams, Rafe, private
Williamson, Edward, private
Willis, David, sergeant
Willis, George, private
Wilson, Daniel, private
Wilson, Samuel, private
Wilson, William, sergeant
Windham, Stephen, corporal
Windham, William, private
Winn, John, private
Wise, James B., private
Withers, Silas, private
Wood, Dennis, private
Wood, Ethan A., captain
Yewell, Joel, quartermaster sergeant
Young, Jesse, private

1st REGIMENT OF MISSISSIPPI VOLUNTEERS

Captain Gerard C. Brandon's Company
Captain Samuel Dale's Company
Captain Benjamin Dent's Company
Captain Philip A. Engel's Company
Captain L. V. Foelckel's Company
Captain William Henry's Company
Captain William Jack's Company
Captain Chas. G. Johnson's Company
Captain Randal Jones' Company
Captain Jos. P. Kennedy's Company
Captain William C. Mead's Company
Captain Hatton Middleton's Company
Captain Hans Morrison's Company
Captain Lewis Paimboiuf's Company
Captain Thos. Posey's Company
Captain John Neilson's Company
Captain James Foster's Company
Captain Abraham M. Scott's Company
Captain Benj. S. Smoot's Company
Captain Archelaus Wells' Company

Abernathe, John, private
Adams, Richard, private
Adams, Thomas, private
Agens, John, private
Agens, William, private
Agiliras, Francisco, private
Aikins, Samuel, private
Akors, Benjamin, private
Alexander, Michael G., private
Alexander, William, private
Alford, Joseph, private
Alford, Robert, sergeant
Allen, David, private
Allen, Drury, private
Allen, John, first lieutenant
Allen, John, private
Allen, John, private
Allen, Josiah, private
Anderson, Allen, sergeant
Anderson, James, private
Anderson, James, private
Anderson, John, private
Anderson, Robert C., second lieutenant
Andrews, Green, private
Andrews, William, private
Anthony, Abraham L., private
Anthony, Joseph, private
Armstrong, Thomas, private
Arnold, Benjamin, Jr., private
Arnold, Benjamin, Sr., private
Arnold, Bridges, private
Ashley, James, private
Atchison, Henry, sergeant
Atkins, Charles, private
Attoy, Dennis, private
Atwater, Asaph, sergeant
Atwood, Thomas, private
Austill, Evan, first lieutenant
Austill, Jeremiah, private
Bagacox, Victor, private
Baggs, Robert, corporal
Bailey, George, private
Bailey, James, first lieutenant
Bainbridge, Thomas, private
Baird, James, private
Baird, John, private
Baird, Samuel, private

Baird, William, private
Baird, William, Jr., private
Baird, William, Sr., private
Baird, William L., private
Baker, Lewis, private
Baldwin, William, private
Baley, Richard, private
Banks, Peregrin, private
Barns, Mark, private
Barra, Francis, private
Barron, John, second lieutenant
Bartlett, Nathaniel, private
Bartley, John, private
Bashford, Robert, sergeant
Battest, John, drummer
Bazer, Edward, private
Beall, Wilkinson, private
Beard, Henry, sergeant
Beasley, Daniel, major
Beason, William, private
Beaty, James C., private
Beauchamp, Baptist, private
Belcher, Branch, private
Bell, Joseph, sergeant
Bell, Ralph, private
Bell, William W., sergeant
Bender, Lott, private
Benge, Harris, private
Bennett, Micajah, private
Bennett, William, private
Bernard, John G., private
Berry, Joseph, corporal
Berryhill, Alexander, private
Biddle, Benjamin, private
Biddlescomb, Jeremiah, private
Bieulet, Joseph, private
Bilbo, James, private
Bishop, Stephen, private
Black, Daniel, corporal
Black, John, private
Black, John S., corporal
Blackwell, James, private
Blair, Thomas, private
Blanton, Benjamin, ensign
Blue, Angus, corporal
Bobbs, Jacob, private
Bonner, James, private

Booth, John, sergeant major
Boozman, Howell, private
Boswell, John, corporal
Bosworth, Richard, sergeant
Bowland, John, private
Bowman, Richardson, first lieutenant
Boyce, William, sergeant
Braden, James, private
Bradford, Leonard, private
Bradley, Bradford, private
Bradley, Luther, private
Brady, Samuel, private
Bragg, John, private
Brandon, Gerard C., captain
Brannan, Thomas, private
Brannon, John P., sergeant
Brant, Lewis W., sergeant
Breard, John, private
Brent, John, sergeant
Brenton, Joseph, private
Brewer, William, private
Bridgement, Thomas, private
Bridges, Benjamin, second lieutenant
Briggs, Johnston, sergeant
Brinkman, George, private
Britt, William S., ensign
Brittle, Thomas M., private
Britton, James, private
Brooks, David, private
Brooks, John, private
Brothers, Lewis, private
Brown, Bartlett, private
Brown, Henry, musician
Brown, John, private
Brown, John, private
Brown, John W., private
Brown, Liberty, private
Brown, Rowling, private
Bruley, Jacob, private
Bruster, James, private
Bruster, Washington, corporal
Bryan, William, private
Bryant, Robert, private
Bullman, John, private
Buntin, Timothy, private
Bullock, James, private
Burgess, Francis, private

Burgess, William B., private
Burk, Martin, private
Burke, James, private
Burnett, Thomas, private
Burns, William, sergeant
Burton, Charles A., private
Burton, Elbert, ensign
Burton, Robert, corporal
Bush, Levi, private
Bush, William, private
Byarse, Henry, private
Byers, James, private
Bynum, Turner, private
Cable, Christopher, private
Cadwell, Aaron, private
Cadwell, William, private
Cain, James B., sergeant
Caldwell, Kean, second lieutenant and adjutant
Caldwell, Thomas, private
Callahan, David, ensign
Caller, Robert, private
Calvet, Alexander, first lieutenant and aide-de-camp
Cameron, Barnabas, private
Camp, John, first lieutenant
Camp, John, private
Campbell, Archibald, private
Campbell, Donald, private
Campbell, James, private
Campbell, John D., private
Cammack, David, private
Cammell, Duncan, private
Canty, William S., sergeant
Carl, James, private
Carlin, James, private
Carmichael, William, private
Carnes, Johnson, private
Carnes, Wells, private
Carrigan, Edward, private
Carson, Joseph, colonel
Carson, Joseph, private
Carter, John, private
Carter, John, private
Carty, Collin, private
Caswell, William, private
Cathel, Joshua, private

Cathel, Levin, sergeant
Caughman, David, private
Caulfield, Francis, private
Chadock, Isaac, private
Chadwick, Isaac, private
Chambers, Michael, corporal
Chambliss, William B., ensign
Chaney, James, private
Chapman, George, private
Charrington, John, private
Cheauveaus, James, second lieutenant
Childers, Ware, private
Chisholm, Cockburn, private
Chislom, Andrew C., first sergeant
Claiborne, Ferdinand L., brigadier general
Clark, Archibald, private
Clark, Henry, private
Clark, James, private
Clark, Samuel, private
Clark, William G., private
Clark, William H., private
Clayton, John Y., private
Clayton, Samuel, private
Cleaveland, Edward, private
Cleaveland, Josiah M., sergeant
Clinton, John, private
Clupper, Phillip, private
Cobb, Frederick, private
Cochran, Cheedle, private
Cockram, William, private
Cogan, William, private
Colbert, Simon, private
Cole, Stewart, first sergeant
Coleman, Daniel, private
Coleman, Levi, private
Collum, David, private
Colson, Samuel, private
Colston, Thomas, private
Colton, Elam, private
Colvin, Talton, private
Colvin, William, private
Conner, George, private
Conner, James, corporal
Conner, John, sergeant
Converse, Wright, sergeant
Cook, Joseph, private

Coolman, George, private
Cooper, George, private
Cooper, John, private
Cooper, Joseph, private
Cooper, Simeon, private
Cooper, William, corporal
Copeland, James, private
Corey, Samuel F., sergeant
Corhel, Nicholas, private
Corkins, David, private
Coulson, Samuel, private
Cousins, Matthew, private
Cox, Thomas, private
Cox, William R., surgeon mate
Crane, Stephen, private
Crane, William, corporal
Crane, William, private
Crawford, Alexander, corporal
Crawford, Hugh, private
Creagh, Gerrard, private
Criswell, Andrew, private
Criswell, Robert, private
Curtis, William, private
Dacosta, Nicholas, corporal
Dale, James, private
Dale, Samuel, captain
Daniel, Nathaniel, sergeant
Daniels, Abner, corporal
Davis, Baxter, sergeant
Davis, Benjamin, private
Davis, Daniel, private
Davis, George, private
Davis, Isaac W., ensign
Davis, Simon, private
Deal, Elias, private
Dean, Daniel, private
Dean, John, Jr., private
Dean, John, Sr., private
Dearman, William, private
Delevan, Cornelius, private
Deloach, William R., first lieutenant and adjutant
Denhart, Augustus, private
Deniston, Andrew, private
Dennis, Asa W., sergeant
Dennis, George P., private
Dennis, Thomas, private

Denson, Isaac, private
Dent, Benjamin, captain
Desha, Benjamin, private
DeVall, John, private
Devanport, John, private
Devin, James, private
Dewell, Lewis, sergeant
Dewitt, James, corporal
Ditzler, Peter, private
Divin, John S., private
Dixon, Hugh, private
Dixon, Thomas, private
Dobbins, Alfred M., private
Dobbs, Jacob, private
Donnelly, James, private
Dorsey, James, private
Dougherty, George, ensign
Doughty, Kitrell, private
Douglass, Jeptha, private
Douthard, John, private
Dowling, Charles, private
Downing, Edward, private
Downing, Nicholas, private
Dozier, Thomas, sergeant
Drake, Edmund, sergeant
Duchur, Victor, private
Dudley, Daniel, private
Dugless, John, private
Duke, Thomas, private
Duncan, Benjamin, private
Duncan, David, private
Duncan, William, private
Dunham, Warren, private
Dunking, Thomas, private
Dunn, John, private
Dunn, Lewis P., corporal
Dunson, William, private
Dupie, Thomas, private
Easley, Edward, private
Easley, John, private
Eaton, Samuel, private
Eavins, Gaddi, private
Eavins, Samuel, private
Ebey, William, drummer
Edgerly, Elijah, private
Edwards, Dabney, private

Edwards, Thomas, private
Egan, William, private
Elder, James, private
Elliott, John, corporal
Elliott, Robert L., corporal
Ellison, Samuel, private
Ellison, Thomas, private
Ellison, William, private
Embree, Jesse, private
Embree, Jonathan, sergeant
Emery, William, private
Emmons, John, ensign
Engel, Philip A., captain
Enos, Eli, private
Ervin, Samuel, private
Espey, Wiley, private
Espinosa, Joseph, private
Espy, Lemuel, private
Ethridge, John, musician
Evans, Elijah, private
Evans, John, private
Evans, Thomas, private
Evans, William, private
Evans, Zachariah, private
Eveleigh, William, private
Everard, Charles, private
Everitt, John, private
Ewalt, William, private
Ewing, Robert B., private
Faite, Peter, private
Faith, Alexander, musician
Farley, Elihu, private
Farris, Samuel S., sergeant
Fell, George, sergeant
Fenton, John, sergeant
Ferguson, Richard, private
Fields, Elijah, corporal
Files, John, ensign
Finch, Christopher, private
Finch, John, private
Finehorn, John, private
Finley, Charles, private
Finley, Norris, private
Finley, Zachariah, private
Fisher, Charles, private
Fisher, Samuel, private

Mississippi Territory in War of 1812—Rowland. 179

Flanigan, John, private
Fleming, John P., private
Flemming, Joseph, private
Fletcher, Jeremiah, private
Flinn, William, private
Flores, Joseph, private
Floyd, John B., sergeant
Foeckel, L. V., captain
Ford, James, sergeant
Ford, William, private
Forget, William, private
Fort, Adison, private
Fortenberry, William, private
Foster, Francis, private
Foster, George, private
Foster, James, captain
Foster, William, private
Fountain, Henry, private
Fox, Washington, corporal
Francis, James, private
Frederick, John, private
French, John, private
Friley, Frederick, private
Fry, Thomas, private
Futch, Onisimus, private
Gallon, Canton, private
Gamble, Robert, private
Gano, Stephen, private
Gardner, Jeremiah, private
Garlington, Edwin, sergeant
Garmany, Washington, sergeant
Garrard, James, private
Garrard, William, private
Garrino, John P., private
Gash, William, private
Gates, Jasper, private
Gatlin, John, private
Gatton, Ignatius, private
Gentry, Elijah, private
Gentry, Elijah, Sr., private
Gentry, James, private
Gibbs, George H., ensign
Gibson, Richard, private
Gillaspie, David, corporal
Gillick, John, private
Gilman, Benare, private

Glass, David, private
Glass, Williamson, private
Glass, Zachariah, private
Godfrey, William, private
Gonsales, John, private
Good, Delanson, private
Goodwin, Robert, private
Gordon, Robert, private
Goss, Henry O. F., private
Gowen, James H., sergeant
Gray, Philip A., corporal
Grayham, James, private
Grayson, Peter, private
Green, Allen, sergeant
Green, Robert, corporal
Green, William, private
Grey, Joseph, private
Grey, Thomas F., private
Griffin, George W., private
Griffin, Isaac W., private
Griffin, James M., private
Griffin, Mitchell, private
Griffin, Patrick, sergeant
Griffin, William, sergeant
Griffis, Thomas, private
Grizzle, Willis, private
Groff, Frederick, private
Groff, Henry C., private
Guest, Samuel, sergeant major
Guest, Westly, private
Gurley, Robert, private
Haggarty, Henry, private
Haggarty, John, private
Haggerty, John, private
Hale, Joel W., corporal
Haley, John, private
Haley, Richard, private
Hall, James, private
Hall, John, private
Hall, John, private
Hall, Matthew, sergeant
Hall, Samuel, private
Hamby, Samuel M., private
Hamilton, Andrew, private
Hamilton, Thomas, private
Hamilton, William, private

Hammon, Thomas, private
Hammond, William, private
Hamrick, Burwell, private
Hand, John B., private
Hardy, Isaiah, private
Harford, Samuel, fife major
Harney, Benjamin F., surgeon mate
Harringill, Joseph, private
Harrington, Hardy, private
Harrington, Hudson, private
Harris, Joseph A., private
Hart, Philip, private
Hawkins, Gilbert D., private
Hays, Mark, private
Hazle, Daniel, corporal
Hazle, Samuel, private
Hazlett, Jacob, private
Head, Benjamin, private
Healy, Daniel, sergeant
Heard, Bailey, first lieutenant
Heard, Joel, private
Hearn, George, private
Hearn, William, private
Heath, Thomas, musician
Heaton, Isaac, private
Hellum, Enos, private
Helms, Henry, private
Henderson, Duncan, private
Henry, John N., private
Henry, Lemuel C. G., private
Henry, William, captain
Henson, James, private
Hide, Harris, corporal
Higgins, John, private
Higgins, Peter, private
High, Martin, private
Hill, James, private
Hill, William, private
Hillebrand, Paul, private
Hillis, John, private
Hinton, William, private
Hixon, Daniel, corporal
Hogg, John, private
Hoggett, Joel, private
Hogue, William, private
Holcomb, Gardner, private
Holcomb, Philip P., private
Holcroft, John, private
Holder, John, private
Holliday, Levi, corporal
Holliday, Richard J., sergeant
Holliday, Simeon, private
Hollister, Francis A., private
Holloway, George, private
Holmes, Thomas, private
Hopkins, Hardy, private
Hopkins, Joseph R., private
Hopkins, Richard, private
Horton, John, private
House, John, private
Howard, Jonathan, private
Howe, Jacob, private
Howell, Archibald, private
Hudson, John, private
Hudson, Westley, private
Huff, William H., private
Hunt, William, private
Hurlock, James, private
Hurry, Richard, private
Hustler, Samuel, drum major
Hutchins, Thomas, private
Hutchinson, John, private
Inman, Richard, private
Irby, Henry, private
Irby, James, private
Ireson, James H., sergeant
Ivey, William, private
Jack, William captain
Jackson, George, private
Jackson, Henry, private
Jacobs, Richard, private
James, Abner, private
James, Almon, private
James, Joseph, corporal
Jetton, Benedict, private
Johnson, Abraham, private
Johnson, Charles G., captain
Johnson, Hugh B., private
Johnson, John, private
Johnson, Peter, private
Johnston, William, private
Joiner, William, private

Jones, Elbert, private
Jones, Hardin, private
Jones, John H., private
Jones, Josiah, private
Jones, Randal, captain
Jones, Russel, private
Jones, Stephen, private
Jones, Thomas, private
Jones, Wiley, private
Jones, William, private
Jones, William, private
Jones, William, private
Jones, William P., private
Jordan, Zachariah, private
Judkins, John, private
Juvenot, Joseph, private
Kaufman, George, private
Keas, William, private
Keel, William, private
Keen, John, sergeant
Kellogg, Theron, first lieutenant
Kelly, Abraham, private
Kelly, Benjamin C., sergeant
Kelly, Jesse, private
Kennedy, Joseph P., captain and brigade major
Kennedy, William, private
Kennedy, William, private
Kerr, John, surgeon
Kief, Thomas, private
Killen, Henry, private
Kimble, Isom, private
Kimble, Ransom, private
King, David, musician
King, John, private
Kingsbury, Daniel, sergeant
Kline, Balthazer, private
Knight, Andrew W. L., private
Knight, Thomas, private
Koen, John, cornet
Koen, Jonathan H., private
Koff, Peter, private
Kregger, John M., private
LaChapelle, Dominic, private
Lambert, Ashley, private
Lambert, Edward

Lang, James, private
Lang, William, private
Langford, David, private
Langford, John, private
Langham, James, private
Laucks, Michael, private
Laughlin, James, private
Lauson, William, corporal
Law, David, private
Law, James, private
Layson, Robert R., first lieutenant-first quartermaster
Lazarus, Nicholas, private
Lazarus, Thomas, sergeant
Leavell, Joseph, private
Leblane, Victor, private
Lee, Charles, sergeant
Lee, James Bud, private
Lee Joseph, private
Lee, Robert, private
Lefoy, Mathew, private
Lemon, William, private
Lenoir, Robert, private
Leverton, Jacob, private
Lewis, David, private
Lewis, Henry W., musician
Lewis, Jacob, musician
Lewis, John, private
Lewis, William, first lieutenant
Lewis, William, private
Lick, William, private
Lilley, George, first lieutenant
Linder, Daniel, private
Linder, Lewis, corporal
Linsey, John, private
Linsey, Robert, corporal
Linton, William, private
Little, Henry, sergeant
Littleton, William B., private
Lloyd, Henry, private
Lloyd, Samuel, private
Lochridge, Nicholas, second lieutenant
Long, Jeremiah, private
Long, William, private
Lora, Felix, private
Lorimer, Charles V., sergeant

Louck, Andrew, private
Love, James, private
Love, Joseph, private
Love, Robert E., sergeant
Love, William D., private
Low, John, sergeant
Lowman, Cornelius, private
Lowrey, John, fifer
Lowry, James, private
Lowry, James, private
Lucier, Anthony, private
Luckett, James, ensign
Luker, Isaac, private
Luker, Jesse, private
Liker, Joshua, sergeant
Luker, William, private
Lumpkin, Hendrick, private
Lunsford, Solomon, private
Lyles, Richmond, private
Lynch, Matthew, sergeant
Lynch, Stephen, private
Madden, James, private
Malone, Joseph, private
Malone, Michael, private
Maner, Elisha, private
Manichy, James, private
Mannen, Willay, private
Manville, Philip, corporal
Marian, Joseph, private
Marquart, George, private
Marrs, Thomas, private
Marshall, Solomon, private
Martin, Aaron, private
Martin, Alexander, private
Martin, Austin, private
Mason, Abraham D., private
Mason, Charles, corporal
Massey, Drewry, private
Masters, Baptist, private
Masters, John, private
Matheney, John D., private
Mathews, Samuel, private
Mathureb, Loran, private
Matson, Thomas, private
Matthews, Hezekiah, private
Matthews, Lyman, private

May, George, private
May, Patrick, second lieutenant
Mayers, David, private
Mays, Stephen, ensign
Mays, William, musician
McAlpin, James, private
McAlpine, William, corporal
McArthur, James, ensign
McCabe, James, private
McCaleb, Alexander, private
McChesney, David, private
McClam, Solomon, corporal
McClure, John, corporal
McCoy, William, private
McCullough, David, private
McDaniel, John, private
McDonald, Hugh, private
McDonald, Robert, private
McDonald, William, corporal
McDonald, Young R., ensign
McGee, Joseph, private
McGee, Thomas, private
McGinley, Barney, private
McGinley, John, private
McGohan, Peter, private
McGrew, William, second sergeant
McGruder, Walter, private
McGuire, James, private
McKinsey, Levi, private
McLaughlin, Charles, private
McLendon, David, private
McLeod, James, private
McLouthlen, James, private
McManniman, Dennis, private
McMichael, William, private
McMillan, James, private
McNeal, Daniel, private
McNeil, Lochlen H., corporal
McPhail, Randol, private
McRay, Elijah, private
McShane, John, private
McWhinney, William, first corporal
McWilliam, John, private
Mead, Cowles colonel
Mead, William C., captain
Meaux, John T. T., corporal

Mississippi Territory in War of 1812—Rowland. 183

Meeks, James, corporal
Melton, Andrew, private
Melvin, Daniel W., private
Mercer, Raney, private
Merriman, William, private
Merritt, Morris, private
Merson, Emanuel, private
Michael, Francis, private
Micheaux, Daniel B., private
Middleton, Hatton, captain
Miller, Jesse, private
Miller, Joash, private
Miller, John, private
Miller, William, private
Milligan, James, private
Miner, Jacob, private
Minton, Joshua, private
Mitchell, John, private
Mitchell, Nathaniel, private
Mitchum, George, private
Mitchum, Richard, private
Moncrief, Benjamin, private
Moncrief, Caleb, private
Monk, William, corporal
Montgomery, Andrew, first lieutenant
Montgomery, Jacob, fifer
Montgomery, John, private
Mooney, Isaac, private
Moore, Boyle, sergeant
Moore, Charles, second lieutenant
Moore, Edward, sergeant
Moore, John, sergeant
Moore, Thomas, private
Moran, John B., private
Moran, William, corporal
Morgan, George, private
Morgan, Isham, private
Morgan, John, private
Morgan, Joseph, private
Morgan, Thomas, private
Morgan, William, first lieutenant
Morris, John, private
Morris, John, private
Morris, John, private
Morris, Joseph, private
Morris, Leroy, private
Morrison, Hans, captain

Morrison, Hugh, private
Morrison, James, private
Morrison, John, drum major
Morton, Hugh, private
Mosely, Thomas, private
Mosely, Thomas B., private
Mosely, William, corporal
Mountjoy, John, sergeant
Mulkey, Ellis, private
Mullin, Timothy, private
Murphy, Benjamin, private
Murphy, John, private
Murphy, Willis, corporal
Murray, Samuel M., private
Murrell, Charles W., private
Mygott, Austin R., musician
Myles, Isaac A., corporal
Myles, John E., private
Myles, Joseph, private
Nabb, Charles B., private
Nance, David, private
Naters, James, private
Neal, James, private
Neal, John D., private
Neilson, Jeremiah, private
Neilson, John, captain
Nelson, Jesse, private
Nettles, John, private
Newman, Dixon, private
Newman, Hezekiah, private
Newman, Jonathan, private
Nicholas, Daniel, private
Nicholas, Thomas, private
Nichols, Benjamin, private
Nicholson, Peter, private
O'Donnald, James, private
Ogden, Alexander, sergeant
Oglethorpe, John N., private
O'Guin, John, private
O'Hara, Alexander, private
Oneal, Michael, private
Orear, Robert, private
Orourk, Timothy, private
Osborn, Spruce M., second lieutenant
Osborne, Audley L., first lieutenant and adjutant
Otis, James, musician

Otty, John, private
Owens, Alexander, private
Pace, Isham, private
Page, Lewis, private
Page, Nehemiah, private
Paimboeuf, Lewis, captain
Painter, Edward, private
Palmer, Aaron, private
Parish, Hezekiah, corporal
Parish, Joseph, private
Parker, John, private
Patton, James, corporal
Paxton, John R., private
Pearson, John, private
Pearson, Reuben, private
Peet, Curtis, private
Penticost, George W., private
Penton, William, corporal
Perkins, Ezekiel, private
Pernell, John M., corporal
Perrett, James, private
Perrett, John, private
Perrett, Robert, private
Perry, Francis, private
Perry, George, private
Perry, Peter, private
Peters, Thomas W., private
Peterson, David, private
Petty, William, private
Pevy, Nehemiah, fifer
Pharis, Samuel, private
Philips, Robert, private
Phillip, Frederick, private
Phillips, Abraham H., private
Phillips, Daniel, sergeant
Phillips, George, private
Phillips, Iredell L., private
Phillips, Isham B., sergeant
Phillips, John, private
Phillips, Lewis, private
Phillips, William E., corporal
Phillis, Jacob, private
Pierce, Lewis, private
Pipkin, Moses, private
Pitchford, Augustin, sergeant
Pitner, John, private
Pittard, Abner, private
Pollard, Joseph, sergeant
Pollock, Charles, private
Porter, John C., private
Posey, Thomas, captain
Potter, John, corporal
Potts, Fleet, private
Poupnell, John Vincent, private
Powell, Archer, corporal
Powell, John, private
Powell, Lewis, private
Powell, William, private
Power, John, private
Powers, Josiah, private
Powers, Nathaniel, private
Prescott, Andrew, private
Presnall, Absolom, private
Presnell, Elijah, private
Price, Charles, private
Price, Edmund, private
Price, James, private
Price, James, private
Price, John, private
Price, Jonathan, private
Proctor, Aaron B., saddler
Pullum, Levy, private
Pyburn, Jacob, private
Rachford, John, sergeant
Rains, John, private
Ramoue, Michael, private
Randal, Thomas, corporal
Rankin, Thomas B., cornet
Rankins, Duncan, private
Ray, Henry, private
Ray, James P., private
Reams, Sterling, private
Reaves, William, private
Red, James E., private
Reed, William, private
Revere, Peter, private
Reviere, John, private
Reynolds, David, private
Reynolds, James, private
Reynolds, Reuben, fife major
Rhodes, Jacob, private
Rhodes, John, private

Mississippi Territory in War of 1812—Rowland. 185

Richardson, Asa S., private
Richardson, Isaac, private
Richardson, Philip, private
Rickards, Archibald, private
Ripley, Samuel, corporal
Riviere, Henry L., second lieutenant
Roberts, John, private
Robertson, James, private
Robertson, Joshua, private
Robertson, Richard, private
Robertson, Thomas, private
Robinson, Aaron, private
Roddridge, Joseph M., private
Rodgers, John, private
Rodgers, John D., first lieutenant
Roe, Benjamin, private
Roe, John, private
Rogers, Hendirck, private
Rogers, William, private
Rollins, John, private
Roney, John, private
Rosheur, David, drummer
Ross, George T., lieutenant-colonel
Ross, Nimrod, private
Ross, Walter R., quartermaster sergeant
Row, James, private
Rudder, David, private
Rule, William, private
Rushing, William, private
Russ, Sylvester, private
Russell, Ervin, private
Russell, John, private
Russell, William, private
Russom, Malchiah, private
Russom, Wilson, private
Ryals, Archibald, private
Ryan, Edmond, private
Ryan, Michael, private
Sage, Nathan, private
Sails, William, private
Salters, Jacob, private
Saltgiver, Andrew, private
Salvage, Benjamin F., first lieutenant
Sanders, William D., corporal
Sands, John B., private
Sansom, William, corporal

Sarber, Jacob, private
Sarter, George, private
Savell, Moses, corporal
Saxon, Charles, private
Saxon, John, private
Scanlon, Patrick, private
Scealy, Gideon, corporal
Schacht, John G., sergeant
Schecho, Alexander, musician
Scolfield, Jessee, private
Scott, Abraham M., captain
Scott, James F., sergeant
Scott, Thomas, private
Scotthorn, Nathaniel, private
Scruggs, Edward H., corporal
Scruggs, Richard W., private
Sermans, Edward, private
Shafer, John, private
Shane, Offe, private
Shane, Teddy, private
Shanover, John, private
Sharp, Samuel, private
Shaw, James, private
Shaw, Zacharias, fifer
Shepherd, David, musician
Sheridan, Thomas, private
Sheridan, William, private
Shilling, Abraham, private
Shipton, Peter, private
Shopshire, William, private
Short, Eli, private
Short, James, private
Short, John, corporal
Short, Michael, private
Shuffield, Joshua, drummer
Shuffield, Stephen, private
Shuffield, William, sergeant
Shull, John, private
Shults, John, private
Sibert, John, corporal
Sillcox, John, private
Silva, Antonio, private
Simmons, James, private
Simmons, Jonathan, private
Simmons, Stephen, musician
Simms, Peyton, private

Simpson, Charles, private
Simpson, John, corporal
Sims, Elias, private
Slater, William, private
Smiley, Archibald, private
Smith, George, drummer
Smith, John, private
Smith, John, private
Smith, Neal, private
Smith, Rees, corporal
Smith, Richard L., sergeant
Smith, Thomas, private
Smith, Whitmal, sergeant
Smith, William, private
Smith, William, Private
Smoot, Benjamin S., captain
Snead, William H., private
Snyder, John, private
Songquest, Jacob, private
Sorrels, Walter, private
Southard, Joseph, private
Spence, Richard, private
Spikes, Jonas, private
Stanley, Jordan, sergeant
Stark, Christopher, private
Stean, James, private
Stean, Newberry, private
Sted, Benjamin, private
Steele, Robert, sergeant
Steers, Edward, sergeant
Steers, James, private
Steers, William, corporal
Stephens, Hugh, private
Stephens, James, private
Stephens, John, private
Stephenson, Isaac, private
Stephenson, Jonathan, private
Stevens, William, private
Stewart, James, private
Stewart, Norman, private
Stewart, Robert, private
Stewart, Thomas, private
Sticker, John, private
Stinson, Burrell, private
Stocker, James S., Corporal
Stoker, William, private

Stowell, Abel, private
Stowell, Benjamin, ensign
Stricker, John, private
Stringer, William, private
Strong, Cyprian, sergeant
Strother, French H., corporal
Stroud, James, private
Sturney, Peter, private
Sullivan, Daniel, private
Sullivan, Daniel, private
Swan, Robert, ensign
Swatzfelter, Adam, private
Swetland, Daniel, private
Swigley, James, private
Talbert, Lewis, private
Tarver, Jonathan, private
Taylor, Benjamin, private
Taylor, Isom, private
Taylor, John F., sergeant
Taylor, John T., sergeant
Taylor, Joseph, private
Thomas, Henry, private
Thomas, Joseph, private
Thomas, William, private
Thompson, James, ensign
Thompson, James C., private
Thompson, John, private
Thompson, Thomas, private
Thornton, John, private
Thornton, Michael, private
Thornton, Mitchell, private
Thrasher, Samuel, private
Tilley, Josiah, private
Tinnin, Alexander, private
Tinnin, Asa, private
Tinnin, William, private
Tolbert, John, private
Tomlinson, Arthur, private
Trent, Henry, private
Trinary, John, private
Trowbridge, John, corporal
Tudeck, Joseph, private
Tuley, John, private
Turner, Joseph, private
Turner, Larkin, private
Turney, George, private

Mississippi Territory in War of 1812—Rowland. 187

Turner, John, private
Turney, Peter, private
Tysch, Jordan, corporal
Upton, John, private
Urich, John, private
Ussery, Richard, private
Vanesse, Jacob, private
Vantine, John C., private
Varner, John, corporal
Vashinder, James, private
Vaughn, John, private
Vaughn, Reuben, private
Vaughn, Thomas C., ensign
Verdon, Godfrey, private
Villiers, Gilbert, private
Vining, John, private
Vintner, John, private
Vinzant, Berry, private
Voials, Benjamin, private
Wade, Henry, private
Wadsworth, Theodore, private
Waggoner, Joseph, corporal
Waid, John, private
Walker, Alexander, private
Walker, Andrew, private
Walker, John, private
Wallace, David, private
Wallace, James, private
Wallace, Oliver, private
Walters, John, private
Waltman, Valentine, private
Ward, John C., private
Warner, John D., private
Washam, Jeremiah, private
Washburn, Henry, private
Watkins, David, sergeant
Watson, John, private
Weaks, William P., private
Weaver, Benjamin H., private
Weaver, Christopher, private
Webb, Thomas, private
Weed, John, private
Weekley, Beford, private
Welch, George, private
Welch, John, sergeant
Welch, John V., private

Wells, Archelaus, captain
Wells, Charles, corporal
Wells, Robert B., private
Wells, William B., private
Welsh, James, private
Wentworth, Stephen, private
West, Aquilla H., sergeant
Wheeler, Joseph, private
Whitaker, Abraham, private
White, James, private
White, James M., private
White, John, private
White, John, private
White, William, private
Whitemore, Nicholas, private
Whitmore, William, private
Whitworth, Abraham, private
Wight, John M., sergeant
Wilcox, Benjamin, private
Wiley, Thomas, private
Wilkinson, John, sergeant
Wilkinson, Thomas, private
Williams, Bird, private
Williams, Isham, private
Williams, Henry, private
Williams, Herron, private
Williams, Jacob, sergeant
Williams, John, corporal
Williams, John, private
Williams, John, private
Williams, John R., corporal
Williams, Jonathan, private
Williams, Stephen, private
Williamson, James, drum major
Willis, Reason, private
Wilson, Benjamin, private
Wilson, James, private
Wilson, Matthew, private
Wilson, Samuel, private
Wilson, William, sergeant
Windham, Samuel, private
Wingate, Martin, private
Witherington, Gabriel, private
Wood, John, private
Woods, John, private
Wooley, Stephen, private

Wooten, William, private
Wooton, Daniel, private
Wright, John, private
Wright, William H., sergeant

Yancey, Thomas, corporal
Yokum, Allen, private
Young, George, private
Young, Henry, private

6TH REGIMENT (1814-1815) OF MISSISSIPPI MILITIA

Anderson, Allen, private
Bass, Alexander, private
Beard, John, private
Berry, Thomas, sergeant
Bowling, John, private
Boyakin, Kinchen, private
Boyakin, William, private
Brady, Samuel, private
Brown, Ardin, private
Brown, Edward, private
Brown, James, private
Bryant, Lewis, private
Callahan, James, private
Carr, Henry, private
Childress, David, private
Chronister, Matthias, private
Cody, John, private
Coker, Bryant, private
Coleman, Philip, private
Coulson, Samuel, private
Cox, Collin, private
Cox, George, private
Cox, Thomas, private
Crane, Mayfield, private
Curry, John, private
Dawkins, Silas, private
Dew, Perry, private
Farley, Elihu, private
Fox, John, private
Gaines, William, private
Galbraith, Nevin, private
Gandy, Edmund, private
Gaston, Ebenezer, private
Graham, William, private
Hailey, John, private
Hailey, Richard, private
Hall, William, private
Hanes, John, Jr., private
Harrison, Samuel, private
Hays, John, sergeant

Heard, Bailey, captain
Henry, Claiborne, corporal
Howell, Joseph, private
James, Edward B., private
James, Henry, private
Jarvis, Joseph, armourer
Joiner, James, private
Jones, Thomas, private
Keel, William, private
Landrum, William, private
Lefoy, James, private
Lefoy, Matthew, private
Lyon, Spencer, private
May, David, private
May, Robert, private
McCrae, Christopher, corporal
McDowell, William; private
McLeod, Alexander, first lieutenant
McMillen, William, musician
McNeice, John, private
Moseley, John T., private
Pearson, John, private
Perkins, William, private
Philips, Iredel L., corporal
Philips, Isham, first sergeant
Philips, John, private
Philips, Ransom, musician
Philips, Richard L., private
Philips, Thomas, private
Pollard, Joseph, sergeant
Potter, Robert D., third lieutenant
Rankins, James, private
Rankins, John K., corporal
Reed, John, private
Reeves, Eli, private
Robertson, Aaron, private
Rollins, Isaac, private
Ross, Nathaniel, private
Russell, Irvine, private
Saterthite, Samuel, private

Mississippi Territory in War of 1812—Rowland. 189

Sauserman, John, private
Smith, Thomas, private
Sneed, William, private
Stanley, Jordan, private
Stephens, John, private
Sterrett, Ralph, second lieutenant
Stone, Samuel, private
Syms, James, private
Tanner, John, private
Taylor, James, private
Thompson, James C., private
Tilley, Josiah, private
Tinnin, William, private

Turner, John, private
Upton, John, private
Walker, Andrew, private
Walker, Felix, private
Walker, John, private
Wamuck, Francis, private
Wamuch, Jesse, private
Wells, Byas, private
Wells, Thomas, private
West, Aquila H., sergeant
Williams, Joshua, ensign
Williams, Stephen, private

7TH REGIMENT (PERKINS' BATTALION) OF MISSISSIPPI MILITIA

Captain Joseph Acklen's Company
Captain Peter Barnett's Company
Captain Samuel Bullen's Company
Captain James Burleson's Company
Captain Thomas Eldridge's Company
Captain James Grafton's Company
Captain Jonathan Gray's Company
Captain James Hamilton's Company
Captain William Johnston's Company
Captain Elisha F. King's Company
Captain James Neelley's Company
Captain John T. Rather's Company
Captain Abraham Roberts' Company

Abanathy, David, private
Acklin, Joseph, captain
Adair, William, private
Adams, Francis, corporal
Adams, James, private
Adams, John, private
Adams, Robert, private
Adare, John, private
Aday, Booz, private
Aday, John, private
Adkins, James S., private
Agin, William, private
Alexander, Jourdon, private
Alexander, Mathew, private
Alford, David, sergeant
Allen, Alexander, private
Allen, Eli, private
Allen, Philip, private

Allen, William, private
Allison, James, private
Allison, William, private
Alman, John, corporal
Anderson, Daniel D., private
Anderson, James, sergeant
Anderson, Solomon, private
Anderson, William, private
Applewhite, Thomas, corporal
Arbough, Jacob, sergeant
Ard, Abraham, sergeant
Ard, James, first lieutenant
Ashbarn, Lewis, private
Ashborn, Aden, private
Ashburn, Andrew, private
Ashburn, Bird, private
Ashworth, John, private
Aswell, Solomon, private

190

Atkins, Thomas, corporal
Atkinson, John, private
Atkinson, Littleton S., second lieutenant
Auyan, John, private
Avertegas, Charles, private
Bailey, Zachariah, private
Baily, David, corporal
Baird, William L., private
Baldridge, Francis, private
Ballew, David, second lieutenant
Barber, Samuel, private
Barefield, Roger, private
Barnel, Joel, private
Barnet, Amos, corporal
Barnett, Peter, captain
Bass, Frederick, private
Bayless, Hezekiah, private
Beard, Samuel, private
Belcher, Branch, private
Bell, Elijah, private
Bell, Francis, private
Bell, James H., second lieutenant
Bell, Thomas, private
Bennet, John, private
Bernard, William, private
Berry, Robert, first sergeant
Berry, Young, sergeant
Beysore, John, private
Biggs, David, corporal
Bilbo, William R., private
Birdwell, George M., corporal
Birmingham, Hugh, private
Black, Alexander, private
Black, Hambright, private
Black, William, ensign
Blackburn, John W., private
Blackman, Lewis, lieutenant
Blackman, Samuel, private
Blair, Andrew, private
Blalock, Jeramiah, private
Blankenship, Calip, private
Blankenship, William, private
Block, George, private
Bly, John, private
Blythe, John, private
Boils, William, private
Boling, Wylie, sergeant

Boren, Mordecai, private
Borsby, Reaves, private
Bosheart, David, private
Bosli, John, private
Boyd, William, private
Bradley, Bradford, corporal
Bradley, John M., private
Bradshaw, Robert, private
Briley, Joseph, private
Britton, James, private
Brooks, John, private
Brooksher, —— —— ——, private
Brown, Elijah, corporal
Brown, James, private
Brown, John Jr., private
Brown, John, Sr., private
Brown, William, private
Bruin, Peter, corporal
Bryant, Robert, private
Bullen, Samuel, captain
Bullick, James B., corporal
Bunch, John, ensign
Burks, Jeremiah, private
Burks, Rowland, private
Burks, Samuel, private
Burleson, Aaron, private
Burlison, Edward, private
Burlison, James, captain
Burlison, James, Jr., private
Burlison, Jonathan, ensign-lieutenant
Burlison, Jonathan, Sr., private
Burlison, Joseph, Jr., private
Burlison, Joseph, Sr., private
Butler, Samuel, private
Butler, Thomas, private
Byram, Ebenezer, first lieutenant
Byrd, Charles, private
Byrd, John, private
Cabaniss, Charles, private
Calvert, Joseph, private
Calvert, William, private
Campbell, Adam, private
Campbell, Daniel, private
Cannady, Josephus, private
Cannimore, Abram, private
Cannimore, David, private
Carnes, Thomas, private

Mississippi Territory in War of 1812—Rowland. 191

Carothers, Robert, private
Carpenter, Owin, private
Carpenter, Solomon, sergeant
Carrell, Joseph, corporal
Carroll, Benjamin, private
Carroll, Luke, private
Carson, Andrew, private
Carter, Matia, private
Carter, William, private
Cary, James, private
Castelan, John, private
Caston, Green G., second lieutenant
Catterson, Patrick, private
Cawley, Jacob, private
Chambers, James, corporal
Chambers, John, ensign
Chambliss, William R., first lieutenant
Chetum, Thomas R., sergeant
Childers, Elisha, private
Childers, Jesse, private
Childers, William, private
Childres, James, ensign
Childres, Lewis, private
Christain, Allen, private
Cissna, Charles, private
Clark, Archibald, private
Clark, James, private
Clark, John, private
Clect, John, first sergeant
Clemm, David, private
Clemm, Mason, private
Clements, Edward, lieutenant
Cleveland, Edward, corporal
Clifton, Alexander, sergeant
Clonch, Love, private
Cloud, Joseph, private
Clounch, John, private
Cloyd, James, private
Cloyd, Samuel, private
Coatney, Jonathan, private
Cobb, Briant, sergeant
Cobb, James, private
Cobb, Stancil, sergeant
Cockram, Burl, private
Coil, James, private
Coil, Samuel, private
Cole, Stewart, sergeant

Coleman, Noah, private
Coleman, Richard, private
Coleman, Samuel, sergeant
Coley, Zachariah, private
Conley, Thomas, private
Cook, Tyre, private
Coolman, George, private
Cooper, Benjamin, private
Cooper, John, private
Cooper, William, private
Corbitt, Walter, private
Corps, George, corporal
Cotten, Peter I., private
Cotton, James, sergeant
Couch, Thomas, lieutenant
Coursey, William, private
Coward, Hardy, private
Cowin, John, corporal
Cox, Moses, private
Craft, Frederick, private
Craft, James, private
Craiger, John, private
Craker, Abraham, private
Craker, John, private
Craton, George W., private
Crisp, Reden, private
Crossley, George, private
Crothers, William, private
Crouch, David, private
Crouser, Richard, private
Crowley, William, private
Crowson, David, private
Crowson, William, private
Cruise, Henry, private
Culwell, Absolum, private
Cuningham, James, private
Cunningham, John, sergeant
Cup, John, corporal
Currie, John, private
Curtis, Reuben, corporal
Cutler, Robert, sergeant
Dailey, Alexander, private
Dailey, Joseph, corporal
Daniel, Anderson, private
Daugherty, William, sergeant
Daughtry, Briant, private
Davidson, Andrew, private

Davis, Elijah, private
Davis, James, private
Davis, John, private
Davis, John J., sergeant
Davis, Samuel, third lieutenant
Davis, William, sergeant
Day, Jonathan, private
Debo, Stephen, ensign
Delasmeat, John, private
Denman, James, private
Dennison, Joseph, private
Derrick, Adam, private
Derrick, Simon, private
Derrick, Tobias, private
Dick, — — — —, waiter
Dobbs, William, private
Doherty, Joseph, private
Donaho, William, private
Dorsey, Richard, corporal
Dowling, Charles, private
Downsy, Robert, private
Dredden, Jonathan, private
Drewer, Antonia, private
Dugan, Samuel, private
Dupee, Thomas, corporal
Dutton, Jerrod, private
Earl, William, sergeant
Easley, Charles, private
Easley, Joseph, private
East, David, private
East, Jesse, private
Eckford, John, private
Edwards, Clarkston, private
Edwards, James, private
Edwards, Joseph, private
Edwards, Nathan, private
Elder, Andrew, private
Elder, Samuel, private
Eldridge, John R. B., first sergeant
Eldridge, Thomas, captain
Elliot, Andrew, private
Elliot, William, private
Elliot, Willis, private
Elliott, John, sergeant
Elliotte, Amos, private
Ellison, Isaac, private
Ellison, Thomas, private
Ellison, William, private
Enceminger, Samuel, private
Erwood, William, private
Ethridge, Samuel, private
Ethridge, William, private
Evans, Andrew B., private
Evans, Joseph, private
Evans, Nathaniel, private
Evans, Thomas, sergeant
Fairbanks, Benjamin, corporal
Farr, Robert, private
Farr, Thomas, private
Felder, David, ensign
Fellow, Henry G., private
Ferguson, Joseph, private
Ferrell, James, private
Ferrell, John, private
Finch, John, private
Fine, William, sergeant
Finton, Matthew, private
Flanigan, William, private
Fleming, William, private
Flippo, William, private
Forgerson, James, private
Forgett, William, private
Forrest, William, private
Foster, John, private
Fowler, Thomas, private
Frizby, Daniel, private
Fry, Solomon, private
Gage, Richmond, private
Gaither, James, private
Gaither, Thomas, private
Gamble, James, private
Gamble, William, private
Gardner, Isaac, private
Gardner, John, private
Garlington, Edwin, private
Garlington, James, private
Garner, John, private
Gassfort, Stephen, private
Gatlett, Mitchell, private
Gaugue, Aaron, private
Gaugue, John, private
Geron, Solomon, sergeant

Gibson, John, private
Gilbert, John, private
Gill, Thomas, private
Gillen, John, private
Ginn, Jesse, private
Girtman, Bartholmew, private
Glasscock, Elijah, private
Goff, William, private
Goodsen, Benjamin, private
Goodson, David, private
Goodson, James, corporal
Goosean, Charles, private
Gorden, Thomas, private
Gordon, James, corporal
Gordon, John M., corporal
Grafton, James, captain
Graham, Charles, private
Graham, George, quartermaster sergeant
Grant, Thomas, private
Graves, Thomas, private
Gravet, Jesse, private
Gray, David, corporal
Gray, Jonathan, captain
Grayham, John, private
Grayham, Nimrod, private
Grayson, Lewis, private
Grayson, Robert, private
Green, Berry, sergeant
Green, James, private
Green, Jesse, private
Green, John, private
Green, Rubin, private
Griffeth, Isaac, corporal
Griffin, Person B., sergeant
Griffith, Abner, private
Groomes, Isaac, private
Groomes, Richard, private
Guarrinan, John, sergeant
Guice, Absalom, private
Gullet, Richard, private
Gunnels, Joseph, private
Gwin, Arthur, private
Hadden, Thomas, private
Hadon, William, private
Ham, Harvil, private

Hambrick, Joseph, private
Hamilton, James, captain
Hamner, Turner, private
Hanigan, William, private
Hannah, James, private
Hannah, John, private
Harbeson, John S., private
Hargrove, Andrew, private
Harkness, Richard, private
Harlin, James, private
Harper, James, private
Harrington, Hudson, private
Harris, William, private
Hart, William, private
Hastings, Robert, private
Hathorn, William D., private
Havard, Thomas, private
Havenor, William, ensign
Havis, Thomas, second lieutenant
Hays, John, second sergeant
Head, Abram, private
Heart, Warren, private
Hemby, James, private
Hendrick, Aron, private
Henry, John, private
Henson, John, corporal
Herrald, James, private
Herron, Jacob, private
Herron, Samuel, private
Hicklin, Robert, private
Hicks, John, private
Hicks, Richard, private
Hill, Bardwell, private
Hill, Eligah, private
Hill, John, private
Hill, Thomas, private
Hill, William, private
Hillard, James, corporal
Hillebrand, Phillip, private
Hilton, John, private
Hinds, Biram, second lieutenant
Hines, Benjamin, private
Hixon, Daniel, private
Hoakes, Samuel, private
Hobson, John M., private
Hodge, Hezekiah, private

Hodge, James, corporal
Hodges, Fleman, private
Hodges, Joshua, ensign
Hodges, Seth, corporal
Holland, Absalom, corporal
Holland, Charles M., corporal
Holland, Tilman, private
Hollaway, John B., sergeant
Holmark, George, first sergeant
Holmes, James, private
Holt, William, private
Honey, Thomas, private
Horn, Harmon, private
Horton, Thomas, private
Hosea, John, private
Hudson, Howel, private
Hudson, Peter B., private
Hughes, James, corporal
Hughes, Joseph, private
Humphrey, William, private
Humphreys, Lewis, private
Hunt, William R., third corporal
Hurlong, Jacob, private
Huston, Archible, private
Huston, James, private
Ice, Frederick, private
Ice, Thomas, private
Ilix, John, private
Inman, Ezekiel, private
Irby, John, private
Irwin, James, second lieutenant
Irwin, James, private
Irwin, William, private
Isaac, ————, private waiter
Jack, ————, servant
Jack, John, private
Jackson, Henry, private
Jackson, Hyram, private
Jacobs, Silas, corporal
Jarlinton, Edwin, private
Jenkins, James, private
Jobe, Nathan, private
John, ————, private waiter
Johns, James, private
Johnson, Luke, private
Johnson, William, private

Johnston, Blassingham, private
Johnston, Solomon, private
Johnston, William, captain
Jones, Frederick, private
Jones, George, private
Jones, Hardin, corporal
Jones, Henry, private
Jones, Jacob, fifer
Jones, John, private
Jones, Stephen, private
Jones, William B., private
Jordan, John, corporal
Jordon, Anthony, private
Jordon, James, private
Jordon, Jesse, private
Kanemore, Jesse, private
Kavenor, William, first ensign
Keen, David, private
Keeth, David, private
Kelly, Joseph, private
Kelly, William, private
Kemp, Thomas, private
Kenedy, Henry, private
Kennedy, Martin, private
Kennemore, John, private
Kennemore, Stephen, private
Key, Henry, private
Killingsworth, Henry, private
Killingsworth, John, private
King, Elisha F., captain
King, George, third lieutenant
King, George R., corporal
King, Henry, first lieutenant
King, James, private
King, John, sergeant
Kirklin, Phemas, private
Kirkpatrick, Edward, private
Knight, Andrew, private
Koon, William, musician
Lacey, Bowlin, private
Lamberson, John, private
Lancaster, Edward, private
Langford, David, sergeant
Langham, Samuel, sergeant
Langham, Solomon, private
Lark, Joseph, private

Mississippi Territory in War of 1812—Rowland. 195

Lasiter, Jacob, sergeant
Lassley, John, private
Law, Wyatt, private
Lawler, Eli, private
Lawler, Isaac, private
Lawler, John, sergeant
Lawrence, Elisha, private
Lawrence, Jacob, private
Lay, James, corporal
Lay, William, private
Lazrus, William, private
Ledbetter, Daniel, private
Ledbetter, Ephraim, private
Ledbetter, Joseph, private
Lee, Abel, private
Lee, Gershorn, private
Lee, Robert, private
Leedy, Henry, private
Legget, James, private
Legran, Malechi, private
Lewis, Charles A., private
Lewis, Enuch, private
Lewis, Isham, private
Lewis, Joshua, private
Lewis, William, private
Light, George, private
Linch, William, sergeant
Linder, Lewis, sergeant
Lindsey, John, corporal
Lindsey, Thomas, private
Lindzey, Elijah, private
Linzey, James, private
Lloyd, John, private
Long, John, corporal
Love, John, private
Love, William, private
Lowry, Edward, private
Loy, George, corporal
Lucus, John, private
Luker, Joshua, private
Luisk, John H., private
Luster, James, private
Luster, John, private
Luttrell, Vincent, private
Lynch, Timothy, private
Lyming, Joel, private

Lynn, John, private
Mackey, Jonathan, private
Mackey, David, private
Macoy, John, private
Magers, Isaac, private
Mahan, William, private
Malone, John, corporal
Malone, Solomon, sergeant
Malone, William, second sergeant
Mannan, James, private
Mansin, Nathaniel, private
Marshall, Lewis, private
Marshall, Thomas, private
Martin, Jeremiah, corporal
Martin, John, private
Martin, Nathan, private
Martin, Richard, private
Mathews, George, private
Mathis, Azor, private
Maxville, James, sergeant
Maxwell, David, private
Maxwell, James, private
May, David, private
May, John, private
May, Patrick, lieutenant
McAnulty, John, private
McBride, Dugal, private
McBroom, Thomas, private
McCall, Duncan, private
McCartney, Andrew, private
McCartney, Robert, private
McCartney, William, private
McCay, John, private
McClorg, Samuel, private
McCormic, Rody, private
McCulley, Andrew, private
McCutchen, Joshua, private
McDonald, William, private
McDowell, William, private
McDuffee, George, private
McFerrin, William, private
McGahey, James, private
McGawen, William, private
McGinty, Reuben, private
McGlamery, Loven, private
McKamey, James, private

McKinney, Isaac, private
McKinney, Robert, private
McKinsey, Alexander, private
McKinsey, John, private
McKneely, George, private
McLary, William, private
McLendon, James, private
McLeymore, Presley, private
McLin, Alexander, first sergeant
McMahan, William, corporal
McMahon, William, private
MaMane, Charles, private
McMurtery, John, private
McNease, Samuel, private
McWhorter, Benjamin, private
McWhorter, Cyrus, sergeant
McWhorter, Hance, private
McWilliams, Andrew, private
McWilliams, William, private
Meaux, Richard, sergeant
Medford, Jonathan, private
Megahha, Robert, private
Metcalf, Edward, private
Miller, George, private
Miller, James, private
Miller, Joseph, private
Miller, Martin, private
Miller, Moses, private
Milton, Henry, private
Minix, Samuel, private
Minor, John, private
Minton, Joshua, private
Mitchell, John, private
Montgomery, Hugh, private
Montgomery, John, private
Moon, John, private
Moon, John, Jr., private
Moon, Samuel, private
Moone, Nathaniel, private
Moore, James, private
Moore, Jeffries H., first lieutenant
Moore, John, private
Moore, Joseph, private
Moore, William C., sergeant
Mooreland, William, private
Morgan, Harbert, private

Morgan, Luther, private
Morris, Edmond, private
Morrow, James S., sergeant
Mowery, John, corporal
Mullins, James, private
Mullins, William, private
Murphey, Samuel, private
Murphy, George, private
Murphy, Vincent, private
Murry, John, private
Murry, John, private
Myers, George C., private
Nail, Andrew, drummer
Neal, David, corporal
Neel, John, private
Neelley, James, captain
Neely, Thomas, corporal
Nelson, James, private
Nelson, Thomas, private
Nesmith, Thomas H., private
Nichols, James, private
Nichols, Simon, private
Nicholson, John, private
Nicholson, Wesley, private
Nixon, Uriah, private
Noblin, William, private
Norwood, Richard, private
Odum, Parker, private
O'Neal, Mitchel, private
Ooten, Jeremiah, private
Orr, James, third lieutenant
Osbury, John, private
Ostean, Thomas, private
Owen, Ezekiel, first lieutenant
Owens, David, private
Owings, Calep, sergeant
Pace, Isham, private
Pace, William, private
Page, Lewis, ensign
Parker, David, private
Parker, Isaac, private
Parker, Isom, private
Parker, John, private
Parker, Joseph, private
Parris, Francisco, private
Paterson, Anejust, private

Paterson, Dunson, private
Patrick, Jackson, private
Patterson, Josiah, private
Patterson, Leonard, sergeant
Patterson, William private
Patton, William, private
Payne, Martin, private
Pearce, Joel, private
Peavey, Wade H., private
Pence, John, private
Perkins, Peter, lieutenant-colonel
Person, William, private
Peter, — — — —, waiter
Peterson, David, private
Pettis, John, private
Peyatt, Samuel, private
Phillips, Jeremiah, private
Pickett, Lewis, private
Pike, Jacob, private
Pilaut, William, private
Pirvis, John, private
Pittard, Abner, private
Pittman, Hiram, private
Pittman, John, private
Pool, William, private
Poole, Adam, corporal
Poole, David, private
Porikett, Jacob, private
Porter, John, private
Porter, John C., private
Postell, Edward, corporal
Potts, George, private
Powell, Joseph, ensign
Powell, William, private
Prestidge, Samuel, private
Provance, John, private
Province, Thomas, private
Purden, James R., private
Qarons, Thomas, private
Quine, Elemuel, corporal
Raborn, Mark, private
Ragan, Benjamin, private
Ragen, John, private
Ragsdale, William, private
Raimer, Adam, corporal
Rainbolt, Elisha, private

Rains, Stephen, private
Rather, John T., captain
Ratliff, John, private
Ray, Martin, first sergeant
Ray, Samuel, private
Read, C. N., surgeon
Read, John, private
Redden, Elemuel, private
Renno, Lewis, sergeant
Reter, Hezekiah, private
Reynolds, John H., private
Reynolds, Thomas, private
Rhea, Samuel, private
Rhodes, Hazel, private
Rice, Aron, corporal
Rice, Daniel, private
Rice, Joel L., private
Rice, John, private
Rice, Joseph, corporal
Rice, Spencer, private
Rife, William, private
Right, Richard, M., private
Roach, William, private
Roades, John, private
Roberts, Abraham, captain
Roberts, Daniel, private
Roberts, Isaac, private
Roberts, Joab, private
Roberts, John, private
Robertson, George, private
Robertson, Joseph, third lieutenant
Robertson, William, private
Robinett, William C., private
Robinson, Eli, third lieutenant
Robinson, John, private
Robinson, William, private
Roche, John H., private
Rochell, John, private
Rodgers, George, private
Rodgers, John, private
Rodgers, Reuben, corporal
Rogers, James, private
Rogers, Robert, private
Roland, Thomas, private
Roller, Jacob, private
Roller, John, private

Rolls, Claudius, private
Romedus, Joseph, private
Ross, Ely K., major
Rotine, Isaiah, private
Rountree, Seborn, first sergeant
Rupe, William, private
Rush, Elijah, private
Rush, Joseph, private
Russell, George, sergeant
Sailing, Henry, private
Sailing, William, private
Sam, — — — —, waiter
Sandell, Daniel, private
Saxon, John, private
Scarborough, Allen, private
Scarborough, David, private
Scaton, Samuel, private
Scaton, William, private
Sceal, Anthony, private
Sceal, Bluford, private
Scism, John, private
Scott, Thomas, private
Scott, William F., private
Sears, John, private
Seaton, John, private
Sebott, Lewis, private
Self, William, private
Sellars, Silas, corporal
Sellers, John, private
Sells, William, private
Selser, Isaac N., sergeant major
Sevier, John, sergeant
Shankle, Abraham, private
Sharp, Archer, private
Sharp, Joseph, private
Shaw, Thompson, B., private
Shell, Jacob, private
Shelton, Stephen, private
Sherkey, Allen, corporal
Shields, Jonathan, private
Shoemaker, James, private
Shott, Caleb, private
Simmons, John, private
Simmons, Jonathan, private
Simpson, William, private
Sims, Josiah, private
Sims, Michael, private
Sims, Samuel, private
Sively, Jessy, private
Sively, John, private
Skinner, Samuel, private
Smalling, Robert, private
Smith, Ambrose, private
Smith, James H., private
Smith, John A., private
Smith, Lewis, private
Smith, Pliny, private
Smith, Richard, private
Smith, Whitmal, private
Smith, William, private
Smith, William, private
Smith, William H., private
Smylie, Andrew, private
Snall, William, private
Snow, John, sergeant
Sorrels, Allen, corporal
Sorrels, Samuel, sergeant
Spigel, David, private
Springer, John, private
Spurlock, David, private
Standlee, Thomas, private
Steegar, Edward, private
Stephens, Isaac, private
Steward, David, private
Stewart, William, private
Stone, Eli, private
Stone, Frederick P., private
Stone, Jesse, private
Storton, Jonathan, private
Strain, Thomas, private
Street, William, corporal
Stringfellow, James, private
Sullivan, Daniel, private
Swaney, Edmund A., private
Tackett, George, private
Tapley, Evan, private
Tatum, John, sergeant
Taylor, Argyle, first lieutenant
Taylor, Brice, private
Taylor, Charles, private
Taylor, Hardin, private
Taylor, Joel, private

Taylor, Larkin, private
Temples, Loyd, private
Templeton, George, private
Terrell, Hiram, sergeant
Thomas, Charles, private
Thomas, John, private
Thompson, Alcemene, private
Thompson, Coleman, corporal
Thompson, John L., ensign
Thompson, Shem, third lieutenant
Thompson, William, private
Thorn, Presly, private
Thornton, Martin, private
Thresher, Robert, sergeant
Thurston, James, private
Tiegue, William, private
Tinder, Abel, private
Tipton, Jacob, private
Tipton, Samuel, private
Tipton, Shedrick, private
Todd, James, private
Towd, James, private
Treadwell, Reuben, private
Trentham, Robert, private
Trepho, Michael, private
Trimble, Archibald, private
Trimble, John, private
Trimble, Moses, private
Trotmon, Samuel, private
Trotmon, William, private
Trux, George, private
Tucker, John, private
Tucker, William, private
Tullis, James, private
Turnay, Felix, private
Turnbow, Jacob, private
Turnbow, Robert, private
Turner, Donaldson F., private
Turner, Sugars, private
Turner, William, private
Turvin, Richard, private
Tweedy, Thomas, private
Tyrone, Adam, private
Tyrone, John, private
Vance, Samuel, sergeant
Vance, William, private

Vandaver, Hollingsworth, private
Vanic, Joshua, private
Vanic, Levin, private
Vonoy, John, private
Vaughan, Robert, private
Vaughn, Benjamin, private
Vaughn, Melkigah, private
Vaughn, Minoah, private
Vaughn, William, private
Vickory, Aaron, private
Vincent, Amos, sergeant
Vining, John, sergeant
Vinzant, Berry, private
Waddy, Samuel, first lieutenant
Wainwright, John, private
Walker, James B., sergeant
Wall, Daniel, private
Wallace, Joel, private
Wallis, Joel, private
Wallis, Nazara, private
Wallis, Thomas, private
Ward, Jonathan, private
Wardlow, Alexander, private
Warford, Benjamin, private
Warner, Archibald, private
Waters, John, private
Waters, Joseph, private
Waters, Samuel, private
Waters, Tilman, private
Watson, William, private
Weaver, Daniel, private
Weaver, Elijah, second lieutenant
Webb, Jacob, private
Wells, Benjamin B., private
Wells, George, private
Wentsworth, Stephen, private
Wetherel, Theophilus, private
Wheat, Hezekiah, private
Wheat, Joseph, private
Wheeler, Joseph, private
White, Isaiah, private
Whitiker, Abraham, private
Whitour, Joshua, private
Whittington, John, private
Wilcox, James, private
Wilkinson, Stephen, private

Willborn, James, private
Williams, Bazil, private
Williams, Henry, private
Wilmouth, David, private
Wilson, John, private
Wilson, Samuel, private
Windham, Thomson, private
Windham, William, private
Wingfield, Austin, private
Winsted, William, private
Winston, William H., adjutant
Winters, Daniel, private
Wise, Nathan, private
Witherington, Gabriel, private
Wood, James B., first lieutenant
Woodall, Thomas, private
Woodard, Jesse, private
Woodburn, James, private
Woods, William, musician
Woods, William B., private
Woodward, John, corporal
Woodward, Thomas, private
Wright, Alexander, sergeant
Wright, John, private
Wright, Robert, private
Wright, William, private
Wright, William, sergeant
Yarborough, Joel, private
Yates, Lewis, private
Yocum, Jesse, private
York, John, private
Young, Daniel, private
Young, Edward, private
Young, Ewing, ensign

13TH REGIMENT (NIXON'S) OF MISSISSIPPI MILITIA

Captain John Bond's Company
Lieutenant William Bond's Company
Captain David Cleveland's Company
Captain Moses Collins' Company
Captain Francis B. Lenoir's Company
Captain James McGowen's Company
Captain James Phillips' Company
Captain Henry Quin's Company
Captain Harmon M. Runnel's Company
Captain William Smith's Company
Captain William Spencer's Company

Addison, Hiram, private
Akin, John, ensign
Alexander, Isaac, private
Allen, Barnabas, sergeant
Allen, Garret, private
Allgood, Wiet, private
Andrews, James, private
Andrews, William, private
Applewhite, Stephen, private
Ard, Thomas, private
Armstrong, Abner, private
Armstrong, Jesse, private
Armstrong, Jonathan, private
Ashton, Henry, private
Askue, Henry, private
Bagley, William, sergeant
Bailey, James, private
Bailey, Thomas, private
Ball, Sampson E., private
Ballard, Lewis, private
Ballard, Nathan, private
Ballard, Reuben, private
Banks, Levi, private
Barksdale, Collier, private
Barret, George, private
Batson, James, private
Batson, Peter, private
Batson, Seth, private
Batson, Thomas, private
Beard, William, private
Beasley, William, private
Becot, Labon, sergeant
Bell, Thomas, private
Berry, James, private

Blue, Angus, sergeant
Blue, Daniel, private
Bond, Gedion, corporal
Bond, Henry, private
Bond, James, private
Bond, John, captain
Bond, Robert, private
Bond, William, lieutenant
Bohannon, Wily, private
Braddy, William, private
Breland, Hillery, sergeant
Brent, Charnel, private
Brent, John, private
Brent, Merideth, ensign
Brent, Thomas, private
Bridges, Sampson, private
Brister, John, private
Brown, Daniel, private
Brown, John, private
Brown, Moses, sergeant
Brown, Robert, private
Buckaloo, John, private
Buckaloo, Richard, private
Buckley, James, private
Bullin, William, private
Bullock, David, private
Bullock, James, private
Bullock, Silas, private
Burge, Nathaniel, private
Burge, Washington, private
Burns, Reason, sergeant
Butler, Luke, private
Cagle, John, private
Calbert, Richmon, private
Canady, Nathen, private
Carpenter, John, private
Carpenter, William, private
Carson, John, Jr., private
Carson, John, Sr., private
Carter, Allen, private
Carter, Burrel, sergeant
Carter, George, private
Carter, Hardy, private
Carter, Marcus, E., corporal
Carter, Michael, private
Carter, William, lieutenant
Catching, Jonathan, private

Catching, Joseph, corporal
Catching, Philip, private
Chesnut, David, private
Cleveland, David, captain
Clower, Daniel, private
Clower, John, private
Coats, Pollard H., private
Collins, Joshua, private
Collins, Moses, captain
Collins, Seabourn, private
Cook, Green, private
Cook, Green B., private
Cook, Matthew, private
Cooper, Hambleton, private
Cooper, John, private
Cooper, John, private
Cooper, Joseph, private
Cooper, William, private
Cooper, William, private
Coore, John, corporal
Cossey, Solomon, private
Cothin, Asea, private
Crawford, William, sergeant
Croft, Jesse, private
Cutrer, John, private
Danaway, Joseph, private
Davis, I. W., sergeant major
Davis, John, private
Davis, Samuel, corporal
Davis, Zacheus, corporal
Day, James, private
Deer, John, private
Denman, Joel, private
Denman, Thomas, private
Dickerson, Caleb, private
Dickerson, John, private
Dickerson, Thomas, private
Dickson, David, Jr., surgeon
Dillon, Clarkson, private
Dillon, Theophilus, private
Dillon, Willis, trumpeter
Doddle, James, private
Drake, Britain, private
Dukes, Jeptha, private
Dukes, Simmion, sergeant
Dunahoo, Daniel, private
Dunahoo, John, sergeant

Dunahoo, William, private
Dunkley, Richard, private
Dunn, John, private
Edmondson, Amos, private
Elliot, William, private
Elliott, Samuel, private
Ellis, George, private
Ellis, Owen, corporal
Ellis, Stephen, private
Ellis, William, private
Fairchilds, John, private
Fairchilds, Lofton, private
Fatheree, Readen, private
Fatheree, Hilliard, corporal
Fathereee, Levi, ensign
Felder, John, private
Fergerson, Aaron, private
Fergerson, Eli, private
Fergerson, Moses, private
Fielder, William, private
Flippin, Merrit, private
Ford, David, private
Ford, Preserved, private
Foxworth, Stephen, private
Garrel, Horatio, private
Gates, Joshua, private
Ginn, Jeptha, private
Gipson, James, private
Gipson, William, private
Goff, Nathaniel, private
Golman, Bedey, private
Golman, William, corporal
Golman, Young, private
Graham, William, private
Grantham, Daniel, private
Grantham, Matthew, private
Graves, Isaac, private
Graves, James, private
Graves, John, ensign
Green, John, private
Green, John, private
Green, Leonard, private
Hains, Noble W., private
Hall, Wyatt, private
Hambleton, Thomas, sergeant
Harrington, Thomas, private

Harvey, John, Jr., private
Harvey, John W., sergeant
Harvey, Nehemiah, second lieutenant
Harvey, Thomas, private
Harvey, Thomas, Sr., private
Harville, Edward, private
Harvy, Thomas P., private
Heard, Thomas, sergeant
Helton, John, private
Herrington, Hardy, private
Hill, Harty, private
Hollingworth, Isaac, corporal
Holmes, Liberty, private
Honea, Wilks, private
Hoover, Christian, private
Hoover, John, private
Howell, Henry, private
Howell, Samuel, private
Hubert, David, private
Hufman, Daniel, private
Hunly, John, private
Isaacks, Elijah, private
Isaacks, Samuel, private
Isle, William, corporal
Isles, Demsy, private
Jackson, Andrew, private
Jacobs, Walter, private
Jenkins, Allen, private
Jenkins, Davis B., private
John, — — — —, private waiter
Johns, John, private
Johnson, George, sergeant
Johnson, John, private
Jones, Britain, private
Jones, Lewis, private
Jones, Samuel W., private
Jones, Thomas, private
Jones, William C., private
Kinchin, Henry, private
King, David, private
King, James, private
King, Jessee, private
King, John, private
King, John F., private
King, William, private
Kinchen, John, private

Mississippi Territory in War of 1812—Rowland. 203

Kinchen, Mathew, private
Kirkland, Obediah, ensign
Lea, Alexander, private
Lee, James, corporal
Lee, Major, private
Lemmons, James, private
Lenoit, Francis B., captain
Lewis, Arthur, private
Lewis, Britton, private
Lewis, William, private
Lewis, William, private
Loftin, Ezekiel, private
Lott, Abraham, private
Lott, Arthur, Jr., private
Lott, Arthur, Sr., private
Lott, John, Jr., private
Lott, John, Sr., private
Lott, Luke, private
Lott, Nathan, private
Lott, Simon, sergeant
Lott, Solomon, private
Lott, William, Jr., lieutenant
Lott, William, Sr., private
Love, Robert, sergeant
Lovin, Bailey, private
Low, John, private
Lowe, Lunchford, corporal
Lumkins, Hendrick, private
Magee, Daniel, private
Magee, Elisha, private
Magee, Fleet, private
Magee, George, private
Magee, Henry, private
Magee, Jacob, private
Magee, John, private
Magee, John, private
Magee, Nehemiah, private
Magee, Robert, private
Magee, Sire, private
Magee, Solomon, private
Magee, Willis, private
Marshall, Matthew, private
Martin, Aaron, private
Martin, Cornelius, private
Martin, Derrell, private
Martin, William, private

Massey, Benjamin, private
Mathewes, John, private
Mathewis, Shadrach, private
Matthews, Silas, private
May, Benjamin, private
May, Berry, ensign
May, Etheldredge, private
May, Green, private
May, John, private
May, Joseph, private
May, Joseph, private
McAnulty, James, private
McAnulty, Robert, private
McAnulty, William, corporal
McComb, William M., private
McCrary, Matthew, private
McCullie, Benjamin, private
McCullie, James, private
McCullie, Mathew, private
McDaniel, John, private
McElvin, Moses, private
McElvinn, John, private
McGowen, Hugh, private
McGowen, James, captain
McGowen, William, private
McGraw, James, private
McGrew, Alexander, private
McGuffee, Alfred, private
McGuffee, John, major
McKinsey, David, private
McNeal, Hector, private
Merrel, Edmund, private
Merret, Joel, corporal
Mikell, James, private
Mikell, John I., corporal
Mikill, John I. (see John I. Mikell), corporal
Miller, Jacob, private
Minor, John, private
Mitchell, Wright, private
Mixon, Cornelius, corporal
Mixon, John, private
Mixon, William, private
Moke, Andrew, private
More, William, private
Morgan, David, private

Morris, Selathiel, private
Moses, ————, private waiter
Myers, Isaac, private
Netherlin, Levi, private
Netherlin, William, private
Nichols, David, private
Nichols, Noah, private
Nixon, George Henry, lieutenant-colonel
Noble, Levi, lieutenant
Noble, Mark, private
Norman, Hiram, private
Norman, James, private
Norris, Acquilla, private
Oats, John H., private
Odam, William, private
Odum, Richard, private
Oneal, Ransom, private
Peak, Stephen, adjutant
Pelatta, Francis, private
Perkins, Samuel, private
Petty, Presley, private
Phillips, Elias, private
Phillips, James, captain
Phillips, Thompson, private
Pleasant, Washington, corporal
Pope, Benjamin, private
Pope, James, private
Prescott, Michael, private
Prescoat, Nathan, private
Prescoat, Willis, private
Prestredge, Howel, lieutenant
Prestridge, John, private
Prestridge, Robert, private
Prestridge, Samuel, private
Price, Stephen, private
Prichard, William, first lieutenant
Pullin, John, private
Quin, Daniel, lieutenant
Quin, Henry, captain
Ragland, Henry, private
Raiborn, James, private
Ralls, Harris, private
Ratliff, James, private
Rawls, Briant, private
Rawls, Charles, private
Rawls, Jabez, ensign

Rawls, James, sergeant
Read, James, corporal
Redman, Jesse, private
Redmon, Wilson, private
Reives, Alfred, private
Reives, John, private
Reives, Thomas, sergeant
Richmon, Andrew, private
Rizer, Adam, private
Roberts, James, private
Roberts, Thomas, private
Robertson, Nathan, private
Robertson, Reason, private
Ross, John, private
Ross, Richard, private
Rowel, Lewis, private
Rule, Thomas, corporal
Runnels, Harmon M., captain
Runnels, Hiram G., sergeant
Runnels, Howell W., quartermaster
Rutland, Asa, private
Sadler, Isaac, private
Sandal, Daniel, private
Sanders, Travis, private
Saville, Aaron, private
Seale, Daniel, sergeant
Seale, Eli, fifer
Seale, Lewis, private
Seale, William, private
Shaves, John, private
Silmon, Elias, private
Simmons, John, private
Simmons, Josephus, private
Simmons, Ralph, private
Simmons, William, private
Simmons, Willis, private
Simpson, Samuel, private
Sims, Robert, private
Slaughter, David, private
Slaughter, George, private
Slaughter, John, private
Slaughter, Richard, private
Slaughter, Robert, private
Slaughter, William, corporal
Smith, Alexander, private
Smith, Eli, private

Mississippi Territory in War of 1812—Rowland. 205

Smith, Ezekiel, private
Smith, Henry, major
Smith, Hugh, private
Smith, Isham, lieutenant
Smith, James, private
Smith, J. Carter, private
Smith, Jeremiah, private
Smith, John, private
Smith, John, private
Smith, Levi, private
Smith, Thomas, private
Smith, William, captain
Smith, William, sergeant
Smith, William, private
Somner, Owen, sergeant
Sones, Henry, private
Sorrel, Washington, sergeant
Sparks, Richard, ensign
Spencer, William, captain
Steen, James, private
Steen, Nathaniel, sergeant
Steen, Robert, ensign
Steen, William, corporal
Sterling, Allen, sergeant
Sterling, John, Jr., private
Sterling, John, Sr., private
Stigler, Benjamin, sergeant
Stigler, George, private
Stone, Marvel, private
Stovall, Charles, quartermaster sergeant
Stovall, Gilbert, private
Stovall, John, corporal
Stovall, Lewis, private
Strickland, Robert, private
Strong, John, private
Strong, Thomas, private
Summerall, Jesse, corporal
Tarver, James, private
Taylor, Daniel, private
Taylor, John, corporal
Tellis, John, private
Tellis, Silas, private
Terrill, Philomon, private
Thomas, Charles, private
Thomas, Daniel, sergeant
Thomas, James, private

Thompkins, Thomas, private
Thompson, Archibald, private
Thompson, Jesse, first sergeant
Thompson, Simeon, private
Thornhill, William, private
Tilley, Drury, private
Tolar, Henry, private
Tomlinson, Jacob, lieutenant
Tompkins, John B., private
Toney, James, private
Trailor, Matthew, private
Trailor, William, private
Tynes, Fleming, private
Tynes, Minor, private
Vardaman, Jeremiah, private
Varnado, Leonard, private
Varnado, Moses, private
Walker, Charles, private
Wallace, Oliver, private
Wallis, Thompson, private
Warren, Daniel R., lieutenant
Warren, John, private
Warren, John Jr., private
Warren, Joseph, private
Warren, Joseph, private
Warren, Solomon, private
Waterhouse, John I., private
Watson, Harrison, private
Weatherby, George W., sergeant
Weathersby, Isham, private
Welcher, Duke W., private
Wells, John, private
Wells, Nathaniel, major
Westfall, Samuel, private
Williams, John, private
Williams, Reuben, private
Williams, Samuel, private
Williford, John, private
Woldredge, William, private
Woodall, William, private
Woods, John, private
Wright, Reuben, corporal
Young, Green, private
Youngblood, Benjamin, private
Youngblood, Henry, private

14TH REGIMENT (McBoy's) OF MISSISSIPPI MILITIA

Captain Benj. Dubroca's Company
Captain McKinsey's Company
Captain Samuel H. Garrow's Company
Captain Chas. L. Aland's Company

Acre, Samuel, private
Alexander, Francis, private
Alexander, Joseph, private
Antonio, Joachim, private
Antonio, Joseph, private
Arrosa, Joseph, private
Baird, Joseph B., private
Barlow, Aaron, private
Barnett, Ulysses, private
Barriel, Joseph, private
Blair, Thomas, private
Bloc, Andre, private
Brewer, Cornelius, corporal
Byrne, Patrick, private
Cahall, Barney, private
Canadien, Francis, private
Cardenas, Joseph, private
Caro, Sebastian, corporal
Cartier, John, private
Chance, Henry, private
Chasting, Baptiste, private
Chastong, Zenon, private
Chaston, Auguste, private
Chastong, Eugene, private
Chinault, William, surgeon
Chistang, Edoi, private
Clements, — — — —, private
Conway, James, private
Cook, John, private
Cook, Nicholas, sergeant major
Damour, Laine, private
Darling, Dennison, private
David, Pierre, private
David, Simon, private
Davis, E., private
Denton, Thomas H., sergeant
Devol, Daniel, ensign
Dolives, Sifroy, private
Dubroca, Benjamin, captain
Dubroca, Eli, private
Ducos, Pierre, private

Duff, William, private
Dumoiy, Augustine, private
Duncan, Alexander, Jr., private
Dunwooddie, — — — —, private
Durette, Joseph, private
Durette, Zedon, private
Estava, Don McGill, private
Fisher, William, private
Fisher, William, Jr., private
Frazee, Carman, corporal
Garrow, Samuel H., captain
Girard, Francis, private
Grant, Edward, private
Haines, Samuel, private
Hobart, Pete. H.. lieutenant
Honore, Colin, private
Hope, George, private
Hopewell, William, private
Huston, Robert, private
Jack, George, private
Killen, Samuel H., sergeant
Kreps, Placide, private
Kreps, Stephen, private
Labat, — — — —, private
Lalande, Charles, captain
Laurendine, Edward, private
Loran, Daniel, private
Lucien, Pierre, private
Lyon, William, private
Martin, Domingo, private
McBoy, Diego, major
McBoy, William, private
McCandless, Joseph, private
McGuire, James, private
McIntire, Duncan, private
McKinsey, Michael, captain
McLoskey, Philip, adjutant
Mitchell, Robert, private
Mitchell, Thomas, private
Mottus, Silvain, private
Newbold, Thomas G., corporal

Mississippi Territory in War of 1812—Rowland. 207

Nicola, Tildea, private
Nicola, Cilvain, private
Ortis, John, private
Page, Jacob, private
Paul, Joseph, private
Perault, Michael, private
Plumley, William, corporal
Randols, David, private
Randon, David, corporal
Robinson, David C., private
Roland, David, private
Rose, John, private
Saint, John, corporal
Savanah, John, first lieutenant
Saxton, — — — —, private
Simon, Felix, private
Simon, Maximilian, private

Simon, Romin, private
Simon, Sylvester, private
Smith, Gabriel, private
Smith, John, private
Smith, John, Sr., private
Soreta, Joseph, private
Soucier, Edward, private
Soucier, Siforier, private
Spillman, — — — —, private
Staltz, William, private
Taylor, George, sergeant
Thornton, Joshua, private
Thornton, William, private
Troulle, Alexis, private
Ward, Michael, sergeant
Whitehead, William, private
Wilkins, Washington, private

15th Regiment (Johnson's) of Mississippi Militia

Anderson, John, private
Beddingfield, George, private
Boyakin, Soloman, private
Braden, James, private
Dradley, John, private
Brown, Bartlet, private
Brunson, Josiah, private
Cassity, Hugh, private
Cavenah, William, corporal
Clarke, William B., private
Clingaman, Henry A., private
Colson, Samuel, private
Coxe, William, private
Curtis, John D., ensign
Daffin, James, second lieutenant
Daniel, James, private
Deloach, Benjamin, private
Dewitt, James, private
Dorcey, James, private
Easley, Samuel, first lieutenant
Ford, James, private
Foster, George, private
Franklin, Thomas, private
Gentry, James, private
Gill, James, private
Gray, Bazzel, private
Green, James, third lieutenant

Green, James, private
Green, William, private
Hall, Armistead, private
Hammond, Lemuel, private
Hammond, Matthias, private
Hammond, Sherrard, private
Hays, William, private
Hicks, Matthew, private
Hill, John, first sergeant
Hogg, John, private
Holdman, Joseph, private
Hosea, Thomas, private
Howel, Henry, private
Jacob, — — — —, servant
James, Allman, private
Johnson, John, private
Johnson, Thomas, private
Jones, Elbert, private
Kelly, John, private
Kelly, Orson, private
Kirkham, Benjamin, private
Landrum, Jesse, private
Landrum, William, private
Lawrey, John, musician
Luker, Jesse, private
Mabry, Walter, sergeant
Matlock, Thomas, sergeant

208

McCane, John, private
McGrew, Alexander, private
McNeill, L. H., sergeant
Milsted, John, private
Mimms, Thomas, private
Mitchell, William, corporal
Mixon, James, private
Montcrief, Caleb, private
Morgan, George, private
Mott, Asa, private
Mott, Lovelace, captain
Odum, Richard, corporal
Ogwynn, John, private
Ousley, John, private
Pearce, Lewis, private
Pearson, Leonard, sergeant
Perry, Darling, private
Perry, Francis, private
Pervis, John, private
Phillips, Daniel, corporal
Phillips, William, private
Price, James, private
Price, Meredith, private
Prothro, Thomas, private

Rabia, Kinchen, private
Ray, Henry, private
Ray, John, corporal
Rhodes, John, private
Rodgers, Absalom, private
Rodgers, Hays, private
Rose, William, private
Short, Michael, private
Simmons, David, private
Smith, Edward, private
Smith, John, private
Smith, Reese, private
Spikes, Jonah, private
Stinson, Burril, private
Vaughn, John, private
Walker, James, private
Walker, Matthias, private
Walker, Nathaniel, private
White, Pleasant, private
Willson, Matthew, private
Willson, William, private
Willson, William H., private
Wood, John, private
York, Jabez, corporal

16TH REGIMENT (BURRUS') OF MISSISSIPPI MILITIA

Captain Samuel A. Allen's Company
Captain Daniel Atkins' Company
Captain William Crawford's Company
Captain William Evans' Company
Captain Griffith's Company
Captain Greaf Johnston's Company
Captain Wm. Moseley's Company

Adams, Benjamin, private
Adams, Joseph, private
Adams, Thomas, private
Albright, John, private
Aldridge, William, sergeant
Allen, John A., lieutenant
Allen, Samuel, private
Allen, Samuel A., captain
Allen, William, private
Allen, William S., private
Almon, John, private
Arnold, John, private
Atkins, Daniel, captain

Atkins, Daniel, private
Babb, Asel, private
Bailes, John, private
Baker, John, private
Baker, William, private
Beason, Jahu, private
Bennet, John, private
Berrimon, Burrel, private
Bigham, William, private
Bird, Isaih, private
Birdwell, Moses, private
Black, John, private
Bledsoe, Lewis, private

Bloodworth, Timothy, private
Boggs, Samuel, private
Bogs, John, private
Boggs, John O., private
Boling, Alexander, private
Bonds, James, private
Boon, Isaac, private
Boren, John, private
Bossley, John, corporal
Bounds, Solomon, private
Box, Michad, private
Bradwaters, Charles, private
Brag, Thomas, private
Bragg, Benjamin, corporal
Bragg, William, private
Broils, George, private
Broils, Jacob, private
Brown, John, private
Brown, Leonard, private
Brown, Thomas T., private
Brunson, Larkin, private
Brunson, Samuel, private
Bryan, William B., private
Buckner, John, first sergeant
Buie, John, private
Burchfield, Thomas, private
Burks, Benjamin, private
Burrow, William J., private
Burrow, William, Sr., private
Burrus, Charles, lieutenant-colonel
Cain, Samuel, private
Busby, Reves, private
Campbell, John, private
Campbell, Theophilus, fifer
Cannon, Skip, private
Capshaw, David, private
Carriel, Benjamin, private
Carroll, William, private
Casey, John, private
Cavott, Thomas, private
Chilcoath, William, private
Childress, Jesse, sergeant
Childress, John, sergeant
Childress, William, private
Clark, Gilliam, private
Clark, Samuel, private
Clark, Thomas, sergeant

Clem, Benjamin, private
Clem, Jesse, private
Clemens, Jacob, private
Coal, Martin, private
Cofman, Daniel, private
Coley, James, second lieutenant
Connor, Jacob, private
Cook, Benjamin, private
Cook, John, private
Cook, Randal, private
Cook, Robert, private
Cooper, George, private
Cornelius, Ira., private
Cotton, Abner, private
Cotton, Loftin, sergeant
Cottrell, John, private
Craig, Adam H., private
Crawford, Alexander, corporal
Crawford, William, captain
Crowder, Robert, private
Curuthers, Redrick, private
Curuthers, Robert, private
Cummings, Levi, private
Cuoy, Charles, private
Daley, Joseph, private
Daniel, William, private
Davis, John, private
Davis, Richard, private
Davis, Samuel, lieutenant
Davis, William, private
Day, David, private
Dean, Samuel, private
Dearman, William, private
Doughty, William, private
Dublin, James, private
Dublin, John, private
Duncan, Charles, private
Dunehue, Joseph, private
Dupre, William, corporal
Durkins, Smith, private
Eddins, John, private
Eddins, Theophilus, corporal
Eddins, Washington, sergeant
Eden, Samuel, private
Edmonson, William, second major
Ellington, Garland, private
Elliott, Thomas S., private

Ellison, Lewis, private
Emery, John M., private
Erwin, William, corporal
Esters, Champion, private
Evans, William, captain
Fields, Moses, corporal
Finch, William, private
French, Amos, private
French, Benjamin, private
Gailey, Andrew, private
Gallaspy, James, private
Gambol, James, sergeant
Ganda, John, private
Garrett, William, private
Gibson, Aaron, sergeant
Gillace, Dougald, private
Goor, Bledsoe, corporal
Gragg, Henry, private
Gray, Thomas, sergeant
Green, Benjamin, private
Greenhaw, Jonathan, private
Greenhaw, William, private
Griffith, Isaac, sergeant
Griffith, Stephen, captain
Grooms, William, private
Guin, Henry, private
Guin, William, private
Hamilton, Asa, corporal
Hancock, Benjamin, private
Harbin, James, private
Hardy, John, private
Hardy, Jonathan, private
Hargrove, Valentine, adjutant
Harper, Edward, private
Harper, John, private
Harper, Robert, private
Harris, Matthew, private
Hartgrove, James, private
Hatton, Allen, private
Hawkins, Thomas, private
Helms, John, private
Henderson, Pleasant, private
Hester, John, sergeant
Hester, William, private
Hitchcock, Denton, private
Hodges, Allison, private

Holland, John, private
Holland, Tilman, private
Holmes, James, private
Holmes, Jesse, private
Hood, Frederick, corporal
Howard, John, private
Howard, Samuel, corporal
Howard, Thomas S., private
Hubbard, Ezekiel, private
Huder, Michael, private
Hughs, Thomas, private
Hunt, George W., first sergeant
Hutchison, Thomas, corporal
Ingram, Samuel, private
Ingram, William, private
Isbell, Jabas, private
Jackson, Jacob, private
Jackson, John, private
Jackson, Sterling, private
Jackson, William, private
John, Asahel, private
Johnson, Burrel, ensign
Johnson, Greaf, captain
Johnson, Henry, corporal
Johnson, Nehemiah, private
Jones, John, private
Jones, Moses, private
Jourdan, Jesse, private
Kennedy, Lexington, private
Kent, Elbert, private
Kent, William, ensign
King, Abraham, ensign
King, Elijah, private
King, Henry, lieutenant
Kinsey, James, corporal
Lancaster, Thomas, private
Landrith, Thomas, private
Lasey, Caleb, sergeant
Lay, Simeon, private
Lee, Isaiah, private
Lemon, Reson, private
Lenard, John, private
Leveston, Samuel, private
Levinston, Anthony, private
Livingston, Jesse, private
Loid, William, private

Loy, Henry, private
Magby, William, private
Manson, William, private
Martin, James, private
Martin, Joel, private
Martin, Nathaniel, private
Martin, Rial, private
Martin, William, private
Martindel, James, private
Martindel, Thomas, private
Mathews, George, private
Mathews, James, private
Mathews, John, private
Mathews, Joseph, sergeant
Mathis, George, sergeant
Matthews, Charles, private
Matthews, John, private
Matthis, George, private
McBroom, Stephen, private
McCrachran, Daniel, private
McCachron, Veill, private
McCain, James, private
McCain, John, private
McCartey, Jacob, private
McCowey, Samuel, private
McGehee, Zachariah, private
McGlamery, Sovereign, private
McGowan, Prewett, corporal
McIfee, Moses, private
McKinney, John, private
McKinney, Lynch, private
McMillan, Absalom, private
McMurtery, John, private
McPhail, John, private
McRay, Silas, sergeant
Mechum, Banks, private
Megee, John, private
Mendingall, Eliasha, lieutenant
Merrimoon, Woody, private
Michell, James, private
Miller, David, private
Miller, Garland B., private
Miller, Henry, private
Millikin, James, private
Mills, William, private
Milon, Bartlet, private

Mitchel, Randol, private
Mitchel, William, private
Mitchel, William, private
Modrell, Robert, private
More, Joseph, private
More, John, private
Morice, John, private
Morriss, Elisha, corporal
Morrow, James, private
Morrow, Thomas, private
Morrow, William, private
Moseley, William, captain
Mosier, Daniel, private
Mosier, Joel, private
Moys, George C., private
Mullins, James, private
Mullins, Thomas, private
Murfrey, John, private
Murphey, John, private
Murphey, Thomas, private
Murrell, Jeoffrey, private
Murrell, Richard, private
Nabors, William, private
Nelloms, Jacob, private
Nichols, Thomas, private
Nixon, Uriah, private
Norman, Barney, private
Norman, Elisha, private
Norwood, John M., private
Ominet, James, private
Paise, James, private
Parkman, Joseph, private
Patterson, Archibald, private
Patterson, Daniel, private
Peer, Daniel, private
Pennington, Jacob, private
Philips, Duncan, private
Philips, Parky, private
Phillips, Glen, private
Pierce, Richard, corporal
Plant, Charles, private
Poor, Jeremiah, private
Poor, Martin, private
Power, Edgel, corporal
Power, John, private
Power, Thomas, sergeant

Prewit, William, private
Priest, James, private
Priest, Samuel, private
Raney, Zebelon, private
Redding, George, private
Redin, Leman, private
Renno, Robert, private
Rice, Spencer, private
Riddle, George, corporal
Riddle, Uriah, private
Roberts, William, private
Robertson, Eli, sergeant
Rodgers, Lemuel, private
Rodgers, Samuel, private
Rogers, James, private
Romins, James, corporal
Roper, Green, private
Sanders, Henry, private
Sanderson, Elijah, private
Sanderson, James, sergeant
Sanderson, Lewis, sergeant
Sasune, Littleberry, private
Scallion, John, private
Scruggs, James S., private
Sebott, Lewis, private
Sharpe, George, private
Sheckles, William, private
Simons, Jonathan, private
Shickle, Joseph, private
Simmon, Dudley, private
Simons, Zachariah, private
Siscoe, Jacob, private
Slaughter, James, private
Slaughter, William, private
Smith, Abraham, private
Smith, Asa, private
Smith, Isaih, private
Smith, Jacob, private
Smith, James, private
Smith, Nathaniel, lieutenant
Smith, Robert, private
Speeks, Hiram, private
Speeks, Richard, private

Speeks, Willie, private
Speer, Moses, private
Spurrs, William, private
Staggs, Thomas, private
Stephens, James, private
Steward, John, private
Sulcey, Henry, sergeant
Taylor, Isaac, sergeant
Taylor, Larkin, drummer
Therill, David, private
Thomas, Moses, private
Thomerson, John, private
Thompson, Swan, private
Tidwell, David T., private
Tilman, Daniel, private
Trump, Green H., sergeant
Turnbo, Robert, sergeant
Turnbow, Jacob, private
Tyrone, Jacob, corporal
Vaughn, Robert, private
Vaught, John, private
Vaught, William, private
Vickers, Joseph, private
Vining, Wade H., private
Walker, Robert, private
Weaver, Elijah, ensign
Wells, Humphrey, private
West, George, private
Wilkerson, Meredith, private
Williams, William, lieutenant
Williamson, Parkey, corporal
Wilmouth, David, corporal
Wilson, Harden, sergeant
Wilson, John, private
Wilson, Thomas, ensign
Winn, Robert, private
Witt, Lewis, private
Woke, David, private
York, Joseph, corporal
York, John, private
York, Uriah, private
Young, Henry, private

Mississippi Territory in War of 1812—Rowland. 213

18TH REGIMENT (1814-1815, OF MISSISSIPPI MILITIA CAPTAIN JOSEPH VELLIO'S COMPANY)

Barabino, T. O., private
Bayard, Ant, sergeant
Carragan, James, lieutenant
Carver, Elihu, major
Cibelot, M., corporal
Courteau, Ih., private
Demetry, — — — —, gunner
Domingon, H. T., sergeant
Favre, Charles, private
Favre, F., private
Favre, I., private
Favre, I. B., private
Fayard, Laurt, private
Labat, J., private
Ladner, Bazile, private
Ladner, Carlos, corporal
Ladner, E., private
Ladner, F., private
Ladner, John, private

Lafontaine, C., private
McCall, Duncan, first lieutenant and quartermaster
Mitchell, — — — —, private
Morin, J. B., private
Morin, John, private
Morin, P., sergeant
Nicaise, Chs., private
Nicholas, John, private
Petit, T., private
Sancier, P., private
Sancier, Ph., private
Saucier, T., corporal
Saucier, T. F., private
Taulme, I. B., ensign
Turin, Felix, gunner
Veillo, Joseph, captain
Wilkinson, Ths., private

CARSON'S REGIMENT OF MISSISSIPPI MILITIA

Adcock, John, private
Alexander, Joseph, private
Alexander, Jourdan, private
Allen, David, private
Austill, Jeremiah, sergeant
Baimbridge, James, private
Baldwin, Benjamin, quartermaster sergeant
Baldwin, William, private
Bates, John, private
Bazer, Edward, corporal
Bazer, Thomas, private
Bemus, James, corporal
Binge, Harris, sergeant
Bird, William, private
Blackwell, David, private
Blackwell, James, private
Bowie, John, private
Boykin, Burrel, private
Boykin, Kinchin, private
Bridges, Benjamin, private
Brown, James E., private
Brown, Solomon, ensign

Browning, William, private
Buchanan, George, surgeon
Buford, John, private
Busby, John, private
Busclark, William, sergeant
Campbell, I. H., private
Carmichael, William, coporal
Carney, John W., private
Carson, Adam, corporal
Carson, Joseph, colonel
Carter, Hezekiah, private
Cartwright, Peter, captain
Cavenah, William, private
Churchwell, James, private
Cobb, James, private
Cochran, William, sergeant
Coleman, Jesse, private
Cooper, John, private
Cox, Colin, private
Crane, Jeremiah, private
Crane, John, private
Crane, Lewis, Jr., private
Crane, Lewis, Sr., private

Curry, John, private
Curry, Willie, private
Daffin, James, private
Dawkins, Silas, private
Denly, James, private
Denly, John, private
Denson, Isaac, first sergeant
Denson, Joseph, private
Devereux, Charles H., captain
Diven, John S., private
Dooly, John, private
Dupreast, James, private
Espey, Wiley, sergeant
Evans, Jehu, private
Evans, John L., private
Evans, Josiah, sergeant
Farr, James, private
Fisher, Samuel, private
Foster, Levy, private
Fox, John, private
Fox, Washington, private
Gaines, Joab, private
Garvin, John, private
Gillespy, Joseph, private
Gilmore, James, private
Glover, Richard, private
Gordon, Isaac, private
Graves, Joshua, private
Griffin, John, private
Griffin, Moses, private
Grimes, Willis, private
Hall, John, private
Hall, William, private
Ham, John, private
Hambrack, James, corporal
Hand, John B., private
Harris, Claiborne, private
Harris, John, private
Harrison, Robert, private
Hays, John, private
Heaton, Isaac, private
Helverson, Peter, private
Herrington, Hutson, private
Hillis, John, private
Hoven, John, private
Hybert, Henry H., private

Irby, Charles, private
Irby, James, corporal
Irvin, Hugh, private
Jenkins, James, private
Johnston, Isaac, private
Johnston, Joseph, private
Joiner, James, private
Keel, William, private
Kennerly, George, private
Ker, Henry, private
Koin, John, private
Landrum, Benjamin, private
Lefoy, James, private
Lipscomb, Abner S., lieutenant
Lister, Josiah D., captain
Matthews, Samuel, private
Matthews, William, private
McCarty, Neal, private
McCloud, Alexander, private
McDanold, Archibald, private
McGee, Thomas, private
McGrew, Bonaparte, private
McGrew, William M., private
McLendon, David, corporal
Melton, Andrew, private
Melton, William, private
Miller, Michael, private
Mills, James, private
Milstead, Abraham, private
Milstead, Joseph, private
Milstead, William, private
Moore, Charles, ensign
Moore, Gibson, corporal
Moore, John, sergeant
Moore, Thomas, sergeant
Moseley, John T., private
Mott, Asa, private
Murrell, William, private
Myles, John, private
Myles, Josephus, corporal
Myrick, Lyttleton, sergeant major
Nabours, Lewis, private
Nail, Joel, private
Newman, John, private
Newman, Jonathan, sergeant
Olberson, Joshua, private

Mississippi Territory in War of 1812—Rowland. 215

Outon, David, private
Pace, Isom, private
Page, Miah, sergeant
Patton, Joseph, private
Pearson, John, corporal
Perkins, William, private
Perry, Wilson, private
Pew, Isaac, private
Pew, Reison, private
Phillips, Iredal, second sergeant
Pickering, Moses, private
Powe, Thomas, private
Powell, William, private
Price, James M., private
Price, John, private
Raglin, David, sergeant
Randon, David, corporal
Rankins, James, private
Rankins, John, private
Rankins, William, private
Rawlins, Mark, private
Reed, John, private
Reeves, Ezekiel, private
Renfrow, James, private
Roberts, Joseph, private
Robinson, Aaron, private
Robinson, Aaron, private
Robinson, Amus, private
Robinson, Jonah, private
Robinson, William, private
Rodgers, John D., lieutenant
Rogers, Frederick, private
Rogers, Thomas A., lieutenant and adjutant
Rollins, James, private
Russel, James, private
Saffold, Reuben, captain
Shaw, James, private
Shoemate, Daniel, private
Sibert, John, sergeant

Smith, Daniel W., private
Smith, Thomas, private
Sossaman, John, private
Standley, Jordan, first corporal
Stean, Newbury, private
Sterrett, Ralph, first lieutenant
Stewart, James, private
Stiggins, George, sergeant
Stringer, William, second corporal
Sulivan, Stephen, private
Terrill, Edward Y., private
Thompson, Thomas, private
Tilman, Desire, private
Tilley, Josiah, private
Toulman, Theophilus, ensign
Upton, John, private
Varner, John, corporal
Wager, David, corporal
Walker, Daniel, private
Walker, John, private
Walker, Matthias, private
Walker, Tandy, private
Walton, James K. T., private
Ward, Bartley, private
Watts, John E., private
Watts, Josiah, captain
Weathers, Henry, private
Wells, Archilaus, private
Wells, Charles, sergeant
Wells, Thomas, private
Wells, William B., private
Welsh, George, private
White, David, ensign
Williams, John, private
Williams, Thomas, private
Willson, M. D., private
Woodyard, John, private
Woodyard, Walter, private
Worley, John B., private

COLONEL CLAIBORNE'S REGIMENT OF MISSISSIPPI MILITIA

Captain Gerard C. Brandon's Company
Captain William Elliott's Company
Captain Philip A. Engel's Company
Captain Jacob Guice's Company
Captain Philip Hill's Company
Captain Randal Jones' Company
Captain Zachariah Lea's Company
Captain Lewis Paimboeuf's Company
Captain John H. Shanks' Company

Abby, Consider, sergeant
Adams, Samuel, private
Aldred, Ezra, corporal
Alexander, Michael G., corporal
Alexander, Robert, first lieutenant
Ally, Seth, private
Armstreet, Aaron, private
Armstrong, William, private
Atwood, Thomas, private
Austin, Ozias, first lieutenant
Bagley, William, sergeant
Baker, Lewis, private
Baldridge, Alexander, private
Baldwin, Hiram, first lieutenant
Barkley, Samuel C., private
Barrow, Francis, private
Bayley, James, private
Beason, William, private
Beaty, James C., private
Beauchamp, Baptist, private
Beckworth, Jonathan, private
Bedlescomb, Jeremiah, private
Bell, Drury, private
Bell, Joseph, sergeant
Bell, Thomas, private
Bell, Wilkinson, private
Bender, Lott, private
Bennett, William, private
Bernard, William, private
Berry, Joseph, corporal
Berry, Martin, private
Berry, Young, sergeant
Bethany, Matthew, private
Black, Alexander, private
Black, Daniel, private
Blanton, Benjamin, private
Blanton, William W., first lieutenant

Boatright, William, private
Bolls, John, private
Bond, Thomas, private
Bonner, James, private
Boothe, John, private
Bower, George Wm., private
Bowman, Richardson, first lieutenant
Boyce, Peyton, private
Boyd, James, private
Boyd, John, private
Boyd, William, private
Braden, Joseph, sergeant
Brady, Samuel, private
Brandon, Gerard C., captain
Brant, Lewis W., corporal
Brashears, Benjamin, private
Brashiers, James, private
Brasue, Nicholas, private
Brent, John, private
Brice, William, private
Britton, James, private
Brother, Lewis, private
Brown, Henry, corporal
Brown, Isaac, private
Brown, John, private
Brown, John, private
Brown, Jonathan, private
Brown, Joseph, private
Brown, Thomas, private
Bruner, William, sergeant
Brusty, Benjamin, private
Buchanan, John, private
Buckallo, Richard, private
Bucklie, William, corporal
Bullin, David, sergeant
Bullock, David, private
Bullock, James, private

Mississippi Territory in War of 1812—Rowland. 217

Burke, George, private
Burks, Leonard W., corporal
Burks, William, private
Burnett, Mark, private
Burns, William, sergeant
Burton, Charles A., private
Burton, Elbert, private
Burton, Robert, sergeant
Bush, William, private
Bush, William, private
Butler, Burwell, private
Butler, Samuel, private
Byrum, George, private
Cable, Christopher, private
Cain, John, sergeant
Calcott, John, corporal
Calcott, Stephen, private
Calvit, Stephen, private
Cammeron, John, corporal
Cameron, James, private
Camp, John, ensign
Campbell, John D., private
Campbell, Silas, private
Canady, David, private
Canady, Honry, private
Canady, Nathan, private
Carmony, William, private
Carter, Joseph, private
Carter, Kinchen, corporal
Cason, Charles, private
Cason, Henry, private
Cassity, Tacity, private
Cater, Josiah, private
Caves, John, private
Cessna, Culbertson D., private
Chambers, Elijah, private
Chambliss, Peter C., second lieutenant
Chambliss, William R., quartermaster sergeant
Chambliss, William R., sergeant
Chapman, George, private
Childers, Ware, private
Cissna, William S., private
Claiborne, Ferdinand L., colonel
Clark, John, private
Cloyd, Joseph, private
Cloyd, William, corporal

Cochran, David, private
Cochran, John, private
Cochran, John, private
Cole, James, private
Collier, Francis, private
Colvin, Talton, private
Colvin, William, private
Conner, George, private
Conner, James, private
Conner, Jeptha L., private
Cook, Green, private
Cook, John, private
Cook, William, private
Coon, Jasper S. M., private
Cooper, James, private
Cooper, John, private
Cordill, John, private
Corey, Samuel F., sergeant
Corner, John, private
Cotton, Able, corporal
Cotton, Haley, private
Cotton, James, private
Courtney, John, private
Couzins, Mathew, private
Coward, Needham, private
Cox, John, surgeon
Crane, James, corporal
Crawford, William, private
Crow, Clark, private
Crow, Levi, private
Cunningham, William, private
Dacosta, Nicholas, private
Daenhart, Augustus, private
Davis, Benjamin, private
Davis, David, private
Davis, James, private
Davis, Martin, private
Davis, Martin, private
Decell, George, corporal
Delany, John, private
Dell, Jacob, private
Deloach, William R., first lieutenant
Demars, Malcolm, private
Dennis, Asa W., private
Dennis, Thomas, private
Devine, Kinsman, private
Dickson, Thomas, private

Dismuke, John, private
Dixon, William, private
Dobbins, Alfred M., private
Dobbs, John H., private
Dougherty, George, sergeant major
Doughty, Edward, private
Douthard, Zedekiah, private
Dowling, Charles, private
Downing, Edward, private
Downs, William, private
Dozer, Thomas, private
Duncan, William, private
Dunn, James, private
Dunson, William, private
Dupie, Thomas, private
Durin, Jonathan, private
Edmonson, Amos, private
Edwards, John, corporal
Edwards, Joseph, private
Edwards, Nathaniel, private
Edwards, Thomas, private
Eldridge, Hollam, private
Elliott, John, corporal
Elliott, William, captain
Elmore, Joseph, private
Engel, Philip A., captain
Evans, Elijah, private
Evans, William, private
Ewing, Robert B., private
Fagan, William, private
Fait, Peter, private
Fake, Thomas, private
Falls, John, private
Fatheree, Hilliard, private
Fenton, John, private
Ferguson, Benjamin, private
Ferguson, Edward, private
Ferguson, William, private
Ferrell, Daniel, private
Fife, Gilbert, private
Fife, Isaac, private
Finnehorn, John, private
Fleming, John B., private
Floyd, John, private
Ford, James, private
Ford, Joseph, private

Forget, William, private
Foster, Randal, private
Fox, Washington, private
Frasher, Ralph, private
Friley, Frederick, private
Furness, John, corporal
Gains, Fountain H., private
Garlington, Benjamin, fifer
Garlington, Edwin, private
Garriday, William, private
Gasaway, Nicholas, private
Gibson, Richard, private
Gilbert, Samuel, corporal
Gillaspie, David, private
Givens, George W., private
Glover, Anderson, private
Glover, David, private
Glover, Peter, private
Godley, Slade, private
Godley, Thomas, corporal
Goleman, William, private
Goleman, Young, private
Goober, Craddock, corporal
Goodale, Samuel, private
Goodrum, John, private
Goodrum, Thomas, private
Goodston, Benjamin, private
Goodston, James, private
Goodwin, Isaac, private
Gordon, George, private
Gordon, James, private
Gowen, James H., sergeant
Gower, Elisha, private
Graddock, Richard, private
Graham, James, private
Graves, James, private
Gray, William, private
Green, James, first lieutenant
Green, John, private
Green, Joseph, private
Greer, Aaron, private
Greer, Aquilla, private
Griffin, George, private
Griffin, Isaac, private
Griffin, James M., sergeant
Griffin, Robert, private

Griffin, William, sergeant
Grissum, Lambert D., private
Groves, James, private
Guest, Samuel, sergeant
Guice, David, first lieutenant
Guice, Jacob, captain
Guice, John A., private
Guice, John H., corporal
Guice, Jonathan, sergeant
Hall, Mathew, private
Hamberlin, Peter, private
Hanna, Josiah, first lieutenant
Hanson, William, private
Harford, Samuel, musician
Harold, Thomas, corporal
Harrigill, Joseph, private
Harrington, Hardy, private
Harrington, Jacob, private
Harrington, Thomas, sergeant
Harris, Levi C., private
Harrison, Nathaniel, private
Harville, Needham, private
Havard, Elijah, private
Heady, Elijah, private
Heath, Thomas, musician
Helms, Henry, private
Hellums, Enos, private
Helvey, Henry, musician
Henderson, Samuel, private
Henry, William H., private
Henson, William, sergeant
Herd, Thomas, corporal
Herrin, Henry, private
Herrin, Jacob, private
Herrin, Samuel, private
Herron, Benjamin, private
Herron, John, private
Higgins, Peter, private
Hill, Alexander I., private
Hill, James, private
Hill, Peter, private
Hill, Philip, captain
Hilliard, James, private
Hilliard, Reubin, private
Hilson, Silas, sergeant
Hixon, Daniel, private

Holland, Alexander G., private
Holliday, Richard I., corporal
Holloway, Lewis, private
Holmes, Ahab, private
Holmes, Drewry, private
Hooper, Thomas, private
Hooter, Jacob, private
Hornsby, Joseph, private
Hope, Adam, sergeant
Hosey, Branson, private
Howard, William, private
Howard, William, private
Howell, Jehu, private
Hudson, Josiah, private
Hudson, Westley, private
Huff, Benjamin, private
Huff, Holloway, private
Huffman, Alexander, private
Hughey, John, private
Hull, Miles, private
Hunter, Thomas, private
Hurley, Thornton, private
Hyland, Christopher, corporal
Hylands, John, sergeant
Ingles, Elliott, private
Ireson, James, private
Irwin, James, private
Jack, William, ensign
Jackson, Henry, private
Jacobs, Richard, private
James, Joseph, private
Jayne, Daniel, private
Jett, James, private
Johns, David, private
Johns, Thomas, private
Johnson, Peter, private
Johnson, William, corporal
Johnston, John, private
Johnston, Samuel, private
Jones, Abraham, private
Jones, Harden, private
Jones, James, private
Jones, John H., private
Jones, John S., private
Jones, Moses, private
Jones, Randal, captain

Jones, Samuel, private
Jones, Thomas, private
Jordan, Charles H., private
Juvenot, Joseph, private
Kean, Thomas, ensign
Keith, Alexander, private
Keller, George, private
Keller, Joseph, private
Kellogg, Theron, ensign
Kennedy, David, private
Kennison, Nathaniel, private
Kenton, Simon, private
Kenton, William, private
Kerr, John, surgeon mate
Kinchen, Mathew, first lieutenant
King David, musician
King, William, ensign
Kirk, Michael, corporal
Kirkham, Spencer, private
Kirkland, Richard, private
Kline, Balthazar, private
Knight, Joseph, sergeant
La Chapelle, Dominic, private
Lambert, Abner, private
Lambert, Ashley, private
Landrum, William, private
Langford, David, private
Law, David, private
Lawhorn, John, private
Layson, Robert, sergeant major-ensign
Lea, Major, private
Lea, Zachariah, captain
Leak, Austin, private
Leak, William, first lieutenant
Leatherman, John, private
Lee, Charles, private
Lee, James B., private
Lee, James, private
Lee, John, private
Lefoy, Mathew, private
Lender, Daniel, private
Leonard, Jacob, private
Levertson, private
Lewis, Nicholas, private
Linder, Lewis, corporal
Lindsey, Robert, private

Llewellyn, Compton G., first lieutenant
Lobdell, James, private
Lochridge, Nicholas, ensign
Long, James, sergeant
Long, James P., private
Long, Jeremiah, private
Long, Philip P., private
Louk, Andrew, private
Love, Joseph, private
Low, John, sergeant
Lowe, Frederick, private
Lowe, Lunsford, private
Lucas, Robert, private
Lucket, James, first sergeant
Lusk, George, private
Lyon, Spencer, private
Lacky, William, private
Madden, James, private
Mann, Simpson, private
Mannen, Jeremiah, private
Manning, Silas, private
Manville, Philip, private
Mark, Samuel, private
Marler, James, private
Marrs, Thomas, private
Marshall, Reuben, private
Marshall, Solomon, private
Martin, Aaron, private
Martin, Christopher, private
Masey, Drury, Jr., private
Mason, Charles, private
Massey, Drury, Sr., private
Master, Baptist, private
Master, John, private
Masterson, Vatchel, private
Mathews, Samuel, private
Mathews, Westley, private
Matthews, Lyman, private
Maxwell, George, private
May, David, corporal
May, William, sergeant
McAleb, Alexander, private
McAlpin, Duncan, private
McCartney, James, private
McCarty, James, private
McClendon, John, private

Mississippi Territory in War of 1812—Rowland. 221

McCune, Archibald, private
McDaniel, Daniel, private
McDaniel, John, private
McGehee, Archibald, sergeant
McGeniss, William, private
McGhee, James, private
McGhee, Samuel, private
McGohan, Peter, corporal
McGowen, James, first lieutenant
McKean, James, private
McLaughlin, John, private
McLaughlin, William, private
McLeod, James, private
McLin, William, private
McMillion, John, private
McNeal, Archibald, private
McNeal, William, private
McNeefe, William, private
Merriday, James, private
Metts, Jacob, private
Metts, Tobias, private
Miller, George, corporal
Miller, Thomas, private
Minton, Joshua, private
Mitchell, Andrew, private
Mitchell, William, sergeant
Monday, Littleton, private
Monger, Thomas, private
Montgomery, Andrew, first lieutenant
Montgomery, John, private
Moore, John, corporal
Morgan, John, private
Morgan, Laburn, private
Morgan, Shadrick, private
Morgan, William, private
Morris, John, private
Morrison, John, drum major
Murfee, Morris, private
Murphey, Wiley, private
Murphy, Benjamin, private
Murphy, Nathaniel, sergeant
Murphy, Samuel, private
Murray, Christopher, private
Murray, Thomas, musician
Mygott, Austin R., fifer-corporal
Neal, James, private

Nelson, James, private
Newson, William, private
Nicholas, James, private
Nichols, Benjamin, private
Nicholson, Samuel, ensign
Old, James, private
Oliphant, James, private
Osborne, James, sergeant
Ostin, Ozias, first lieutenant
Owens, William, private
Paimboeuf, Lewis, captain
Painter, Edward, private
Pate, William, private
Patton, Francis, private
Patton, William
Paxton, John R., private
Payson, Robert, ensign
Pearce, Edmund, private
Pentecost, George W., private
Perkins, Isaac, private
Petit, Lewis, private
Petty, William, private
Peyton, Joseph E., sergeant
Phelps, Samuel, private
Phillis, Jacob, private
Philips, Thomas, private
Pierce, John, private
Pinson, Daniel B., private
Pitchford, Augustin, private
Pitman, Julius, private
Platner, John L., private
Platner, William, private
Pleasant, Washington, private
Potter, John, private
Powell, William, private
Prestage, John, private
Prestrage, Samuel, private
Price, Benjamin, private
Price, Jonathan, corporal
Quine, Lemuel, private
Quine, Mordecai, private
Quine, Robert, corporal
Rains, Stephens, private
Rains, William, private
Ralls, Harris, private
Ralls, James, private

Randall, Hiram, private
Randall, Isham, private
Raybourn, Mark, private
Reed, John, private
Reed, William, private
Reynolds, James, private
Rhambart, Zachariah, private
Rheams, Lemuel, sergeant
Rhodes, Jacob, private
Richards, Archibald, private
Riley, Stephen, private
Ring, Mark, private
Ripley, Samuel, corporal
Robert, Redding, drummer
Roberts, Abraham, sergeant
Robinson, Raymond, major
Robinson, William, private
Robinson, Younglove, private
Rollins, Benjamin, private
Ross, Daniel, private
Ross, Nimrod, private
Row, John, private
Rowe, Benjamin, private
Rush, Elijah, private
Rushing, Matthew, private
Rushing, William, private
Russell, Hugh, private
Russell, John, private
Salters, Jacob, private
Salvage, Benjamin F., first lieutenant and quartermaster
Samson, Andrew, sergeant
Sanders, Joseph, private
Sanders, Keatland, private
Saunders, James, sergeant
Saunders, James, corporal
Saunders, William D., private
Scott, Casen, private
Scott, James F., sergeant
Scott, John W., private
Scott, Nehemiah, private
Scurry, Eli, private
See, Howell, private
Seward, Belloup, private
Shafer, David, private
Shanks, John H., captain
Shannon, James, private
Sharkey, Allen, private
Sharkey, Patrick, sergeant
Sharp, Samuel, private
Shaw, Thompson, private
Shelby, Moses, private
Shields, Benjamin, ensign
Shipton, Peter, private
Short, Eli, private
Shuffield, Isham, private
Shuffield, Kinchen H., private
Shull, John, private
Sibley, Benjamin, private
Sibley, West, private
Simmons, George, private
Simmons, Isaiah, private
Simmons, John, private
Simms, Peyton, private
Smallwood, Elisha, private
Smith, Henry, private
Smith, James, private
Smith, Laban, private
Smith, Whitmal, corporal
Southard, Joseph, private
Spillman, Ellis E., ensign
Spurlock, David, private
Spurlock, Drury, private
Steel, Robert, private
Steele, Robert S., sergeant
Stephens, James, private
Stephens, John, first lieutenant
Stephenson, Jonathan, private
Sterling, James, private
Stewart, John, private
Steward, Robert, private
Stockton, Samuel, private
Stoker, Henry, private
Stoker, Matthew, private
Stoker, William, private
Stone, Frederick, private
Strange, Littleberry, private
Strodart, George, private
Stroud, Dixon, private
Stroud, James, private
Stuart, Thomas, private
Sugg, William, private

Sutton, Stephen, private
Swain, James, private
Swan, Robert, sergeant
Swearingame, Joel, sergeant
Tanner, Cullen E., corporal
Taylor, Brice, private
Taylor, Thomas, private
Terry, John, private
Tharp, Jesse, private
Thomas, William, private
Thomkin, Thomas, private
Thompson, Archibald, private
Thomspon, Joab, private
Thompson, John, private
Thompson, John, private
Thompson, Richrd, private
Thornhill, Robert, private
Tines, Minor, private
Tomlinson, Jacob, first lieutenant
Tooten, William, private
Trefox, Charles, private
Trimble, Walter, private
Tullis, Thomas, private
Tyson, Jordan, private
Upton, John, corporal
Urie, Robert, private
Vance, William, corporal
Varnell, Richard, private
Vaughn, Thomas C., private
Verdon, Godfrey, private
Vickery, Aaron, private
Vining, John, private
Waggoner, Joseph, corporal
Waid, William, private
Walden, William, private
Wallace, Oliver, private
Warren, Daniel, private
Warren, Joseph, private
Warsaw, John, private
Washburn, Henry, private
Watson, George B., private
Weaks, Zadock, private
Weatherby, George Wm., first lieutenant
Weatherly, John, private
Weeve, Frederick, private
Welch, John, quartermaster sergeant
Wells, John, private
West, William, private
Weygatt, David, private
White, Henry, private
White, Jacob, private
White, Joel, ensign
White, Joseph, private
White, Nelson, private
Whitworth, Abraham, private
Wigley, Job, private
Wilcox, Benjamin, private
Wilcox, John, private
Williams, David, private
Williams, Elias, private
Williams, Jacob, private
Williams, John, private
Williamson, James, musician
Willis, Reason, private
Wilson, Abel, sergeant
Wilson, Benjamin, private
Wilson, John, private
Wilson, Matthew, private
Wilson, Samuel, private
Wilson, William, private
Winnborne, David, sergeant
Wood, John, lieutenant-colonel
Wood, John, private
Wood, William, private
Woods, Joseph, private
Worsham, Joseph S., first lieutenant and adjutant
Wright, John, private
Wright, William H., private
Yokum, Allen, private
Young, George, private
Young, Peter, private
Zeagler, John, private

Major Dale's Battalion of Mississippi Militia

Austill, Evan, captain
Bedingsfield, George, private
Creaugh, Gerard W., first lieutenant
Daffin, James, adjutant
Dale, Samuel, major
Dodd, Jessey, private
Dukes, H., private
Elliot, Charles, private
Finley, Norris, private
Fisher, Charles, private
Ford, James, sergeant
Foster, William, private
Gentry, Elijah, private
Gentry, James, sergeant
Glass, John, private
Hammond, Jacob, private
Harbert, William, first sergeant
Harrell, Hardy, private
Hearn, William, corporal
Hicklin, Robert, sergeant
Hunt, William, private
Jetton, Benedix, private
Jones, Absalum, private
Matlock, Thomas, private
McGee, Joseph, private
Miles, John, private
Mosely, Thomas B., corporal
Mosley, William, private
Odum, Richard, private
Pearson, John, sergeant
Rodgers, Absolom, private
Rodgers, Hays, private
Simmons, David, private
Schomota, — — — —, private
Talbot, John, corporal
Talbot, John Jr., private
Talbot, Joseph, private
Vaughn, John, private
Wilson, Matthew, private
Wilson, William, private
Wilson, William H., private

Major Smoot's Battalion of Mississippi Militia

Captain William Bate's Company
Captain Samuel Dale's Company
Captain John Jones' Company
Captain Josiah D. Lister's Company

Alexander, Jordan, private
Allen, David, private
Allen, Drewry, private
Angle, John, private
Arnold, Jesse, private
Austin, Evan, first lieutenant
Austin, Jeremiah, private
Baimbridge, Thomas, private
Bankson, John, private
Bates, William, captain
Benge, Harris, private
Billow, Hopson, private
Bilbo, James, private
Booth, John, private
Bosworth, Richard, sergeant
Braden, James, private
Brashears, Jesse, private
Brown, James, private
Brown, John, sergeant
Brunston, Josiah, private
Busby, John, private
Chapman, Joseph, private
Christian, Cary, sergeant
Christmas, Noel, private
Churchwell, James, private
Coody, John, private
Copeland, Isom, private
Crain, Martin, private
Crawford, John, private
Crear, Jerrard W., second lieutenant
Currie, John, private
Dale, James, private
Dale, Samuel, captain
Davis, Simeon, private
Denson, James, second lieutenant
Drinkard, Allenton, private

Mississippi Territory in War of 1812—Rowland. 225

Drinkard, Francis, private
Dubose, Amos, corporal
Due, Perry, private
Easley, Edward, private
Easley, Samuel, private
Emmonds, John, ensign
Evans, Henry, ensign
Evans, Josiah, first lieutenant
Fenley, John, private
Figures, Thomas, private
Gates, Joshua, private
George, Reuben, private
Gordon, Alexander, private
Glass, David, private
Glass, John, private
Gray, William B., private
Green, Daniel, private
Green, James, private
Green, James, Sr., private
Green, William, private
Grizzle, Willis, private
Harris, Silas, private
Heard, Bailey, first lieutenant
Helveston, Peter, corporal
Henderson, Robert, private
Henson, John, private
Herbert, William, sergeant
Herrington, Isaac, private
Hicklin, Robert, corporal
Hogan, Lemuel, private
Hoskins, Henry, private
Housley, Charles, private
Hughes, Isom, sergeant
Huston, Archibald, private
Jiles, William, private
Johnson, James, ensign
Jones, Efford L., private
Jones, Elbert, private
Jones, John, captain
Jones, Wiley, private
Jones, William, private
Landrum, Barnes, private
Lary, Daniel, private
Lister, Josiah D., captain
Matta, Soa, private
May, Patrick, lieutenant and adjutant

McConnell, Thomas, sergeant
McFareen, William, private
McGee, James, private
McLaughlin, Edward, private
McLeod, Alexander, ensign
McNeil, Lochlin H., private
Moffitt, Eli, private
Moody, Joel, private
Monroe, Neal, private
Montcreaf, Benjamin, private
Morgan, George, private
Morton, Hughes, private
Mosely, William, private
Murrell, Zachariah, private
Nail, Joel, private
Norris, Notley, private
Ogletharp, John, private
Patton, Thomas, corporal
Pearson, John, private
Pearson, Reuben, private
Penticost, G. S., private
Phillips, Daniel, sergeant
Pierce, John, private
Pollard, Joseph, corporal
Randon, Peter, private
Ray, Henry, private
Reaves, Eli, private
Reed, John, private
Roberts, Isaac, private
Roberts, John, private
Rogers, Absolom, private
Ross, Nathaniel, corporal
Sapp, Jason, private
Serrett, Ralph, ensign
Short, John, sergeant
Slay, John, private
Smith, Edmund, private
Smith, Neale, surgeon mate
Smoot, B. S., major
Stafford, Abraham, private
Terrell, Brian, private
Thede, Soloman, private
Thomas, John, private
Thompson, John, private
Thornton, William, private
Tisdale, William, private

Tool, David, corporal
Toulmin, Theophilus, first lieutenant
Vaughan, William, private
Vaun, John, private
Walker, Felix, private
Wall, Absalom, second lieutenant
Wall, Thomas, sergeant
Walley, Goldsbury, private
Welch, Henry, private
Welsh, James, private
White, Drury, private
Williams, George, corporal
Wooten, Jeremiah, private
Young, John, private

LIEUTENANT-COLONEL NEILSON'S DETACHMENT OF MISSISSIPPI MILITIA

Captain David T. W. Cook's Company
Captain John Joor's Company
Captain William A. Lucas' Company
Captain Nathan H. Luse's Company
Captain Samuel K. Sorsby's Company
Captain Francis Wood's Company

Adams, Joseph, private
Adams, Thomas C., sergeant
Aldridge, George, private
Aldridge, Sylvester, private
Anden, George, private
Anderson, Ephraim, private
Anderson, Henry, ensign
Anderson, Frederick, private
Anderson, Robert C., sergeant
Anderson, William, corporal
Armstreat, Philip, sergeant
Armstrong, William, private
Arnold, Isham, private
Arnold, Richard, private
Applewhite, James, private
Ashly, John, private
Austin, John, private
Austin, William, private
Bacon, John, sergeant
Badgett, David, private
Baldridge, John, private
Baldwin, Levi, private
Barcley, Glass C., private
Barkee, David, private
Barnes, Pittkin, sergeant
Barns, John, private
Barron, Thomas, private
Bass, Jeremiah, private
Bassett, William, sergeant
Baty, Francis, private
Beard, Adam, private
Bennett, David, private
Bennett, William, private
Berry, David, private
Best, Abraham, private
Betis, Julius, private
Black, Alexander, private
Boles, James, private
Booker, Samuel, private
Booker, William, private
Boothe, Shelly, private
Bosman, Samuel, private
Bowling, Jesse, private
Boyd, Augustus, private
Boyd, John, private
Boyd, William, private
Bradley, Archibald, private
Bradshaw, Peter, private
Bradway, Ebenezer, private
Brannon, Thomas, private
Brannon, William, private
Brieland, Daniel, private
Briley, Job, private
Briscoe, Parmenas, major
Brister, George, private
Brown, John, private
Brown, Joseph, private
Brown, Lampkin W., private
Brown, William, private
Brown, William, private
Brunaugh, Martin, sergeant
Buckley, William C., private

Buckman, Henry, private
Buckner, David, private
Burge, Christopher, private
Burnes, John, sergeant
Burnham, Gabriel, private
Burke, John E., private
Burks, William, corporal
Burton, Charles A., private
Burton, John, third lieutenant
Burton, Thomas, private
Bush, Isaac, private
Butler, Henry, private
Calcoat, Stephen, private
Caldwell, R. S., private
Calhoon, John, private
Campbell, Silas, private
Carman, Asa, private
Carmany, William, private
Carnis, David, private
Carr, John H., private
Carr, Joseph, private
Cason, Charles, private
Cassells, Benjamin, private
Cassells, Reuben, private
Cater, James, private
Caton, Michael, private
Chaddick, Richard, private
Chaddick, William, private
Chambers, Elijah, corporal
Chambliss, Peter C., ensign
Chaney, George W., private
Chism, Samuel F., private
Coarsey, James, private
Cochran, Edward, private
Collier, Vines L., private
Collins, Henry, private
Collins, John, private
Cook, David T. W., captain
Cook, John, private
Cook, John, private
Clanton, James, private
Clark, Daniel, private
Clark, Wilson, private
Clarke, Lewis, corporal
Cole, Mason G., private
Cole, William, private
Colville, Andrew, private

Cook, Abel, private
Cooper, Martin, private
Corbet, Abel, private
Crawford, Richard, sergeant
Crow, James, private
Curry, Peter, private
Curtis, Richard, private
Dancer, Ulric M., private
Dassy, Silas, private
Davis, Hugh, second lieutenant
Day, David, private
Dean, John T., private
Dey, Robert, private
Dismuke, Joseph, private
Divine, William, private
Donoho, Charles, private
Downs, George, private
Downs, Hiram, private
Downs, Jeremiah, first lieutenant
Downs, Joseph, private
Draughan, Elbert, corporal
Ducker, John, private
Dunn, David, private
Dunn, William, private
Duval, William B., private
Edwards, John, private
Egbert, John, private
Elkins, Ralph, private
Ellis, William, private
Ethridge, Godfrey, private
Everett, John, private
Ewell, James, private
Fake, John, private
Fant, John T., private
Farley, Stephen E., private
Farmer, Joseph D., private
Farmer, William, private
Farmer, William, private
Ferry, John, private
Fleming, William, J. B., sergeant
Fletcher, Lemuel, private
Fife, John, private
Fitzgerald, James, private
Flynn, Thomas, second lieutenant
Fowler, William, private
Frank, — — — —, waiter
French, Robert, private

Fridley, John, private
Frisby, William, private
Gaines, David, private
Gaines, Young, private
Galbreath, Lauvhlin, private
Galbreath, Robert, private
Gale, Thomas M., private
Gardner, John, private
Gardner, William, private
George, Isaac, private
Gibbs, Franklin W., private
Gile, William, private
Gillas, Norman, private
Glover, Matthias, private
Goodale, James, private
Goodwin, John, private
Goodwin, William, private
Goodshorn, John, private
Grafton, Daniel, first lieutenant
Graham, Richard, corporal
Griffin, Isham, private
Guise, Ephraim, private
Guise, John H., corporal
Hadden, Robert, private
Hall, John, private
Hall, John E., sergeant
Hallowel, William L., private
Hammett, Absolum, private
Harkness, Henry, private
Harrell, James, first lieutenant
Harson, John, private
Hawthorn, William, private
Henson, James, sergeant
Herbert, William, corporal
Hezekiah, servant
Hickenbottom, William L., private
Hickman, Isaac, private
Hickman, William, private
Hicks, James, private
Higdon, Daniel, second lieutenant
Hill, William, private
Hoggatt, Philip, first lieutenant and quartermaster
Holliman, Jacob, sergeant
Holly, Joseph, private
House, Henry, private

Hubbert, James, private
Hull, Thomas M., private
Hunter, Field P., sergeant
Hutchinson, James, private
Hutson, George, private
Hux, Benjamin, private
Hux, William, private
Hylan, John, first lieutenant
Inmon, Levi, private
Jackson, Henry, private
Jacob, ————, servant
Jacobs, Francis, private
Jansen, Egbert, surgeon
Jarome, James, private
Jenkins, William, private
Johnson, Hugh B., corporal
Jones, Charles, private
Jones, David, drummer
Jones, Henry, private
Jones, Isaac, private
Jones, Richard, private
Jones, William, private
Jones, William, private
Jones, William, private
Joor, John, captain
Keen, Thomas, private
Kelly, Hugh, private
Kenedy, Cade L., private
Kennedy, David, private
Kennison, Nathaniel, private
Kiger, Michael, corporal
King, Charles, private
King, Elisha, private
King, Richard, sergeant major
King, Samuel, ensign
Kinnison, Nathaniel, sergeant
Kirkham, Thomas, first lieutenant
Kitchens, Benjamin, private
Kizer, John, private
Knowland, James, corporal
Knox, Andrew, private
Knox, John, corporal
Lamb, Henry, private
Lambert, David, corporal
Lambright, David, private
Land, Benjamin, private

Mississippi Territory in War of 1812—Rowland. 229

Laneheart, Jacob, corporal
Lee, Thomas, private
Leek, John, private
Lilly, Mills, private
Lohorn, John, private
Long, Jeremiah, private
Love, William D., private
Lucas, William A., captain
Luse, Nathan H., captain
Lyon, Daniel, private
Manning, William, private
Martin, Henry, private
Mashborn, Enoch, private
Matthews, Zech, private
Maxey, Radford B., corporal
Maxwell, William E., corporal
Mays, Stephen, private
McAllister, John, private
McAlpin, Alexander, private
McAltie, Thomas, private
McCall, Thomas, private
McCartney, Lewis, private
McConnell, Robert B., private
McCormick, William, private
McDaniel, John, private
McDaniel, Jonathan, private
McEwen, Archibald, private
McGee, Jonathan, private
McGinty, Joseph, private
McGlaughlin, William, private
McCoy, Daniel, corporal
McCoy, Jesse, private
McKey, Hugh, private
McLoughlin, Charles, private
McLoughlin, Patrick, sergeant
McMorris, William, private
McNeely, Paul, private
McNeil, Neil, private
McNely, John, private
Merrill, Elijah, corporal
Mills, Edmond, private
Mitchell, Benjamin, corporal
Mitchell, Bluford, private
Mitchell, Joel, private
Montgomery, Andrew, first lieutenant and adjutant

Montgomery, John, private
Moore, Henson, private
Moore, James, private
Moore, Jesse, private
Moore, John, private
Moore, Parsons, private
Moore, William, private
Morgan, James, private
Morgan, John, private
Morris, John, private
Mowry, George, quartermaster sergeant
Murphy, Morris, private
Murrah, Morgan, private
Nathaniel, ————, servant
Neal, James, private
Neal, James, private
Neeland, Middleton, private
Neilson, David, lieutenant-colonel
Nelson, Hugh, private
Nettles, James, private
Newman, Hezekiah, private
Newman, Thomas, private
Nicholls, Julius, private
Nugent, Lewis, private
Obriant, John, private
Ogden, George, second lieutenant
Oglesby, John, private
Oglesby, Sabert, private
Oglesby, William, private
Oliphant, James, private
Oliver, Robert, private
O'Neal, Peter, corporal
Ostean, Gabriel, private
Parham, Peterson, corporal
Parker, David, private
Parker, John, private
Peck, Benjamin, sergeant
Penton, William, private
Perry, John, private
Pervis, John, private
Pharis, William, private
Phillips, Isaac, corporal
Pickett, Lewis, private
Plaster, Thomas R., sergeant
Plutner, Stephen, private
Porter, John, first lieutenant

Porter, William S., private
Powers, Benjamin, private
Prescott, Andrew, private
Price, Joseph, private
Prichard, William, private
Prince, ————, waiter
Quine, Henry, private
Quine, William, private
Quine, William, private
Ragsdale, Elijah, private
Rankin, Christopher, second lieutenant
Reed, Caleb, private
Reynolds, Thomas, private
Rhoades, Andrew, private
Rice, Jesse, private
Richards, Thomas, private
Roberts, Robert, private
Robinson, Seth, private
Ross, David, private
Roundtree, Reuben, private
Rushing, Hugh, private
Rushing, William, private
Russel, John, private
Ryan, Cornelius W. B., private
Sam, ————, servant
Sanders, James, private
Sapp, Dill, private
Saunders, Joseph, private
Saxon, Joshua, private
Saxon, Samuel, private
Scott, Bumberry, private
Searcy, Ransom, private
Sellers, Isaac, private
Segrist, Lewis, private
Sexton, Samuel, private
Shannon, James, sergeant
Shaw, Saxton, private
Shelly, Lewis, private
Sheridan, Thomas, private
Shilling, Abraham, private
Shirky, Lewis, corporal
Shirky, Patrick, corporal
Shropshire, John, private
Shuffield, Stephen, private
Shuffield, William, private
Sibley, William, private

Simmons, Joseph Y., private
Simms, Peyton, private
Sisson, Eldridge, private
Sisson, James, private
Slocum, Charles C., private
Smith, James, private
Smith, John M., private
Smith, Samuel, private
Smith, Thomas, private
Sorsby, Samuel K., captain
Spires, Robert, private
Stafford, James T., private
Stark, John, private
Steel, James, sergeant
Stephens, Briton, private
Stephens, Daniel, private
Sterdwan, Pleasant, private
Sterling, James, private
Sterling, Robert, private
Sterns, Peter, private
Stevens, Henry W., private
Stewart, William, private
Stiles, Chilion F., private
Strain, David, private
Strickland, Henry D., private
Sturdivant, Henry, private
Sturdivant, William R., private
Stutts, William, private
Swayney, Edmond, private
Sweat, Johnston, private
Tanner, James, corporal
Taylor, Isaac, private
Taylor, William, private
Templeton, Joseph, private
Thompson, Robert, private
Tichner, Abram, private
Tidwell, John, private
Tillery, William, private
Toney (negro), waiter
Tribble, John M., private
Triplett, Daniel, private
Turney, John, private
Ursrey, John, private
Ursrey, Richard, private
Usher, William, private
Vandevall, John, corporal

Mississippi Territory in War of 1812—Rowland. 231

VanHouten, Cornelius, sergeant
Vickroy, Nathan, private
Vicks, Burwell, private
Vining, Jepthah, private
Vinson, William, private
Waddle, Jacob, private
Wade, William C., private
Walker, Alexander, corporal
Walker, John B., ensign
Wall, Elisha, private
Wall, Howell, private
Weatherspoon, John, private
Webber, Robert, private
Welch, Nathan, private
Wells, Abraham, private
Wells, Edmond, private
Wells, Noel, private
Wheat, William, private
Whitacar, Isaac, private
White, Benjamin, private
White, Benjamin, private
White, Larkin, ensign
White, Richard, sergeant
White, Robert, private
Whitehurst, J., private
Whittington, James, private
Whittington, Willey, private
Wiley, Hugh, private
William (negro), waiter
Williams, Asa, private
Williams, John L., private
Williams, Lemuel, private
Wilson, Samuel, private
Windham, Stephen, sergeant
Wise, Brunton, private
Wood, Denniss, private
Wood, Francis, captain
Wood, Joseph, private
Woolforth, Michael, private
Wren, John, corporal
Wright, Jesse, private
Wright, John, corporal
Wroe, William O., sergeant
Young, Samuel, private

Major Swayze's Detachment of Mississippi Militia

Swayze, Nathan, major
Titus, — — — —, waiter

Captain John A. Allen's Company of Mississippi Militia

Allen, John A., captain
Baker, Nathan, private
Baker, William, private
Baltimore, — — — —, waiter
Bayles, Jessee, private
Bayles, John, private
Bayles, Wyley, drummer
Bell, Samuel, private
Birdwell, George W., sergeant
Bland, John, corporal
Bratton, Hugh, private
Bratton, Martin, private
Cheatham, Wyatt, sergeant
Cock, Jessee, private
Cock, John, private
Crayton, Gloud W., corporal
Dalton, Samuel, private
Galyan, Abner, fifer
Galyan, Laybourn, fifer
Hodges, Elison, private
Hogland, Anthony, private
Hooker, John, corporal
Houston, James, private
Jones, Jeremiah, private
Long, James, private
McCall, Alexander, private
McCall, Robert, private
McKee, Robert, private
Moses, — — — —, waiter
Parr, John, corporal
Parton, Leonard, private
Paulley, Elijah, private
Riddle, George, private
Riddle, John, private
Scaggs, Wyley, private
Seals, Anthony, private

Seals, Bluford, private
Smith, John A., private
Smith, William, private
Staggs, Zachariah, drummer
Taylor, Harden, sergeant
Taylor, Joel, corporal
Townsend, Eli, private
Townsend, Johnson, corporal
Vaughn, Peter, private
Walker, Israel, private
Wells, John, private
White, James A., private
White, Mitchel, private
White, William, private

Captain Green's Company of Mississippi Militia

Anderson, John, private
Armstreet, Aaron, private
Aswell, Hiram, private
Barclay, Abraham, private
Bass, William, private
Beck, David, sergeant
Bob, —— ——, servant
Boots, John, private
Bradshaw, Willis, private
Brown, Elisha, corporal
Brown, John A., private
Brown, Roland, private
Brown, Wiley, private
Burge, Neil, private
Burns, James, private
Burton, Charles A., private
Burton, Pleasant, private
Burton, Thomas, private
Cain, William, private
Callihan, David M., second lieutenant
Carter, James, private
Caston, William R., private
Clawson, Thomas, private
Cockram, John, private
Cole, William, private
Comly, Charles, private
Conner, James, corporal
Cotton, Eli, private
Coursy, James, private
Crow, John, private
Crow, Levi, private
Curry, Jacob, private
Daugherty, James, private
Davis, John, third lieutenant
Davis, John, private
Dickson, Hugh, private
Dixon, Thomas, sergeant

Dublin, —— ——, servant
Eby, William, private
Falls, John, private
Fletcher, Lionel, private
Freeman, James, private
Fuller, Benjamin, third lieutenant
Funk, Jacob, private
Galbreath, William, private
Germany, Washington, private
Gibson, George, private
Gibson, Jesse, private
Green, James, captain
Grimlair, Henry, private
Hails, John, private
Hamberlin, Jacob, private
Hamberlin, Stephen, private
Harrigill, Benjamin, sergeant
Hawthorn, William, private
Healy, Daniel, corporal
Henly, Nery, private
Hess, Nelson I., sergeant
Hewitt, Jonathan, private
Hogg, William, private
House, Henry, private
Hudnal, Ezekiel, private
Hutchins, Jesse, private
Irby, Hiram, private
Issue, John, private
Jackson, David, corporal
James, Edward, private
Jeffries, John, private
Jennings, Hiram, private
Joe, —— ——, servant
Johnston, Thomas, private
Jones, George W., private
Jones, Micajah, private
Kay, Gabriel, private

Keller, Peter, private
Kirk, James, private
Knox, Andrew, private
Lambert, Abraham, private
Landram, Burton, private
Landsberry, John, private
Lannagan, William, private
Lehr, John, ensign
Long, Jeremiah, private
Love, W. D., private
Lum, Israel, private
Manning, Jeremiah, private
Marlow, Allen, private
Martin, Daniel Wm., private
Martin, John, private
McCaleb, Thomas F., third lieutenant
McCarroll, Charles, private
McCartney, Lewis, private
McDonald, Benjamin, private
McDonald, Peter, private
McDowell, James, first lieutenant
McGee, Charles, private
McKee, James, private
McKee, Samuel, private
McLaughlin, John, private
Melvin, Daniel W., private
Miles, Lemuel, private
Millar, John, private
Moore, John, private
Murphy, Wiley, private
Murphy, William, private
Neelands, Middn., private
Neighbours, Zedekiah, private
Nelson, James, private
Newman, Isaac A., ensign
Nichols, Henry, private
Odum, Abraham, private
Oglesby, James, private
Old, Thomas, private
Osborn, John, private
Parker, Miles, private
Patterson, William, private

Pickett, John, private
Price, Martin, private
Rawls, Luke, private
Ray, William, private
Romedis, John, private
Row, John, private
Rundell, Joshua, third lieutenant
Rush, John, private
Rushton, James, corporal
Scisson, James, private
Sexton, Daniel, private
Shropshie, Walter, private
Smith, William, private
Sorrells, Walter, private
Sparks, Samuel, private
Stokes, Thomas, private
Tankersly, Fountain, private
Tedder, William, private
Therrell, Edmund, private
Thomas, John, private
Turner, Arthur, private
Turner, Robert, private
Twilley, Joseph, corporal
Usher, William, sergeant
Walton, Timothy, private
Westner, Samuel, private
Wheeler, Amos, private
Whipps, Nathan, private
White, William, private
Whitney, John, private
Whitney, John, private
Whittington, Aaron, private
Wigley, Thomas, private
Williams, William, private
Williams, James, private
Wilbourn, Ralph, private
Wilds, John D., sergeant
Wiley, George, corporal
Wilson, Daniel,
Wright, Jesse, private
Wright, Joseph, private

NOTE: Non-applicable portions of this Index have been lined out.

INDEX.

A

Acklen, *Capt.* Joseph, 189.
Adair, *Gen.* ——, 134, 137.
Adams, Henry, cited, 92, 103, 109, 115.
Adams, John, comparison of Jackson with, 152; ~~opposition to administration of, 241.~~
Adams, R. H., manager of ball in honor of Jackson, 152.
~~Adams, Gen. Wirt, 265.~~
Aetna, U. S. brig, 114.
Alabama, settlement of Mississippi Territory, 18.
~~Alabama, University of, orders to burn, 264; cadet corps of, 264-265.~~
Alibamos, tribe belonging to "Red Sticks," 32.
Aland, *Capt.* Chas. L., 206.
Allen, *Lieut.* Drury M., officers and men of company of, 162.
Allen, *1st Lieut.* John, 38.
Allen, *Capt.* John A., officers and men of company of, 231-232.
Allen, *Capt.* Samuel A., 208.
Allen's Company of Mississippi Militia, officers and men of, 231-232.
Alligator, U. S. naval tender, 107.
Anaconda, brig, attack of, on Fort Bowyer, 95.
Anderson, ——, historian, cited, 29.
Anderson, *2d Lieut.* R. C., 38.
Annide, British frigate, 101.
~~Apafallaya, Indian town, 271.~~
Archer, R., manager of ball in honor of Jackson, 152.
Armat, Thomas, member of committee, 156.
Armstrong, ——, at battle of Burnt Corn, 37.
Asia, British frigate, 101.
Atkins', *Capt.* Daniel, 208.
Atossees, tribe belonging to "Red Sticks," 32.
Austill, *Capt.* Jeremiah, at Fort Madison, 61, 61n; command of boats by, 64-65.

B

Bailey, Daniel, at massacre of Fort Mims, 47.

Bailey, *Capt.* Dixon, celebrated half-breed, 35; at battle of Burnt Corn, 36-37; encounter with Weatherford at Fort Mims, 46n; 59, home of, 64.
Bailey, *1st Lieut.* James, 38; at massacre of Fort Mims, 47; in command at Fort Sinquefield, 59.
Baker, *Capt.* ——, 119.
Baldwin, ——, at battle of Burnt Corn, 37.
Ball, historian, cited, 39n, 43.
Ball, T. H., letter to, 45n.
~~Bancroft, George, cited, 269.~~
Barnett, *Capt.* Peter, 189.
Baron, *2d Lieut.* Charles, 38.
Bates, *Lieut.-Col. Com.* William, 17th Regiment, Jackson county, 90.
Bates, *Capt.* William, 224.
Bartram, historian, cited, 34n.
Beale, *Capt.* ——, of Orleans Rifle Company, 119; takes British by surprise, 121; at battle of New Orleans, 140.
Bealle, James, escape of, from massacre at Fort Mims, 50n
Beard, ——, story of, 63.
Beasley, *Maj.* Daniel, commissioned major, 38; at Fort Mims, 44; death of, 46.
Becket, *Capt.* ——, captain of volunteer company, 27.
Bedford, British frigate, 101.
Bell, J., manager of ball in honor of Jackson, 152.
Belle Poule, British frigate, 101.
Bellevue, *Lieut.* ——, in command of marines at battle of New Orleans, 134.
Beluche, *Capt.* ——, 113.
Benton, Thomas H., duel with Jackson, 55.
Berkeley county, Virginia, 14.
~~Bienville's Cotton Gin Port Fort, 275.~~
Bingaman, *Col.* Adam L., appointed secretary of committee, 156.
Bingaman, J. F., manager of ball in honor of Jackson, 152.
Birmingham Age Herald, cited, 50n.
"Black drink," description of, 31n.

235

236

Bladensburg, battle of, troops from, 101.
Blanchard, Charles K., aide-de-camp to *Gov.* Holmes, 90.
Blanton, *Ensign* Benjamin, 38.
Blennerhassett, Harmon member of vigilance committee, 52.
Blount, *Gov.* ——, letter to, 67; letter to, 83.
Bluche, *Capt.* ——, command of battery 3 by, at New Orleans, 133.
Blue, *Maj.* ——, 88; in attack upon Pensacola, 98; punishes Spaniards, 100.
Bond, *Capt.* John, 200.
Bond, *Lieut.* William, 200.
Bourne, Dr. Edward Gaylord, of Yale College, cited, 269.
Bowman, *1st Lieut.* Richard, 38.
Bowyer, *Maj.* John, 25.
Boyd, Gen. ——, of Martinsburg, 237.
Boyd, Mrs. Nancy, sketch of, 237.
Boyle, *Capt.* Thomas H., officers and men of company of, 162.
Boyles, *Mrs.* ——, cited, 47n.
Boyles, *Col.* William, of Mobile, 47n.
Bradberry, ——, loses life, 63.
Bradberry, *Capt.* James, officers and men of company of, 162.
Bradbury, ——, at battle of Burnt Corn, 37.
Bradford, Elemuel, escape from massacre at Fort Mims, 50n.
Bradley, Aaron, escape from massacre at Fort Mims, 50n.
Brandon, *Capt.* Gerard C., 174, 216.
Breedlove, ——, at battle of New Orleans, 135n.
Brewer, ——, cited, 81.
British, at Pensacola, 84; attack on Fort Bowyer by, 95; fleet at Negril Bay, 101–102; plans to attack New Orleans, 114–115.
Britt, *Ensign* William S., 38.
Browne, *Gov.* ——, English governor, 34.
Bruinsburgh, store of Jackson's at, 14n.
Bryant, William Cullen, poet, cited, 272-273.
Bullard, ——, at battle of Burnt Corn, 37.
Bullen, *Capt.* Samuel, 189.
Bullet, William, on staff of *Gen.* Coffee, 135n.
Burleson, *Capt.* James, 189.

Burnet, Daniel, candidate for lieutenant-governor, 155.
Burnt Corn, battle of, 32; events after, 43.
Burr, Aaron, 12.
Burris, *Lieut.-Col. Com.* Charles, 16th Regiment, Madison county, 90.
Burton, *2d Lieut.* Robert, 38.
Bute County, North Carolina, 24n.
Butler, *Col.* ——, especially commended, 122.
Buttahatchie river crossed by De Soto, 272; beauty of, 273.

C

Cadillac, ——, erects Fort Toulouse, 84.
Caesar, negro, in Dale's famous fight, 65.
Calahan, *Lieut.* ——, 71n.
Caldwell, *2d Lieut.* Kean, 38.
Calhoun, *Dr.* C., 12.
Caller, *Col.* James, letter from, 25; senior military officer, 35; in command at battle of Burnt Corn, 36–37; commander of 6th Regiment, Washington county, 90.
Callihan, *2d Lieut.* D. M., 38.
Calvit, *Lieut.* Alexander, staff aide, 38.
Calvit, *Capt.* James, officers and men of company of, 162–163.
Camp, *1st Lieut.* John, 38.
Campbell, Anthony, cited, 55n.
Carney, Joseph, builder of fort, 42n.
Carolina, U. S. schooner, at battle of New Orleans, 120, 121n, 125, 126.
Caron, sloop, attacks Fort Bowyer, 94.
Carr, Judge ——, of Virginia Court of Appeals, 239, 245; chancellor of state, 246; anecdote of, 246.
Carradine, *Lieut.-Col. Com.* David, 4th Regiment, Jefferson county, 90.
Carroll, *Capt.* W. B., orders sent to, 114.
Carroll, *Gen.* ——, ordered to New Orleans, 108; commands line at battle of New Orleans, 134, 137.
Carson, *Miss* A., invitation to ball sent to, 152.
Carson, *Col.* Joseph, letter from, 25; commander of battalion at Mobile, 28; commissioned major, 38, 39; sketch of, 55n; evacuates Fort Madison, 61, 73; at the capture of the Holy City, 74–75.

Index.   237

Carson's Regiment of Mississippi Militia, officers and men of, 213–215.
Cassell, *Maj.* ——, 73–74.
Cassity, *Capt.* Hugh, officers and men of company of, 163.
Cathell, *Mrs.* ——, widow, from Georgia, 42n.
Cato's fort, location of, 41n.
Chamberlain, *Lieut.* Reuben, 40.
Chambliss, *Lieut.* W. R., escape from massacre at Fort Mims, 50n.
Chauveau, *Capt.* ——, 119; command of battery 7 by, at New Orleans, 133, 134.
Cherokees, friendly party of, at Tallussahatchie, 67.
~~Chesapeake, attack upon, 241.~~
Chester, *Gov.* ——, English governor, 34.
~~Chicasa, forced march to, 273.~~
Chickasaws, traits of, 20.
~~Chickasaw nation, main trail from, 271.~~
~~Chisca Town, Mississippi, De Soto's route to, 269.~~
~~Chisholm, Rev. James, memoir of, 234.~~
Choctaws, branch of the Muscogees, 19; in attack upon Pensacola, 98; ~~dealings with Spaniards, 273.~~
Chotard, *Maj.* ——, especially commended, 122.
Chotard, H., manager of ball in honor of Jackson, 152.
Church Hill, Jefferson county, 16n.
Claiborne, *Gen.* Ferdinand L., patriotism of, 11; sketch of, 13; appointed brigadier-general, 27; assigned to command, 38; constructs Fort Madison, 39; ordered to Fort Stoddart, 39; visits Fort Easley, 41n; headquarters at Mt. Vernon, 42n; correspondence of, 43n; visits Fort Mims, 44; original records of, 46; sorrow of, 52; appeals for action, 53–54; checks advance of Creeks, 54; refuses to interfere between Hinds and Flournoy, 58; orders evacuation of Fort Madison, 61; statesmanship of, 62; desires to rid country of Indians, 66; receives orders from Flournoy, 70; letters from, 71; plans to attack Creek capital, 71–72; conquers the Holy Ground, 74–77; letter from, 78; regard for Jackson of, 83; ill health of, 90; sketch of, 154.

Claiborne, J. F. H., cited, 23, 71, 77, 155, ~~276, 269;~~ manager of ball in honor of Jackson, 152; ~~letter to, 234; memoranda for, 235.~~
Claiborne, *Gov.* William Charles Cole, administration of, 12; second governor of Mississippi Territory, 13; letter to, 91n, 92; apprehensive of safety of New Orleans, 101; appeals to people for defense of New Orleans, 104; protests to U. S. government, 105; guards New Orleans, 115; devotion to American government of, 124; cited, 136; command of river bank by, 145; sketch of 153.
Claiborne's Regiment of Mississippi Militia, officers and men of, 216–223.
Clanton, *Dr.* A. B., cited, 51n.
~~Clarion, 277.~~
Cleveland, *Capt.* David, 200.
Cockrane, *Sir* Alexander, in command of British fleet at Negril Bay, 101; proclamations issued by, 118.
Cocke, *Gen.* John, reinforces Claiborne, 55; blamed for "Hillabee Massacre," 69; attitude of, 83.
Codrington, *Rear Admiral Sir* Edward, British officer, 101.
Coffee, *Gen.* ——, reinforces Claiborne, 55; at battle of Tallussahatchie, 67; at battle of Horseshoe Bend, 80–81; in attack upon Pensacola, 98; ordered to New Orleans, 108; commands left of Jackson's army at New Orleans, 119; ordered to turn British right flank, 120; 135; 137.
Colbert family of half-breeds, 20.
Collins, *Capt.* Moses, 200.
Colson, *Capt.* ——, 113.
Conrad, *Dr.* Daniel, of Winchester, 236; ~~skill of, 253.~~
~~Conrad, D. H., David Holmes: First Governor of Mississippi, 234; 257; letter from, 234–235.~~
~~Conrad, Frederick, family of, 244.~~
~~Conrad, Mrs. Rebecca, sketch of, 236; faithfulness of, to brother, 253.~~
Cook, ——, escape of, from massacre at Fort Mims, 50n.
Cook, *Capt.* David T. W., 226.
~~Coosa Town, Alabama, De Soto's route from, 269.~~
Cornell, Lucy, 47n.

Cornells, Jim, half-breed scout, 44.
~~Cortez, Hernando, comparison of, with De Soto, 272.~~
~~Cotton Gin Port, Choctaw trail to, 271; advance division of De Soto at, 273.~~
Covington, Alexander, of Washington, M. T., 25n.
Covington, Col. Leonard, advice asked of, 25; sketch of, 25n.
Covington, Levin, judge of probate of Adams county, 25n.
Cox, William R., appointed surgeon's mate, 38.
Crawford, Capt. William, 208.
Crawley, Lieut. ——, good service of, at battle of New Orleans, 129; command of battery 4 by, at New Orleans, 133, 134.
Creagh, Walter G., frontiersman, 35; 73.
Creek Confederacy, description of, 33-34.
Creek Nation, assistance of British to, 88; pitable conditions of, after defeat, 88-89.
Creek Indian war, 17; causes of 18-21; Mississippi troops in, 38; capture and destruction of the Holy City, 73-78; surrender of Creeks at Fort Toulouse, 84; signing of peace treaty, 89.
Creek Indians, frontier guarded against, 13; cruelty of, 17; incited to war, 17; country of, 24; trouble expected from, 28; early hostilities of, 30n; friendly party of, at Tallussahatchie, 67; besiege Talladega, 68.
Crockett, Davy, volunteer, 52.
~~Croghan, Col. ——, 237.~~
~~Croxton, Gen. ——, 264, 265.~~
Cunningham, Lieut. ——, commands gunboat, 114.

D

Dale, Capt. Samuel, border hero, 35; at battle of Burnt Corn, 36-37; at Fort Madison, 61; sketch of, 63; famous hand-to-hand fight of, 64-66; 73; at battle of New Orleans, 135; takes news of victory of New Orleans to President Madison, 147; 174, 224.

Dale's Battalion of Mississippi Militia, officers and men of, 222.
~~Dangerfields, family of, 244.~~
Daniels, Private ——, escape of from massacre at Fort Mims, 50n.
Daquin, Maj. ——, 111, 119, 134.
Dougherty, 2d Lieut. George, 38.
Davis, Ensign Isaac W., 38.
Davis, Mrs. Jefferson, 55n.
Davis, Jefferson, 12, 14, 57n; comparison of Jackson with, 153.
Davis, Joseph E., brother of Jefferson Davis, 14.
Davis, Ensign Robert, 38.
~~De Boedma, Lays Hernandez, commissary, 269.~~
de Galvez, Don Bernardo, captor of Pensacola, 20.
de la Ronde, Col. Denis, escape of, 115; sends courier to Jackson, 116, 119.
De Loach, Lieut. W. R., appointed adjutant, 38.
Dent, Capt. ——, at McIntosh Bluff, 31n.
Dent, Capt. Benjamin, 38, 174.
De Soto, rough treatment of Muscogee Nation by, 32-33; ~~route of expedition of, 268-278; comparison of with Cortez, 272.~~
~~Destruction and Reconstruction, cited, 266.~~
Dictator, British frigate, 101.
Dijean, Col. ——, at battle of New Orleans, 142.
Doherty, Capt. John, 157.
Dominique, Capt. —— 113; good service of, at battle of New Orleans, 129; command of battery 3 by, 133.
Donelson, Col. John, father of Mrs. Jackson, 15n.
Drake, ——, historian, cited, 23.
Dreisback, Maj. ——, cited, 75-76.
Dubourg, Rev. Abbe ——, day of prayer appointed by, 147; address of, 148, 148n-149n.
Dubroca, Capt. Benj., 206.
Dunbar, Capt. Isaac, of Jefferson Troop, 131.
~~Dunbar, ——, 234.~~
~~Dunbar, ——, lawyer, of Winchester, 249.~~
Dunn, Capt. Henry, 157.
Dyer, Col. ——, attacks Littefutche, 67.

Index. 239

E

Eaton, ——, cited, 96, 150.
Econachaca, fort erected by Weatherford, 71–72.
Eighteenth Regiment of Mississippi Militia, officers and men of, 213.
Eldridge, *Capt.* Thomas, 189.
Elliott, *Capt.* William, 216.
~~Ellis, *Judge* ——, of Winchester, 249;
253~~
Ellis, R. G., manager of ball in honor of Jackson, 152.
Encyclopedia Britannica, cited, 19n.
Encyclopedia of Mississippi History, cited, 13, 14n, 25–26, 55, 56n, 100, 153, ~~157n.~~
Encyplopedia of United States History, cited, 22.
Engle, *Capt.* Philip A., 38, 174, 216.
~~Ethelville, Alabama, relic at, 275.~~
Evans, *Capt.* William, 208.

F

Farrar, *Capt.* Benjamin, of Mississippi Dragoons, 56n.
Fiftteenth Regiment (Johnson's) of Mississippi Militia, officers and men of, 207–208.
First Regiment of Mississippi Infantry, officers of, 38.
First Regiment of Mississippi Volunteers, officers and members of, 174–188.
Flaugeac, *Gen.* Garrigues, command of battery 6 by, at New Orleans, 133.
Fleming, *Lieut.-Col. Com.* David, 3d Regiment, Adams county, 90.
Fletcher, Josiah, escape of, from massacre at Fort Mims, 50n.
Flournoy, *Gen.* ——, commander of U. S. troops in the south, 32; correspondence of, 43; cold attitude of, 53; finally agrees with Claiborne, 66.
Floyd, *Gen.* ——, commands Georgia volunteers, 55; attacks Autossee, 70.
Foelckil, *Capt.* L. V., 38, 174.
Foote, Henry S., cited, 56.
~~Forrest, *Gen.* Nathan B., promoted to lieutenant-general, 258; tragic incident concerning, 259–262; dispatch from, 263.~~
Fort Barancas, at Pensacola, 99, 100.

Fort Bowyer, at Mobile, 40n; troops sent to, 94; location of, 94n; attack made upon, 95–96; successful attack on, 146.
Fort Burbon, at New Orleans, 104.
Fort Carney, location of, 42n.
Fort Charlotte, at Mobile, 40.
Fort Claiborne, abandoned, 73.
Fort Deposit, cavalry sent from, 67.
Fort Easley, location of, 41n.
Fort Glass, volunteers at, 35; built, 40n.
Fort Jackson, treaty concluded at, 88; supplies ordered to, 110.
Fort Madison, built, 40n.
Fort Meigs, siege of, 20n.
Fort Mims, construction of, 39–40; capture and massacre at, 45–51; those who escaped massacre at, 49n–50n; indignation caused by massacre at, 51.
Fort Montgomery, Jackson assembles troops at, 96.
Fort Pierce, name of, 40n.
Fort Sinquefield, location of, 40n, 58; attack on, 59–60.
Fort St. Leon, artillery sent to, 127.
Fort St. Michael, at Pensacola, 99.
Fort St. Philip, at New Orleans, 104; bombardment of, 145.
Fort St. Stephens, rendezvous of troops at, 26; sketch of, 39n.
Fort Stoddart, brigade organized at, 13; establishment of, 40n.
Fort Strother, erected, 68; supplies ordered to, 110.
Fort Toulouse, erection of, 84; location of, 84n.
Fort White, location of, 41n.
Fort Wayne, treaty of, 20n.
Fort Williams, supplies ordered to, 110.
Fortier, *Col.* Michael, levies negro troops, 110.
Foster, *Capt.* Arthur, officers and men of company of, 163.
Foster, *Capt.* James, 38, 174.
Fourteenth Regiment (McBoy's) of Mississippi Militia officers and men of, 206–207.
Francis, Joseph, "the Prophet," 32; attacks home of Ransom Kimbell, 58; attacks Fort Sinquefield, 59–60; orders prisoners burnt at stake, 72.
Francis, Josiah, threatens Weatherford, 44n.
Free Trader, cited, 155–156.
~~French, B. F., translator, 269.~~

G

Gaines, *Lieut.* Edmund P., 40n.
Gaines, Geo. S., letter to, 30n; unusual leadership of, 52; accompanies Pushmataha, 62.
Gaines, R. M., manager of ball in honor of Jackson, 152.
~~Galloway, Bishop ——, 279.~~
Garrigue, ——, leads volunteers, at battle of New Orleans, 132.
Garrow, *Capt.* Samuel H., 206.
Gayarre, ——, cited, 112–113.
Georgia, volunteers forces from, 55.
Gerald, *Capt.* Samuel, 157.
Ghent, Treaty of, 11.
Gibbs, *Gen.* ——, British officer at battle of New Orleans, 137; mortally wounded, 140.
Gibbs, *2d Lieut.* George H., 38.
~~Gildarts, family of, 244.~~
Gwin, William M., nomination of, for U. S. marshal, 155.
Glass, ——, at battle of Burnt Corn, 37.
Glass, Zachariah, tory Creek, 40n.
Gleig, ——, English historian, cited, 146.
Gordon, *Capt.* James Alexander, 101.
Gorgon, British frigate, 101.
Grafton, *Capt.* James, 189.
Gray, *Capt.* Jonathan, 189.
Great Britain, incites Creeks against Americans, 91; alliance with Spain, 92.
Green, Henry, colonial settler, 14.
Green, *Miss* Malinda Marston, wife of Thomas Hinds, 16, 156; burial place of, 156n.
Green, Thomas Marston, marriage of Jackson at home of, 15.
Green's Company of Mississippi Militia, officers and men of, 232–233.
Greenville, Indian treaty of, 19n.
Griffith, *Capt.* Stephen, 208.
Grove Hill, town of, formerly called Macon, 41n.
Gubbins, *Col.* ——, British officer at battle of New Orleans, 143.
Guest, *Ensign* Samuel, 38.
Guice, *Capt.* Jacob, 216.

H

Haile, William, congressman, 155.
Haines, John, aide-de-camp to *Gov.* Holmes, 90.

Halbert, *Prof.* H. S., historian, cited, 23, 36, 39n, 43, 44, 44n, 49, 50n, 68, 86n–87n, ~~069, 274.~~
Halbert, Zenophon, 274.
Hamilton, *Capt.* James, 189.
Hardy, *Sir* Thomas, British naval officer, 101.
Harper's *Encylopedia of United States History*, cited, 22.
~~Harper's Magazine, cited, 277, 278.~~
Harris, L. C., wounded at battle of New Orleans, 131.
Harris, ——, appointed to meet Jackson, 151–152.
~~Harrison, Lieut. Gov. James T., of Lowndes county, 279, 280.~~
Harrison, *Gov.* William Henry, interview of, 19n.
~~Hastings, Col. John C., 278, 279.~~
~~Hastings, Mrs. Olivia, of Claiborne county, 277, 278.~~
~~Hastings' home on "Hopewell" plantation, 280.~~
Hatterway, *Mrs.* Susan, cited, 46n; escape of from massacre at Fort Mims, 50n.
Hawkins, *Col.* Benjamin, U. S. agent of Indian affairs, 18, 22; sketch of 24n; cited, 34; optimistic views of, 35; views of 44; treaty making of, 89.
Hayden, Isaac, at Fort Sinquefield, 59.
Hayne, *Col.* Arthur P., at treaty making, 89; sketch of, 89n; inspector-general of army, 117.
Heard, ——, 73.
Henderson, *Col.* ——, killed at battle of New Orleans, 130.
Henley, *Capt.* —— commander of the *Carolina*, 120.
Henry, ——, at battle of Burnt Corn, 37.
Henry, Patrick, Jackson compared to. 118.
Henry, *Capt.* William, 174,
Hermes, British sloop, attack on Fort Bowyer by, 95.
Hester, negro, escape of from massacre at Fort Mims, 49n; devotion to white race, 51.
Hill, *Capt.* Philip, 216.
"Hillabee massacre," 69.
Hillis Hadjo, "new made prophet," 44n.
Hinds, *Gen.* Thomas, patriotism of, 11; arrival in Natchez district, 14; appointed chief justice of orphans

court, 16; marriage of, 16; first military service, 17; arrives with Mississippi Dragoons, 55; close association with Claiborne, 62; in Southern District, 66; Jackson looks for support of, 90; begins to realize ambitions, 90; sent to Pearl river, 94; again placed in command of Mississippi Dragoons, 97; in attack upon Pensacola, 98; march to Pensacola, 98; sent to reconnoiter British, 117, 119; renders valuable aid, 122; in forefront of battle, 127; brilliant attacks of, 125; adventure of the ditch, 131; 135; impatience of restraint of, 136; pursuit of British by, 144; appointed brigadier-general, 151n; resolutions passed in honor of, 154; praise of Jackson for, 154; sketch of subsequent career of, 154–155; death of, 155–156.
Hinds' battalion of cavalry, Mississippi Militia, officers and men of, 157–162.
Hinson, *Lieut.-Col. Com.* John, 14th Regiment, Mobile county, 90.
Historical Memoirs, cited, 113.
History of United States, by Henry Adams, cited, 92n.
Hollinger, ——, at battle of Burnt Corn, 37.
Holmes, *Capt.* Andrew Hunter, inspector of regiment, 28; sketch of 237.
Holmes, *Gov.* David, patriotism of, 11; receives letter concerning hostile attitude of Creeks, 25–26; communication to legislature, 26–27; orders for troops, 27; part taken in prosecuting war, 35; strengthens defenses 44; communicates with governors, 52; orders troops 55–56; general orders of, 56; letter of, 57; statesmanship of, 62; aides-de-camp of, 90; message of, 94; letter to *Gov.* Blount, 83; regard for Jackson of, 83; orders of, 145, 146; sketch of, 153; first governor of Mississippi, 234–237; lineage of, 235–237; early life of, 238–241; congressional career of, 241–243; removal to Mississippi Territory of, 243–245; characteristic traits of, 245–246; unhandiness of, 247–250; last visit to Virginia of, 250–255; why never married, 255–257.

Holmes, *Judge* Hugh, difference from brother of, 234; sketch of, 236; 239, 240; horsemanship of, 247; anecdote of, 248.
Holmes, *Col.* Joseph, of Frederick county, Va., 235.
Holmes, Joseph, of Kenawha county, Va., sketch of, 237.
Holmes, *Miss.* Rebecca, sketch of, 236.
Holmes, *Dr.* Thomas G., escape of, from massacre at Fort Mims, 50n.
Holy City of the Creeks, capture of, 73–78.
Holy Ground, battle of, effects of victory of, 77.
Hood, *Gen.* ——, disastrous campaign of, 261.
Hopie Tustanuggee, cited, 44n.
Horseshoe Bend, battle of, 79–83; slaughter at, 82.
Houma Mingo, assistant to Pushmataha, 22.
Houston, *Ensign* Sam, volunteer, 52; at battle of Horseshoe Bend, 81.
Howard, *Gov.* George, of Maryland, 252.
Howell, William B., marriage of, 56.
Hull, *Gen.* William, surrender of, at Detroit, 20n.
Humbert, *Gen.* ——, at battle of New Orleans, 145.
Humphrey, ——, battery of, at battle of New Orleans, 128; leads Baratarians, 132, 133; in command of battery 1, 133.
Humphries, Buck, state representative, 280.
Hunter, *Rev.* Andrew, chaplain at navy yard, 237.
Hunter, *Col.* David, cited, 234; sketch of, 235–236.
Hunter, *Miss* Fanny W., 236.
Hunter, Rebecca, wife of *Col.* Joseph Holmes, 235.
Hutchins, *Col.* Anthony, 13.

I

Iffa Tustunnaga, Creek warrior, 46n.
In Clarke and Its Surroundings, cited, 11.
International Encyclopedia, cited, 11.
Irving, Theodore, 269.

J

Jack, *Capt.* ——, sent to Fort Mims, 39; death of, at Fort Mims, 48.
Jack, negro slave of *Gov.* Holmes, 249.
Jack, *Capt.* William, 38, 174.

242

Jackson, *Gen.* Andrew, campaign in Mississippi Territory begun by, 12; where married, 14; lives in "Old Greenville," 14; sketch of, 14n; early association of with Thomas Hinds, 16; apprised of massacre at Fort Mims, 52; duel with Blanton, 55; letter of, 57; letter of, 67; at battle of Tallussahatchie, 67; erects Fort Strother, 68; raises siege of Talladega, 68; falsely blamed for massacre of Hillabees, 69n; appears mysterious to the Indians, 70; continues war upon Creeks, 78; at battle of Horseshoe Bend, 80–82; at Fort Williams, 83; at Fort Toulouse, 84; concludes treaty with Indians, 88; retires to the "Hermitage," 88; promoted major-general, 89; plans expedition to Pensacola, 91–93; letter from, 91n, 92; disposition of troops by, 94; praises defense of Fort Bowyer, 96; assembles troops at Fort Montgomery, 96–97; plans to defend New Orleans, 101; charms of personality at New Orleans, 102–103; urgent calls for assistance by, 108–109; reviews militia at New Orleans, 111; proclaims martial law, 112; forces of, at New Orleans, 119; personal bearing of, during attack, 123; answer to Packenham, 127; orders buildings blown up, 128; determination of, to resist British advance, 130; discovers British plans, 133; strength of force of, 135; general orders of, 137n; 143; visit to wounded British officers by, 144; conference with *Gen.* Lambert, 145; announcement of victory by, 146–147; reply of, to address of *Abbé* Dubourg, 149n; ill-feeling against, 150; address to, 151; reply to address by, 151; character of, 152–153; 246.
Jackson and New Orleans, cited, 125.
Jackson Highway, 272, 276.
Jackson Military Road, 271, 272.
Jackson, *Gen.* Thomas J., dispatch to 263; 265.
Jefferson, Thomas, 12; Manual of, 236; details of administration of, 241; opposition to policy of, 242.
Jefferson Troop of Horse, 16.
Jim Boy, Creek chieftain, 32; sketch of, 32n.

Johnson, *Capt.* C. G., 38, 174.
Johnson, Chapman, letter of, 241.
Johnson, *Col.* Richard M., of Kentucky, cited, 20n.
Johnson, *Sailing Master* ——, 106.
Johnston, *Gen.* ——, army of, 258, 259.
Johnston, *Capt.* Greaf, 208.
Johnson, *Capt.* William, 189.
Johnstone, *Gov.* ——, English governor, 34.
Jones, ——, escape of, from massacre at Fort Mims, 50n.
Jones, *Rev.* J. G., of Hazlehurst, Miss., cited, 50n.
Jones, *Capt.* John, 224.
Jones, *Capt.* Randall, 38, 174, 216.
Jones, *Capt.* Thomas A P., U. S. naval officer, 106; report of, 107; severely wounded, 107; mentioned by historians, 108.
Jonisdon, Charles H., wounded at battle of New Orleans.
Joor, *Capt.* John, 226.
Jugeant, *Capt.* J., 110
Jugeant, *Capt.* Pierre, 119.

K

Kean, *Maj.* ——, clerk of superior court 248, anecdote of, 248–249.
Keane, *Gen.* ——, British officer, 101–102, 118; resists attack of Americans, 121, 137, 139; wounded, 140.
Kellogg, *1st Lieut.* Theron, 38.
Kelly, *Col.* D. C., of 7th Tennessee Cavalry, 263.
Kempe, *Capt.* James, of Mississippi Dragoons, 55; sketch of, 55n, 157.
Kemper *Col.* Reuben, pursuit of British by, 144; sketch of, 144n.
Kennedy, *Capt.* J. L., letter from, 31n.
Kennedy, *Capt.* Joseph P., brigade-major, 38, 174.
Kennedy, *Maj.* ——, in attack upon Pensacola, 98.
Ker, David, judge of territorial supreme court, 38n.
Kerr, *Dr.* John, staff surgeon, 38.
Kerr, *Surg.-Gen.* ——, American surgeon-general, 143.
Kerr, *Miss* ——, address of, 148.
Kimbell, Isham, of Clarke county, 58.
Kimbell, Ransom, home attacked by "the Prophet," 58.
King, *Capt.* Elisha F., 189.

Index.   243

L

Lacoste, *Maj.* ——, 109, 134.
Lafitte, John, privateer, 112–113; sketch of, 112n–113n.
Lafitte, Pierre, sketch of, 112n–113n.
Lagand, *Capt.* ——, 113.
~~Lamb, Charles, cited, 239.~~
Lambert, *Gen.* ——, succeeds to command of Packenham, 140; abandons position, 143; notified of ratification of peace, 146n.
Landrum's fort, location of, 41n.
La Ronde, *Col.*, pursuit of British by, 144.
Latour, *Maj.* ——, cited, 94n; assists Jackson in plans for defense of New Orleans, 103–104; cited, 109, 121, 123, 135, 142, 147–148.
Latrobe, ——, at battle of New Orleans, 128.
~~Latrobe, J. H. B., letter from, 234.~~
Lauderdale, *Col.* ——, death of, 122, 122n.
Laval, *Maj.* William, death of, 99; sketch of, 99n.
Lavier, *Capt.* Lawson, builder of fort, 42n.
~~Layson, 1st Lieut. Robert, 38.~~
Lawrence *Maj.* William, defender of Fort Bowyer, 94–96.
Lea, *Capt.* Zachariah, 216.
Lee, Robert E., comparison of Jackson with, 152; ~~army of, 258; 259.~~
~~Legrand, Mrs. Margaret, 234; sketch of, 236.~~
~~Legrand, Rev. Nash, eminent divine, 236.~~
Lenoir, *Capt.* Francis B., 200.
~~Leftwich, Hon. Geo. J., of Aberdeen, 273.~~
Lewis, ——, at battle of Burnt Corn, 37.
~~Lewis, negro slave of Gov. Holmes, 249.~~
~~Lewis, Dr. Theodore Hays, cited, 269.~~
Liberty, town of, 12.
Life of General Jackson, cited, 69n, 96.
Lincoln, Abraham, comparison of Jackson with, 153.
~~Lisbon, history published at, 268.~~
Lister, *Capt.* Josiah, 224.
Livingston, Edward, Jackson at home of, 102; sketch of, 102n.
Lizzie, negro, escape of, from massacre at Fort Mims, 50n.
Lackridge, *2d Lieut.* N., 38.
Lockyer, *Capt.* ——, British naval officer, 101; severely wounded, 108.

Lossing, ——, historian, cited, 23.
Louisiana, U. S. schooner, at battle of New Orleans, 125, 126, 127, 128, 130.
~~Love, William A., Reminiscences of the Closing Days of the War of Secession, 258–267; Route of De Soto's Expedition Through Lowndes County, Mississippi, 268–278.~~
~~Lowndes county, Miss., route of De Soto through, 268–278.~~
~~Lowry, Gov. ——, of Mississippi, 279.~~
Lucas, *Capt.* William A., 226.
Luckett, *2d Lieut.* James, 38.
Luse, *Capt.* Nathan H., 226.
~~Luxapalila river, crossed by De Soto, 271; location of, 272; relic found at, 276.~~

M

~~McCalebs, old home of, 278.~~
McCaskey, John, at Powell's fort, 42n.
~~McCook, Gen. ——, capture of bridge by, 263, 264, 265.~~
McDonald, *Ensign* Y. R., 38.
McDougall ——, aide to General Packenham, 140.
McGillivray, Alexander noted halfbreed, 21; sketch of, 21n.
McGillivray, Lachlan, father of Alexander, 21n.
McGillivray William, descendants of, 70.
McGirth, *Mrs.* ——, escape, of from massacre at Fort Mims, 49n.
McGirth family escape of, from massacre at Fort Mims, 50n.
McGowen, *Capt.* James, 200.
McGrew, *Maj.* John, letter from, 25.
McGrew, John, British royalist, 42.
McGrew, William, British royalist, 42n.
McGrew, *Col.* William, killed, 63.
McGrew's fort, location of, 41n.
~~McGuire, Edward, of Winchester, 236.~~
~~McGuire, Mrs. Elizabeth, sketch of, 236.~~
~~McGuire, Hugh Holmes, eminent physician, 236.~~
McKee, *Col.* ——, secures attachment of Chickasaws, 62.
McKinsey, *Capt.* ——, 206.
McQueen, Peter, Creek chieftain, 32.
McRea, *Col.* ——, 119.
~~Martin, Hon. J. McC., True History of Incorporaton of the Industrial Institute and College,~~

~~Located at Columbus, Mississippi, 277-280.~~
Mason, Samuel, noted outlaw, 15.
Massacre at Fort Mims. *See* Fort Mims.
Matthews, Serg. ——, escape of, from massacre at Fort Mims, 50n.
Maumee river, battle on, 13.
Maurice, ——, escape of, from massacre at Fort Mims, 50n.
May, ——, at battle of Burnt Corn, 37.
May, Patrick, 73.
Mays, *Ensign* Stephen, 38.
Mazant *Lieut.* —— commands artillery at battle of New Orleans, 134.
Mead, Cowles, commissioned colonel, 38.
Mead, *Capt.* William C., 38; defeated for congress, 38n; 174.
Meek, *Judge* ——, cited, 50n.
Middleton, *Capt.* ——, sent to Fort Mims, 39; death of, at Fort Mims, 48.
Middleton, *Capt.* Hatton, 174.
Middleton, *Capt.* Hatton, 38.
~~Miller, Gen. T. M., of Warren county, 279.~~
Milton, *Col.* ——, lack of coöperation of, 83.
Mims, Alexander, escape of, from massacre at Fort Mims, 50n.
Mims, David, escape of, from massacre at Fort Mims, 50n.
Mims, Joseph, escape of, from massacre at Fort Mims, 50n.
Mims, *Mrs.* ——, escape of, from massacre at Fort Mims, 50n.
Mims, Samuel, residence of, 43.
Mississippi commands in the war of 1812, Rolls of, 157-233.
Mississippi Dragoons, officers of, 55-56; sketch of, 56; at New Orleans, 116-117; devotion and faithfulness of, 122n; high praise of, by Jackson, 131.
~~Mississippi State College for Women, 277n.~~
Mississippi Territory in the War of 1812, 11, 233; older population of, 12; military situation in 1812, 25-26; troops from, 27-28.
Mitchell, *Gen.* P. L., member of committee, 156.
Mixon, *Col.* ——, sketch of, 56n-57n.
Mobile, included in annexation of Mississippi Territory, 12; ~~Spaniards at, 275.~~

Moniac, —— notable half-breed, refuses to take "blackdrink," 31.
Moniac, Mary, first wife of Weatherford, 47n.
Moniac, Sam, trip with Weatherford, 44n.
~~Morancy, Mrs. Jennie, state librarian, 279.~~
~~Monroe county, Indian mounds in, 273.~~
Monroe, James, express from, announcing declaration of war with Great Britain, 26.
Montgomery, *1st Lieut.* A., 38.
Montgomery, *Maj.* ——, at battle of Horseshoe Bend, 81; first to mount breastworks, 82; sketch of, 82n.
Montjoy, ——, escape of, from massacre at Fort Mims, 50n.
~~Moore, Clarence B., mounds described by, 275.~~
Moore, ——, historian, cited, 23.
Moore, *2d Lieut.* Charles, 38.
Morgan, ——, at battle of Horseshoe Bend, 80.
Morgan, *Brig.-Gen.* David, marches without orders, 123; receives unfortunate instruction, 127; failure to defend line by, 142-143; ordered to advance, 145.
Morgan, *Lieut.-Col. Com.* Jordan, 18th Regiment, Hancock county, 90.
Morgan, *1st Lieut.* William, 38.
M'Pheters, J. A., manager of ball in honor of Jackson, 152.
Morris, A. J., escape of, from massacre at Fort Mims, 50n.
Morrison, *Capt.* Hans, 38, 174.
~~Morton, Mrs. ——, of Charlotte county, Va., 234.~~
Moseley, *Capt.* Wm., 208.
Moshilitubee, assistant to Pushmataha, 22.
~~Moss, Mrs. Gertrude E., sketch of, 237.~~
~~Moss, William, of Fairfax county, Va., 237.~~
Mott's fort, location of, 41n.
Moulton, *Lieut.* ——, at battle of Horseshoe Bend, 81.
Mt. Vernon, forts and arsenals at, 42n.
Munce, *Lieut.* Thomas S., member of committee, 156.
Murray, *Lieut.* ——, death of, 98.
Murrel, *Dr.* ——, carries flag of truce, 117.
Muscogee Nation, sketch of 33-34.

Muscogees, Choctaw branch, 19
Mushshulatubbe, Choctaw chief, letter from, 30n.
~~Mackey, Mrs. ——, of Clarke county, Va., 234.~~
Mad-dog, Indian chieftain, 69.
Madison, *President* James, requisition for troops made by, 94; notification of victory of New Orleans sent to, 147.
Malcolm, *Rear Admiral* ——, British officer, 101.
Manadere, *Lieut.-Col. Com.* Henry, 10th Regiment, Warren county, 90.
Manae, Saml., half-breed, cited, 29n.
Manique, *Gov.* ——, Spanish governor at Pensacola, 43; letter from, 76.
~~Manuel, negro slave of Gov. Holmes, 234, 249; ungratefulness of, 250.~~
Marchand, *Capt.* ——, French officer, 21n.
Marschalk, *Adj. Gen.* Andrew, 90.
~~Marshall, Judge Hunter, of Charlotte, Va., 236.~~
Martin, *Gen.* Joseph, Indian treaties negotiated by, 15n.

N

~~Nancy, negro slave of Gov. Holmes, 249.~~
Nash, Wiley N., of Starkville, 279.
Natchez Almanac, cited, 90.
Natchez District, colonial period in, 12.
Natchez, during colonial period, 12, 14; first capital of Mississippi Territory, 25n.
Natchez trail, 14.
Neelley, *Capt.* James, 189.
Negril Bay, rendezvous of British fleet, 101–102.
Neilson, *Col.* ——, 57
Neilson, *Lieut.-Col. Com.* David, 1st Regiment, Amite county, 90; reinforcements of, 146.
Neilson, *Capt.* John, 174.
Neilson's Detachment of Mississippi Militia, officers and men of, 226–231.
Newman, Algier, of Monroe county, 47n.
Newman, *Capt.* ——, 110.
New Orleans, battle of, 11, 119–146; last day of, 136–145; British losses at, 141; celebration of victory of, 147.

Nichols, *Col.* Edward, British officer, lands troops, 93.
Nichols, ——, at attack upon Fort Bowyer, 96.
Nichols, *Col.* ——, guest of Spanish at Pensacola, 98.
Nixon, *Col.* ——, 56.
Nixon, *Lieut.-Col. Com.* George H., 13th Regiment, Marion county, 90; officers and members of regiment of, 164–174.
Norge, British frigate, 101.
Norris, *Lieut.* ——, in command of battery 2 at battle of New Orleans, 134.
Nuniah Waiya, sacred mound of the Choctaws, 34, 34n.

O

Ogden, *Capt.* ——, 135.
Oglethorpe, treaty with in 1732, 32.
Ohio, army in, 13.
Old Greenville, during colonial period, 12; name of, 14.
Orpheus, British ship, lands arms at Appalachicola, 91.
Orr, ——, delegate from Chickasaw county, 279.
Orr, *Judge* ——, of Lowndes county, 279, 280.
Osborn, *1st Lieut.* A. L., 38.
Osborn, *2d Lieut.* W. M., 38.

P

Packenham, *Sir* Edward, British commander-in-chief, 118; determines to advance, 122; arrival of, 125; sketch of, 126; complains of shooting of sentinels, 127, 130; astonishment of, 132; wounded, 139; death of, 139–140.
Paimboiuf, *Capt.* Lewis, 174, 216.
Painboeuff, *Capt.* ——, captain of volunteer company, 27.
Panthon, *Col.* David, encounter with Weatherford, 47n.
Parker, *Master's Mate* ——, assumes charge, 107.
Parton, author of *Life of General Jackson*, 15; cited, 17, 23, 99, 101, 135.
Patterson, *Commodore* Daniel T., naval commander at New Orleans, 104–105; letter to, 105; announces loss of gunboats, 111; sends gun-

boat to Fort St. Philip, 114; report of, to secretary of the navy, 128–129; 143
Patton's fort, location of, 42n.
Patton, *Lieut.-Col. Com.* James, 9th Regiment, Wayne county, 90.
~~Payne, Dr. J. W. W., of Ethelville, Alabama, 275.~~
Pensacola, Spanish possession of, 20; beauty of, 98–99 capture of, 99–100; ~~Spaniards at, 275~~
Percy *Capt.* ——, British naval officer, 101.
Percy, *Commodore* ——, British officer in command of naval attack upon Fort Bowyer, 95–96.
Percy, Thomas, aide-de-camp to *Gov.* Holmes, 90.
Perkins, *Lieut.-Col. Com.* Peter, 7th Regiment, Madison county, 90.
Perry, *Col.* ——, command of battery 5 by, at New Orleans, 133.
Perry, Joseph, escape from massacre at Fort Mims, 50n.
~~Peyton, Mrs. ——, of Copiah county, 277.~~
~~Philadelphia, book published at, 268.~~
Phillips, *Capt.* James, 200.
Piatt, *Col* ——, especially commended, 122.
Pickens county, De Soto's army in, 270.
Pickett, historian, cited, 23, 28n, 35, 42n, 43, 45, 46, 49, 80, ~~269.~~
Pierce, John, teacher, 40n.
Pierce, William, weaver, 40n.
Pierre, *Maj.* ——, carries flag of truce to Pensacola, 98; 119; commands 7th Regiment at battle of New Orleans, 134.
Piqua, birthplace of Tecumseh, 19n.
Plauche, *Maj.* ——, 119, 134.
Poindexter, George, 14; at battle of New Orleans, 135n; elected governor, 155; ~~234.~~
~~Pollock, Henry, of Baltimore, Md., 234.~~
~~Pontotoc county, Chickasaw towns in, 271, 273.~~
Port Gibson, during colonial period, 12.
Posey, *Capt.* Thos., 174.
Powell, James, at Powell's fort, 42n.
Powell, *Lieut.-Col. Com.* James, 8th Regiment, Baldwin county, 90.
Powell, John, at Powell's fort, 42n.
Princess Sehoy, marriage of, 21n.
Proctor, *Col* Henry, retreat of, from Malden, 20n.

Pushmataha, Choctaw chieftain, 19; assistants of, 22; remains friendly to whites, 54; visits Fort St. Stephens, 62; exults over victory of Burnt Corn, 70–71; at the capture of the Holy City, 73, 76.
Put-in-Bay, battle of, 20n.

Q

Quin, *Capt.* Henry, 200.
Quitman, *Gen.* John A., presiding officer at meeting, 155–156.

R

Ramilies, British frigate, 101.
Ramsey, historian, cited, 23.
~~Ramsey, ——, of Tennessee, 269.~~
Randon, Elizabeth, taken prisoner at Fort Mims, 46n.
Randon, *Lieut.* Peter, escape from massacre at Fort Mims, 50n.
~~Ranjel, Rodrigo, private secretary to De Soto, 269, 271.~~
Rankin, Christopher, 14.
Rapalje, *Capt* ——, 57.
Rather, *Capt.* John T., 189.
"Red Cattle," sobriquet of Creeks, 44.
Red Eagle. *See* William Weatherford.
Red Eagle, the elder Muscogee warrior, 47.
"Red Sticks," tribes belonging to, 32.
Renee, ——, British officer at battle of New Orleans' 140; body found, 143.
~~Reynolds, Reuben O., state senator of Mississippi, 277; opposes bill, 279; withdraws opposition to bill, 279–280.~~
Richardson, *Capt.* J. G., of Mississippi Dragoons, 56, at battle of New Orleans, 135, 157.
Rigdon, Martin, escape of, from massacre at Fort Mims, 50n.
Robards, *Mrs.* Rachel Donelson, bride of Andrew Jackson, 15; sketch of 15n
Roberts, *Capt.* Abraham, 189.
Rodgers, *1st Lieut.* J. D., 38
Roger's fort, location of, 42n.
Robinson, *Lieut.-Col. Com.* Raymond, 5th Regiment, Claiborne county; 90.
ROLLS OF MISSISSIPPI COMMANDS IN THE WAR OF 1812, 157–233.
Ross, *Col.* ——, at battle of New Orleans, 120; commands line at battle of New Orleans, 134.

Ross, *Lieut.* ——, commands company at New Orleans, 134.
Ross, *Capt.* John J. W., 157.
Rowland, *Mrs.* Dunbar, MISSISSIPPI TERRITORY IN THE WAR OF 1812, 9–233.
Rowland, *Hon.* Dunbar, 280.
Royal Oak, British frigate, 101.
Runnels, *Capt.* Harmon M., 200.
Russell, *Col.* ——, 71n.
Russell, ——, at battle of Horseshoe Bend, 80.

S

Saffold, *Lieut.-Col. Com.* Reuben, 15th Regiment, Clarke county, 90.
Salvage, *Lieut.* B. F., appointed quartermaster, 38.
Sargent, Winthrop, administration of, 12.
Sartain, ——, artist, of Philadelphia, 234.
Savary, *Capt.* ——, levies negro troops, 110.
Scott, *Capt.* Abram M., 38, 174.
Scott, *Col.* ——, sent to Fort St. Stephens, 39.
Schuyler, *Capt.* ——, commander of Fort Stoddart, 40n.
Sea-horse, British frigate, 101.
Seekaboo, Shawnee prophet, 44; at massacre of Fort Mims, 48.
Seminoles, British send messages to, 93.
Sessions, Joseph, aide-de-camp to *Gov.* Holmes, 90.
Seventh Regiment (Perkins' Battalion) of Mississippi Militia, officers and men of, 189–200.
Seventh Tennessee Cavalry, Forrest's old regiment, 263.
Shanks, *Capt.* John H., 216.
Shea, John Gilmory, 269.
Shelby, *Col.* Isaac, negotiating Indian treaties, 15n.
Sherman, *Gen.* William T., army of, 258, 259.
Shields, ——, purser, carries flag of truce, 117.
Shipp, Bernard, translator, 268.
Shouler, historian, cited, 11.
Sillers, *Mrs.* Walter, Sr., record presented by, 154.
Sixth Regiment of Mississippi Militia, officers and men of, 188–189.
Sixth Mississippi Regiment of Cavalry, Confederate, 267.

Sixteenth Regiment (Burrus') of Mississippi Militia, officers and men of, 208–212.
Sizemore, Absalom, 47n.
Skinner, *Lieut.-Col. Com.* Josiah, 12th Regiment, Greene county, 90.
Smith, Buckingham, translator, 269.
Smith, James, at Fort Sinquefield, 59; in Dale's famous fight, 65.
Smith, *Capt.* Jedediah, 157.
Smith, Samuel, escape from massacre at Fort Mims, 50n.
Smith, *Ensign* Richard, 38.
Smith, *Capt.* William, 200.
Smith, ——, cited, 143.
Smoot, *Capt.* ——, at battle of Burnt Corn, 36–37.
Smoot, *Maj.* Benjamin, 73–74, 174.
Smoot's Battalion of Mississippi Militia, officers and men of, 224–226.
Somerville, *Lieut.* ——, at battle of Horseshoe Bend, 81.
Songis, *Capt.* ——, 113.
Sophia, British sloop, attack on Fort Bowyer by, 95.
Sorsby, *Capt.* Samuel K., 226.
Spark's *Memories of Fifty Years*, cited, 14n.
Spencer, *Capt.* William, 200.
Spotts, *Lieut.* ——, 119; command of battery 7 by, at New Orleans, 133, 134.
Sprague, J., manager of ball in honor of Jackson, 152.
Steadham, Edward, escape from massacre at Fort Mims, 50n.
Steadham, Jesse, escape from massacre at Fort Mims, 50n.
Stewart, *Lieut. Gen.* ——, cited, 235.
Stiggins, Mary, third wife of Weatherford, 47n.
Stocket, *Lieut.-Col. Com.* Samuel, 2d Regiment, Wilkinson county, 90.
Stowell, *Ensign* Benjamin, 38.
Stubblefield, *Dr.* Clanton, cited, 50n.
Subaltern, historian, cited, 18n, 128, 128n.
Sullivan county, Long Island, 15n.
Stuart, *Judge* Alexander, of Missouri, 239.
Swan, *2d Lieut.* Robert, 38.
Swayze, *Maj.* ——, 57.
Swayze's Detachment of Mississippi Militia, officers and men of, 231.
Sykes, *Judge* E. O., of Aberdeen, 279.
Sykes, *Senator* ——, of Columbus, 280.

T

Tallassees, tribe belonging to "Red Stick," 32.
Tallussahatchie, battle of, 67.
Tate, David, half-brother of Weatherford, 46n.
Tatum, *Maj.* ——, 116.
~~Taylor, Gen. Richard, escape of, 266; cited, 266.~~
Tecumseh, Shawnee chieftain, 17; sketch of, 19, 19n; eloquence of, 21; visit to Creeks in 1812, 22; prophesies earthquake, 22n; second visit to gulf tribes, 23–24; "Dance of the Lakes," taught by, 35; no influence over Weatherford, 44n.
~~Ten Mile School, Indian mound at, 274.~~
~~Tennessee river, Choctaw trail from, 271.~~
Tensas, settlement of Mississippi Territory, 19.
Tenskwatawa, brother of Tecumseh, 19n.
Thames river, battle with Tecumseh on, 20n.
The British Compaigns at Washington and New Orleans, cited, 18n.
"The Hermitage," death of Mrs. Jackson at, 15.
~~The Independent, cited, 274.~~
The Mississippian, cited, 155.
"The Prophet," *See* Joseph Francis.
Thirteenth Regiment (Nixon's) of Mississippi Militia, officers and men of, 200–205.
Thlanie, Sapoth, second wife of Weatherford, 47n.
Throckmorton, ——, at battle of New Orleans, 135n.
Throckmorton, R. L., manager of ball in honor of Jackson, 152.
Thomas, *Gen.* John, reinforces Jackson at battle of New Orleans, 133, 137.
Thomas, *Maj.-Gen.* Philemon, ordered to organize companies at Baton Rouge, 92.
Thompson, *Lieut.* ——, at battle of New Orleans, 130n.
Thornton, ——, British officer at battle of New Orleans, 118, 142.
Thurman, Wild Bill, gambler, 86n–87n.
~~Thurstons, family of, 244.~~

Tippecanoe, battle of, 20n.
Tohopeka, *See* Horseshoe Bend.
Tombigbee, settlement of Mississippi Territory, 18.
~~Tombigbee river, Choctaw trail from, 271; historic trail along, 274.~~
Tonnant, British frigate, 101.
Toockabatcha, ancient capital of Creeks, 22n.
Tookabatchee, Indian chieftain, 69.
Toulmin, *Judge,* letter from, 29n.
Trimble, ——, cited, 131, 136.
Trowbridge, *Sir* Thomas, British naval officer, 101.
~~Tucker, Henry, praise of, 241.~~
Turner, Abner, early settler of West Bend, 41n.
Turner, Edward, 14.
Turner's fort, location of, 41n.
Tustinuggee-Thlucco, Creek chieftain, 22n.

V

~~Vega, Garcillasco De La, cited, 268.~~
Vellio, *Capt.* Joseph, officers and men of company of, 213.
Vicksburg, 14.
Villere, *Maj.-Gen.* ——, ordered to organize companies at New Orleans, 92; house of, headquarters of British, 115, 118.
Villere, *Maj.* ——, made prisoner, 115–116.

W

Wagner, *Lieut.* ——, at Fort St. John, 111.
Wailes, B. L. C., geologist, 25n.
Walker, Robert J., candidate for U. S. senate, 155.
Walker, Tandy, daring backwoodsman, 41n; story of, 63.
War of 1812, Mississippi Territory in the, 11–233.
Ward, *Mrs.* ——, testimony of, 32.
Washington, George, comparison of Jackson with, 152.
Washington, town of, 12, 14; capital of Mississippi Territory, 25.
~~Waverly, on Tombigbee river, 274.~~
Wayne, *Gen.* Anthony, 13n.
Weatherford, Charles, grandson of William Weatherford, letter from, 45n.
Weatherford, Charles, Sr., 45n.
Weatherford, William, noted halfbreed chieftain, 30; receives con-

Index.   249

gratulations, 43; assists in attack on Fort Mims, 43n; humanity of, 45; plans attack on Fort Mims, 45; anecdote of, 47n; marriages of, 47n; defends the Holy City, 74; wonderful escape of, 76; surrender of, at Fort Toulouse, 84–86; story concerning, 86n–87n.
Weeks, Mrs. Alfred, of Louisiana, 236.
Wells, *Capt.* Archilaus, 38, 174.
West, *Ensign* Charles, 38.
Wheeler's *History of North Carolina,* cited, 24n.
White, *Gen.* ——, reinforces Claiborne, 55; blamed for "Hillabee Massacre," 69.
Whitney, J. J., state senator, of Jefferson county, 279.
Wilkins, *Col.* James C., reinforcements of, 146; chairman of memorial committee, 156; officers and men of company of, 163–164.
Wilkinson, *Gen.* James, information given by, 32; cited, 44.
Wilkinson, *Maj.* ——, death of, 140.
Williams, Hon. ——, 253.

Wilson, Gen. ——, of the Union army, 258, 259, 265.
Winchester, *Gen.* ——, ordered to New Orleans, 108; ordered to be vigilant, 110.
Winchester, G., manager of ball in honor of Jackson, 152.
Winchester, *Judge* George, 155; member of committee, 156.
Wirt, William, letter of, 239; cited, 243.
Witherspoon, *Lieut.-Col. Com.* Robert, 11th Regiment, Franklin county, 90.
Wood, *Maj.* ——, bluff named for, 41.
Wood, *Capt.* Francis, 226.
Wood, James, at Fort Sinquefield, 59.
Wood, John, aide-de-camp to *Gen.* Claiborne, 90.
Woodbine, ——, at defense of Fort Bowyer, 96.
Woodruff, *Maj.* ——, in attack upon Pensacola, 98.
Woodville, during colonial period, 12.
Woodward, historian, cited, 30, 89.
Woodward, *Gen.* ——, cited, 44n.

www.ingramcontent.com/pod-product-compliance
Lightning Source LLC
Chambersburg PA
CBHW061440300426
44114CB00014B/1767